CONTEMPORARY STUDIES IN SCRIPTURE

An exciting new series from Greg Kofford Books featuring authors whose works engage in rigorous textual analyses of the Bible and other LDS scripture. Written by Latter-day Saints for a Latter-day Saint audience, these books utilize the tools of historical criticism, literature, philosophy, and the sciences to celebrate the richness and complexity found in the standard works. This series will provide readers with new and fascinating ways to read, study, and re-read these sacred texts.

Beholding
the Tree of Life

Beholding
the Tree of Life

A Rabbinic Approach to the
Book of Mormon

Bradley J. Kramer

GREG KOFFORD BOOKS
SALT LAKE CITY, 2014

Greg Kofford Books
P.O. Box 1362
Draper, UT 84020
www.gregkofford.com
facebook.com/gkbooks

Also available in ebook.

———————————————————

Library of Congress Cataloging-in-Publication Data

Kramer, Bradley J., author.
  Beholding the tree of life : a rabbinic approach to the Book of Mormon / Bradley J. Kramer.
      pages cm
  Includes bibliographical references and index.
  Summary: Using interpretive techniques developed by Talmudic and post-Talmudic rabbis, Kramer shows how to read the Book of Mormon closely, in levels, paying attention to the details of its expression as well as to its overall connection to the Hebrew Scriptures.
   ISBN 978-1-58958-701-4 (pbk.) -- ISBN 978-1-58958-702-1 (hardcover)
  1. Book of Mormon--Study and teaching. I. Title.
  BX8627.K73 2014
  289.3'22--dc23
                                              2014039358

To Richard Dilworth Rust, my teacher, my friend, and someone who has always judged me in a favorable light

Contents

Acknowledgments

Having worked on this project for nearly two decades, I have many people to whom I must give thanks: Von R. Nielsen, my mission president, who encouraged me to learn from Jewish people as well as to teach them; Richard D. Rust, for his scholarly faith and for opening my eyes to the literary richness of the Book of Mormon; Terryl Givens, for providing constant friendship, steadying encouragement, and valuable insights into the writing process and into myself as a writer; Rabbis John Friedman and Leah Berkowitz as well as the other members of Durham's Judea Reform Congregation, for welcoming me into their classes, their services, their homes, and their lives so graciously and so openly as to allow me to glimpse many of the gems of Judaism as well as the beauty and intelligence of their own personal faith; Bishop Matthew Nelson, the Chapel Hill 1st Ward, and the Durham Stake Relief Society, for allowing me to try out many of my ideas in firesides and in conferences and for providing me with valuable feedback and encouragement; Matt Grey, for introducing me to the background required for this effort; Amy-Jill Levine, for sensitizing me to the finer points of Jewish-Christian dialogue and for encouraging me in my work; Dana Pike, for helping me focus my arguments and address possible objections to my points; Abby Parcell and Jason Kerr, for having the fortitude to read through several book-length drafts and the courage to show me where I had gone wrong; Jim and Bette Maxwell, Artha Lubeck, and Anson and M'Liss Dorrance, for their much needed support; C. L. Kendell, for consistently haranguing me to "get the thing done," particularly when my stamina flagged; Loyd Ericson, Emily Allen, and the other fine people at Greg Kofford Books, for working so hard and so quickly to prepare this book for production; my children—Rachel, Hilary, and Nick—for remaining supportive of this project despite hearing about it almost from birth; and finally Nancy Kramer, my wife, for believing in the Book of Mormon and in this project, but especially for believing in me.

people untutored in modern methods of scholarship and
ry but nonetheless so "exquisitely tuned to small verbal
tinuity and to significant lexical nuances" in the Hebrew
at Robert Alter, the latter-day champion of the literary ap-
he Bible, can state that today's "literary student of the Bible
o learn from the traditional [rabbinic] commentaries than from
cholarship."[3]

n that these rabbis took seriously the words of the Hebrew
es; assumed that these scriptures formed a coherent, meaningful,
spired whole; and devoted themselves to scrutinizing every aspect
t whole in order to uncover subtle, sometimes hidden messages from
, why would their approach not work well with other scriptures? And
y would it not work especially well with the Book of Mormon, a scrip-
re that, like the Hebrew Scriptures, tells a story of how a group of Jews
ft their homes, journeyed to a far off Promised Land, attempted to create
a "holy nation," sinned under judges as well as kings, received prophetic
warnings of destruction if they did not repent, failed to repent, and were
ultimately dispersed or destroyed along with their capital city? I think it
does, and I think the remarkable way the Book of Mormon responds to
many of the most prominent principles of rabbinic exegesis demonstrates
the strength of my position.

However, as compelling as this single reason may be, there are others.
For one, although very much an ancient document, the Book of Mormon
was designed particularly and prophetically for three groups of readers,
one of whom, almost by definition, approaches scripture rabbinically—
modern Jews. Moroni, the last writer in the Book of Mormon, writing
around 420 C.E., makes this purpose clear right from the beginning. In
his title page, he describes the Book of Mormon as "an abridgment of the
record of the people of Nephi, and also of the Lamanites" written not just
to the descendants of these people and to the Gentiles but to the Jews as
well, "hid up" to come forth later. Mormon, Moroni's father and principal
compiler of the Book of Mormon, similarly affirms that his work is intended to go to Jews, *not* during the fifth century C.E., his time, but much
later, in God's "own due time" (Morm. 3:17–18; 5:12). And Nephi too,
living nearly a thousand years before both Mormon and Moroni, experiences a vision in which he sees the Book of Mormon going forth unto the
Jews in a far distant era, during an age long after Europeans have come to

---

2. Robert Alter, *The World of Biblical Literature*, 142.
3. Robert Alter, *The Art of Biblical Narrative*, 11.

brilliant readers
scientific inqu
signals of cor
Scriptures th
proach to
has more
modern
Giv
Script
and i
of th
Go
wl
tu

Preface

Behold, great and marvelous are the works of the L
are the depths of the mysteries of him; and it is
should find out all his ways. And no man knoweth
be revealed unto him; wherefore, brethren, despise not
God. (Jacob 4:8)

In many ways, the Book of Mormon has little in commo
foundational texts and classic commentaries of rabbinic Judaism. U
Talmud, it was compiled anciently somewhere in the Americas, not l
in Galilee or in Babylonia. Unlike the Mishnah, it was written in refor.
Egyptian, not Hebrew. And unlike Rashi, Ibn Ezra, and Maimonides, .
authors wrote to help persuade their readers to "come unto Christ" (Jacob
1:7), not to encourage them to live lives consistent with the Law of Moses.
(See the glossary in the back of this book for definitions of unfamiliar terms.)
Why then would anyone want to approach the Book of Mormon rabbinically, differing as this tradition does with the Book of Mormon so radically
in time, locale, language, and purpose?

The best and possibly most "rabbinic" answer I can give is "Why not?"
After all, the Talmudic sages (often referred to simply as "the Rabbis"[1])
as well as the classic Jewish commentators were not contemporaries of
Enoch and Abraham, Moses and Joshua, or Samuel and Jeremiah. They
were not people experientially qualified to shed light on biblical culture,
customs, and religious beliefs. Nor were they trained historians, linguists,
or theologians—degreed scholars whose learned opinions represent the
latest discoveries in Near Eastern archeology, anthropology, and societal
concerns. These rabbis came instead to the Hebrew Scriptures simply as

---

1. Stephen M. Wylen, *The Seventy Faces of Torah: The Jewish Way of Reading the Sacred Scriptures*, 28.

the New World, have waged war against its native inhabitants, and have begun to "prosper" (1 Ne. 13:12–20). None of these ancient writers, obviously, had personal experience with modern Jews or were versed in traditional rabbinic approaches to scripture. However, the fact that all of them were so insistent that their work would have special meaning for modern Jews as well as the fact that they consistently ascribed to it a supernatural gift of persuasion, even "the gift and power of God" (1 Ne. 13:39, Morm. 5:13, Title Page), make it hard not to see Moroni, Mormon, and Nephi as effectively daring their readers to employ the traditional rabbinic interpretive techniques modern Jews use as they engage the Book of Mormon.

Granted, few religious Jews today still consider the Talmud, the Mishnah, the Midrash, and the classic rabbinic commentaries to be religiously authoritative. Only the ultra-Orthodox and the Orthodox believe that the substance of these texts was given orally to Moses at the same time and with the same divine sanction as the written Law of Moses. However, as Stephen M. Wylen, a Reform rabbi, writes, the religious customs and traditions of all modern American Jews, "from holiday celebrations to marriage and funeral customs to the ethical ideals they hold dear" are rooted in these rabbinic writings and therefore require at least some knowledge of them.[4] Familiarity with these writings is particularly valued with regard to the way Jews typically approach scripture. As my own experience with Reform and Conservative congregations confirms, even non-Orthodox rabbis frequently quote Talmudic and post-Talmudic rabbis in sermons, classes, and conversations as they explain the Hebrew Scriptures.[5] Furthermore, *Etz Hayim* and other annotated versions of the Pentateuch commonly used by non-Orthodox congregations include copious amounts of rabbinic as well as historic commentary.[6] Jewish study bibles too, such as the fine volumes published by the Jewish Publication Society and Judaica Press, similarly include numerous quotations from rabbinic sources. In addition, popular books on Judaism written by non-Orthodox Jews for non-Orthodox Jews, such as Jewish Lights' "Way Into" series, also repeatedly cite these sources, all of which populate synagogue libraries or are readily available for purchase from Jewish bookstores and web sites.

Again, many of these modern Jews do not agree with everything that Hillel, Akiva, Ibn Ezra, Rashi, and Maimonides have to say. However, most

---

4. Stephen M. Wylen, *Settings of Silver: An Introduction to Judaism*, 194.

5. Rabbi Morris N. Kertzer, *What Is a Jew? A Guide to the Beliefs, Traditions, and Practices of Judaism that Answers Questions for Both Jew and Non-Jew*, 47–50.

6. David L. Lieber, ed., *Etz Hayim*, xx–xxii.

believe that what these rabbis said is still worth knowing and, to some degree, following. As Morris Kertzer, another Reform rabbi, writes, "All modern Jews take Jewish [rabbinic] tradition seriously, but relatively few adhere to it slavishly. It is our guide from out of the past, to be consulted as we solve problems of the present."[7] Consequently, many Jews today not only study what the ancient rabbis said about the Hebrew Scriptures but approach the Hebrew Scriptures in similar ways. As Rabbi Kertzer continues:

> [We] Jews spend a long time on a page. We do not read rapidly through a biblical text, so much as we read a single verse or two, and then let our eyes meander through various commentaries on the page, playing with the various ways Jews in times past have read the passage before us. . . . [In this way] any given page of the book in our hands is like a guided tour through the inner landscape of the collective Jewish soul: all the way from the ancient Aramaic alternative version of the biblical text itself, to the medieval mystics and rationalists, with stop-off points in classical rabbinic sources along the way.[8]

Given this modern Jewish connection to the rabbinic tradition, it only makes sense to me that a scripture such as the Book of Mormon that is written expressly to modern Jews would connect with the rabbinic tradition—especially since the Book of Mormon applauds such an approach and invites its Gentile readers to learn it and use it as they study the Book of Mormon. Certainly, according to Jacob, one of Nephi's younger brothers, the way some ancient Jews came to their prophetic writings is definitely not to be followed. However, Jacob makes it clear that this group of Jews is limited to ancient, pre-exilic Jews and does not extend to modern or even medieval post-exilic Jews. Using the past or completed tense, Jacob restricts his condemnation to those Jews he had left behind, people who had lived in Jerusalem before his family left that city (sometime after 600 B.C.E.), long before he wrote his book. According to him, it was these inhabitants of the soon-to-be-dispersed Kingdom of Judah who "*were* a stiffnecked people," who "*despised* the words of plainness, and *killed* the prophets, and *sought* for things that they could not understand." It was therefore these ancient Judahites, not later Jews, whom he describes as spiritually blind and who looked "beyond the mark." As he continues, still using the past tense, "for God *hath taken away* his plainness from them, and *delivered* unto them many things which they cannot understand, because they *desired* it" (Jacob 4:14).

---

7. Morris H. Kertzer, *What Is a Jew? A Guide to the Beliefs, Traditions, and Practices of Judaism that Answers Questions for Both Jew and Non-Jew,* 56.

8. Ibid., 56–57.

Nephi too condemns these ancient pre-exilic Jews and uses the past tense to affirm that their "works *were* works of darkness, and their doings *were* doings of abominations" (2 Ne. 25:2). However, Nephi makes it clear that the evils of that generation were not passed on to their descendants, especially those evils that interfered with correct scriptural comprehension. Changing to the ongoing or "incomplete" present tense, Nephi in this same chapter prophetically confirms that later, post-exilic Jews indeed "*do* understand the things of the prophets." In fact their scriptural comprehension is so advanced that Nephi claims that "there *is* none other people that *understand* the things which were spoken unto the Jews like unto them, save it be that they are taught after the manner of the things of the Jews" (2 Ne. 25:5). Since the Book of Mormon is one of those "things" written expressly to modern Jews, it follows that Nephi is here saying that the Book of Mormon should also be approached in a distinctly Jewish manner, both by Jews and by non-Jews who are familiar with this approach.

Beholding the Tree of Life is, consequently, an attempt to do just that, to accept Nephi's invitation to study the Book of Mormon in an ancient and yet contemporary Jewish way. In it, I endeavor to approach the Book of Mormon in a manner that is consistent with the way many religiously serious modern Jews approach their scriptures—rabbinically, using principles put forth by the Talmudic sages, developed by classic medieval Jewish commentators, and emphasized by many contemporary rabbis. Since such an approach is by its very nature both particularistic and holistic, I have divided this book into two parts: one primarily concerned with the textual details of the Book of Mormon and the other with the way the Book of Mormon fits into a larger biblical context. In Chapter One, I introduce several key principles prominent in the rabbinic interpretive tradition and contrast this more literary approach with the more quotation-centered approach suggested by the New Testament. In Chapter Two, I begin to examine the Book of Mormon according to these principles, especially the way the Talmudic and post-Talmudic rabbis approached the Torah inclusively using four distinct hermeneutical levels: the simple level, the allegorical level, the sermonic level, and the mystical level. In Chapter Three, I scrutinize the Book of Mormon's *words* closely according to the first of these interpretive levels. As several Talmudic sages and classic commentators often did with regards to the Torah, I look for phrasings in the Book of Mormon that may seem odd, contradictory, redundant, or simply out of place, and I approach these phrasings not as mistakes or as problems but as prompts to dig more deeply into the text and discover divine messages that would have remained hidden otherwise. In Chapter Four, I acknowledge the help of others in my scriptural efforts, particularly the way the three most prominent writers of the Book of Mormon—Nephi, Mormon, and Moroni—accompany their readers in the text and engage them in a kind of scriptural conversation, again much as Talmudic and post-Talmudic rabbis advised their readers to do when they studied the Hebrew Scriptures.

In Part 2, Chapters Five through Ten, I then build upon these rabbinic techniques to place the Book of Mormon in a similar dialogue with the Hebrew Scriptures. In these chapters, I follow the practice recommended by the Talmudic and post-Talmudic rabbis and join these two sacred volumes together much as readings from the Torah and the Prophets are connected in Jewish congregational readings. And finally in the conclusion, I emphasize that I am presenting my work as a beginning of a discussion, as an introduction of a new and extremely productive way of looking at the Book of Mormon, and not as the ultimate statement of how approaching the Book of Mormon rabbinically could or should work.

My purpose, therefore, in writing this book is not so much to describe in any thoroughgoing or comprehensive way the entire sweep and complexity of rabbinic thought as it relates to the scriptures; rather, it is to extract from this tradition several of its most prominent principles and explain them in such a way as to help readers of the Book of Mormon use these principles to enhance their experience with that sacred book. In this way, I follow the work of Rabbi Norman J. Cohen, Rabbi Avigdor Bonchek, Rabbi Stephen M. Wylen, Rabbi George Robinson, and Rabbi Jacob Neusner (all of whom are frequently quoted in this book) and other Jewish scholars who attempt to similarly educate and equip their readers regarding their study of the Torah. Just as Shubert Spero, professor of Jewish Thought at Bar-Ilan University, said of Rabbi Bonchek's book *Studying the Torah*, I hope this book will be a kind of "do-it-yourself guide" that will lead both "seasoned scholars as well as beginners"[9] to a deeper investigation and appreciation of the Book of Mormon.

Along these lines, I wish to stress that in no way do I consider myself someone who has "mastered" modern Judaism or its foundational texts in any sort of complete or comprehensive sense. I have certainly studied both for many years. However, as a Mormon who has read many books about my own faith by authors who do not share it, I am acutely aware of how off-base outsiders can sometimes be despite decades of honest,

---

9. Avigdor Bonchek, *Studying the Torah: A Guide to In-Depth Interpretation*, back cover.

thorough, and dedicated academic research. I have therefore attempted to augment my "book learning" by attending countless Jewish services, classes, lectures, meetings, and informal get-togethers; as a result, I am not only pleased to count many Jews as close personal friends, but I feel that I have developed a working sense of how some modern Jews approach the Hebrew Scriptures. Nevertheless, I still cannot say that I know *everything* about this very old and very complex tradition. Neither am I certain as to what *all* Jews think about anything, much less their scriptures. It has become very apparent to me that Jews today are such an extremely independent-minded and diverse people that anyone, including fellow Jews, who claims to represent all of them is almost certainly wrong. Consequently, my readers should remember that although the principles put forth in this book generally describe the rabbinic tradition and generally represent how it is understood today, there is much more to this tradition than is contained in this book.

My readers should also be aware that although I am using the term "rabbinic" in this somewhat general, inclusive way, I am also using it in a technical, exclusive sense as well. Strictly speaking, "rabbinic Judaism" refers to that Judaism that considers the Talmud and other related writings religiously authoritative or important.[10] Consequently, Orthodox, ultra-Orthodox, Conservative, Reform, and Reconstructionist Jews are rabbinic, but Karaites, Sabbateans, Frankists, and other Jewish groups that reject the Talmud are not. In addition, since rabbinic Judaism began after the destruction of the Second Temple in 70 C.E., when the tradition reflected in the Talmud was taking shape,[11] all of the various groups that existed before that time are also not rabbinic: not the Alexandrine Jews of Philo's time, not the Jews who were members of the Dead Sea Scroll sect, not the Essenes, the Zealots, or the Sadducees. Even the Pharisees, a group that in many ways served as precursors of rabbinic Jews, are not, strictly speaking, rabbinic Jews. And neither are the Jews of the First Temple—Isaiah, Ezekiel, Jeremiah, Josiah, Hezekiah, Solomon, and David—nor the "pre-Jews" that came before them—Adam, Enoch, Noah, Abraham, Isaac, Jacob, and Joseph—nor the Jews of the Book of Mormon—Lehi, Nephi, Enos, Jarom, Mosiah, and the rest.

---

10. Bernard J. Bamberger, *The Story of Judaism*, 107–8.

11. For a brief introduction to the origins of Rabbinic Judaism as well as the Post-Talmudic era, see Jacob Neusner, *Understanding Rabbinic Judaism: From Talmudic to Modern Times*, 11–23.

To be perfectly clear, although I very much see the text of the Book of Mormon as responding to and even encouraging the use of many fundamental rabbinic interpretive techniques, I do *not* believe that the Book of Mormon writers knew of or consciously employed these techniques in their writings. The rabbinic interpretive approach discussed in this book was developed long after many of these Book of Mormon writers were dead and gone. However, these techniques represent universal principles of effective reading that have been specifically *adapted* for scriptural narratives, and as such they are extremely helpful in approaching the Book of Mormon. In addition to unearthing valuable messages buried deep under layers of divine meaning, these techniques also encourage a better understanding of and a closer relationship with God through aesthetics. By sensitizing readers to the subtle artistry of God's words and by encouraging them to continually explore that artistry, these techniques not only enable readers to potentially receive additional information from God, but they promote an ever increasing appreciation of the love and care and beauty that is behind them. If human beings were indeed created to experience divine joy, as the Book of Mormon states (2 Ne. 2:25), then studying the scriptures in this way can become a way of experiencing that joy and delighting in the scriptures (4:15).

In this book, I present a number of quotations from rabbinic sources. For quotations from the Babylonian Talmud, I have relied on the translation edited by Isadore Epstein and published by Soncino Press.[12] For those from the Mishnah and the Tosefta, I have used versions of these works translated by Jacob Neusner.[13] Following standard practice, I have identified each of these quotations using the tractate it comes from as well as the folio it appears in (for example, Megillah 63a). However, since all three of these works follow the same basic organization and use the same tractate names, I have tried to clarify the source of each quotation by prefacing it with either "BT" for the Babylonian Talmud, "TO" for the Tosefta, or "MI" for the Mishnah. As a result, readers can easily find these quotations in other versions of these rabbinic works. Since Pirkei Avot is often treated as a separate work despite the fact that much of it appears in the Mishnah, I have elected to treat it separately and have used William

---

12. I. Epstein, ed., *The Babylonian Talmud* (London, Soncino Press, 1935–48).

13. Jacob Neusner, *The Tosefta: Translated from the Hebrew with a New Introduction* (Peabody, Mass.: Hendrickson Publishers 2002); and Jacob Neusner, *The Mishnah: A New Translation* (New Haven: Yale University Press, 1988).

Berkson's translation, without identifying it as part of the Mishnah.[14] References to it include chapter and verse (for example, Pirke Avot 1:6) and can be used to locate quotations in other versions. Quotations from other rabbinic sources that cannot be easily found in translation (such as Numbers Rabbah and Pesiktah Rabbah) include references to anthologies and other works where they can be found.

In addition, my readers should also understand that I rely solely on the King James Version of the Bible for my biblical quotations. I do so *not* because I believe this version to be the most accurate, most clear, or most popular translation (especially for modern Jews), but because the Book of Mormon was originally translated into a style very similar to King James English, and therefore the ties between its text and that of the Hebrew Scriptures are most evident when shown in connection with this version. When I divert from this practice or my sources use other versions, I make this plain either in the text or in a footnote. All emphases or italicized words within scriptural quotations are my own.

I also, as is already apparent, do not use the term "Old Testament" in the book. I prefer the term "Hebrew Scriptures." Inherent within the term "Old Testament," as many Jews have pointed out, is an insinuation that Genesis, Exodus, Leviticus, and the rest are worn out, used up, irrelevant, and obsolete. These old books have seemingly been replaced by the more up-to-date gospels and epistles of the New Testament and are therefore not worth the close scrutiny and reverence the rabbinic tradition has historically lavished on them. Since this book attempts to use many of the techniques from that tradition that were developed specifically to reveal the ongoing relevance and beauty of these ancient books, it seems inappropriate to use this traditional Christian term, and it certainly runs counter to the deep respect and regard I have for them.

---

14. William Berkson, *Pirke Avot: Timeless Wisdom for Modern Life* (Philadelphia: The Jewish Publication Society, 2010).

Part 1

Contemplating the Branches

Chapter One

The Fruit and the Tree

And after I [Lehi] had traveled for the space of many hours in darkness, I began to pray unto the Lord that he would have mercy on me, according to the multitude of his tender mercies. And it came to pass after I had prayed unto the Lord I beheld a large and spacious field. And it came to pass that I beheld a tree, whose fruit was desirable to make one happy. And it came to pass that I did go forth and partake of the fruit thereof; and I beheld that it was most sweet, above all that I ever before tasted. Yea, and I beheld that the fruit thereof was white, to exceed all the whiteness that I had ever seen. And as I partook of the fruit thereof it filled my soul with exceedingly great joy; wherefore, I began to be desirous that my family should partake of it also; for I knew that it was desirable above all other fruit. . . . And it came to pass that I beckoned unto them; and I also did say unto them with a loud voice that they should come unto me, and partake of the fruit, which was desirable above all other fruit. (1 Ne. 8:8–12, 15)

Although Lehi's dream is not often associated with a specific scriptural approach, it resonates well with the quotation-centered approach suggested in the New Testament. Scripture is, after all, according to that testament, "a more sure word of prophecy" that when seen clearly becomes "a light that shineth in a dark place" (2 Pet. 1:19). Its words can be perceived as "sweet" (Rev. 10:9), and they can be received with joy as well as with understanding (Matt. 13:20, 23). Moreover, scripture exists to be harvested, in small amounts, and shared with family, friends, and associates, nourishing them spiritually and making them "wise unto salvation" (2 Tim. 3:15). Not to be used for personal or for "private interpretation," it is rather to be used openly, pedagogically, rhetorically, sermonically "for doctrine, for reproof, for correction, for instruction in righteousness" (2 Pet. 1:20, 2 Tim. 3:16). Scripture, in other words, much like Lehi's fruit, represents the "words of eternal life" (John 6:68), which, when distributed freely to others, enable them to come unto God and make their "abode" with him forever (John 14:23).

In keeping with these suggestions, many modern followers of the New Testament "go forth and partake" of the Scriptures, just as Lehi did his heavenly fruit. They scan their Bibles, diligently and devotedly, amassing short, powerful quotations—verses of the day, daily inspirations, and proselyting passages—that enable them to "open [their mouths] boldly," to "make known the mystery of the gospel," and to stand "against principalities, against powers, against the rulers of the darkness of this world, [and] against spiritual wickedness in high places" (Eph. 6:12, 19). Just as the fruit in Lehi's dream both motivates and empowers Lehi to preach unto his children and bid them to "keep the commandments of the Lord" (1 Ne. 8:38), so do these scriptural quotations likewise give their readers "utterance" and enable them "to make known the mystery of the gospel" to all the world (Eph. 6:19).

The Book of Mormon and
the Quotation-centered Approach to Scripture

Given that the Book of Mormon has been subtitled "Another Testament of Jesus Christ," it comes as no surprise that it responds well to a quotation-centered approach. As with the New Testament, scanning the Book of Mormon, even cursorily, yields a multitude of short, impressive statements, which Mormons often memorize and even "master" so that they can repeat them as occasion requires. These statements include divine promises such as "Inasmuch as ye shall keep my commandments ye shall prosper in the land" (2 Ne. 1:20); inspiring resolutions such as Nephi's commitment to "go and do the things which the Lord hath commanded" (1 Ne. 3:7); theological insights such as "Adam fell that men might be; and men are, that they might have joy" (2 Ne. 2:25); as well as ringing assertions such as "wickedness never was happiness" (Alma 41:10) and "charity is the pure love of Christ" (Moro. 7:47).

However, despite the obvious productivity of a quotation-centered approach and its utility in sermons, speeches, and other religious communications, it fails to do justice to the Book of Mormon. After all, the Book of Mormon was not created from or designed around aurally impressive quotations, as was the New Testament. It does not contain gospels, works assembled from oral sources containing "individual incidents from the lifetime of Jesus in set short forms" that, as E. P. Sanders explains, were passed on verbally by preachers in order to communicate single points;[1] nor does it involve ancient epistles, letters written long ago to be read out loud to an equally ancient and overwhelmingly illiterate group of listeners in churches.[2] The Book of Mormon was instead compiled from written sources, carefully preserved, and composed prophetically to be read silently, thoughtfully, reflectively, and repeatedly by very literate and very modern *readers* in a much more private and personal setting—a quiet place where one can "remember how merciful the Lord hath been unto the children of men, from the creation of Adam even down until the time that [they] shall receive these things," "ponder these things" in their hearts, ask God to "manifest the truth of it," and receive an answer "by the power of the Holy Ghost" (Moro. 10:3–4).

From its very beginning, the Book of Mormon was conceived of as a *literary* work compiled from *literary* sources arranged in a *literary* way for a *literate* audience. As soon as Lehi and his family reached their promised land, Nephi was commanded to make "plates of ore that [he] might engraven upon them the record of [his] people." His was to be a record that included "the record of [his] father," "[his] journeyings in the wilderness," his prophecies, as well as "many of [Nephi's] own prophecies" (1 Ne. 19:1). These plates were then passed down from generation to generation, with each recipient responsible for writing in them "their wars, and their contentions, and the reigns of their kings" (Jacob 3:13) until these plates were finally collected, edited, summarized, and added to by Mormon and his son Moroni.

This "abridgement," as Mormon and Moroni called their work (W of M 1:3; Morm. 5:9), however, was not presented publically to congregations of people in their day. Working on the brink of their civilization's destruction, Mormon and Moroni purposely put together a book to be read centuries later by modern readers, by themselves, or with a few close companions (Morm. 3:17–19). It, along with the other writings that they included with their abridgment, was not a work addressed to plurals, Jews and Gentiles, but to singulars, "Jew and Gentile" (Title Page), individual people who are "alike unto God" (2 Ne. 26:33) and for whom Nephi, especially, has charity (2 Ne. 33:8). The Book of Mormon therefore details

---

1. E. P. Sanders, *The Historical Figure of Jesus*, 59–60.

2. For brief discussions on literacy in the ancient world and on how scriptures were used in the ancient Christian church, see Bart D. Ehrman, *The New Testament: A Historical Introduction to the Early Christian Writings*, 54; Robert A. Spivey, D. Moody Smith Jr., and C. Clifton Black, *Anatomy of the New Testament*, 7–8.

the errors of an ancient age in the form of a story to be read by individuals so that "the fulness of the wrath of God" may not come upon them as it did upon the former "inhabitants of the land" (Ether 2:11).

In other words, the Book of Mormon was, as Richard D. Rust writes, "not only planned with a purpose but shaped artistically so that form and content are totally integrated."[3] It includes subtle narrative, epic, poetic, and other literary elements that can only be appreciated as one reads and rereads the book reflectively, carefully, and holistically. The Book of Mormon's deepest treasures are simply not apparent when it is quoted solely in small swatches over a podium or from a lectern. For instance, the effectiveness of quoting King Benjamin's famous statement, "when ye are in the service of your fellow beings ye are only in the service of your God" (Mosiah 2:17) is, to a large degree, dependent upon when it was given, why it was given, and by whom. Here King Benjamin has commanded his people to be gathered together "to hear the words which [he] should speak unto them" (2:1). He has seen "that he must very soon go the way of all the earth; therefore, he thought it expedient that he should confer the kingdom upon one of his sons" (1:9). King Benjamin, in other words, is delivering a coronation speech, perhaps his last speech, and is therefore summarizing the accomplishments of his reign as well as offering advice to his successor. As a result, much of the power of this statement derives from the fact that it was uttered by a "holy man" at the end of his life, a righteous ruler who "did fight with the strength of his own arm" in defense of his people and labored "with all the might of his body and the faculty of his whole soul" to rid them of the many contentions that existed "among his own people" (W of M 1:12, 18).

King Benjamin is then a walking explanation of what this statement means and what following it can accomplish. Not only did he establish "peace in the land" after many years of war (W of M 1:12–18), but he did so by seeking neither "gold nor silver nor any manner of riches." He did not make slaves of his people or force them to serve him but instead labored with his own hands and taught his people "that [they] should keep the commandments of the Lord" (Mosiah 2:12–14). Furthermore, the fact that King Benjamin made this statement to his son Mosiah, who eventually abolished the rule of kings in favor of a more egalitarian system of judges, transforms Benjamin's words from one man's secret of success into a divine law of governance—a law made more clear during the course

---

3. Richard Dilworth Rust, *Feasting on the Word: The Literary Testimony of the Book of Mormon*, 2.

of the Book of Mormon by the examples of kings who did not follow it. King Noah, for instance, a near contemporary of Benjamin's, "did not keep the commandments of God" and laid a heavy tax on his people in order to "support himself, and his wives and his concubines" (Mosiah 11:2–4). He also used this tax to build "many elegant and spacious buildings" including "a spacious palace" for himself with an ornamented "throne in the midst thereof" (vv. 8–9). And as a result, King Noah's people failed to enjoy peace as Benjamin's people did and instead endured much war, internal strife, and captivity—all harbingers of the "continual round of murder and bloodshed" (Morm. 8:8) that eventually envelops the Book of Mormon peoples in the end.

In other words, the Book of Mormon is simply too much of a *book* to be approached simply as a source of quotations. It is a sophisticated literary work where ideas do not exist in isolation, but such things as characterization, setting, description, plot, as well as their placement in the canon relative to other scriptures must be considered in order to be fully understood and appreciated. The Book of Mormon consequently demands a comprehensive, in-depth literary approach. Simply "partaking" of its wisdom in short quotations, as Lehi's dream seemingly suggests, is not enough. Something more extensive is required.

The Book of Mormon and the Rabbinic Approach to Scripture

It is therefore significant that Lehi's dream is not the only visionary experience in the Book of Mormon with scriptural implications, nor is a quotation-centered approach the only scriptural approach the Book of Mormon responds to. Nephi's vision—the way he prepares for it, views it, engages it, and discusses it, as well as what he ultimately gains from it—resonates remarkably with the more literary approach initiated by Talmudic rabbis, developed by medieval rabbis, and promoted by many contemporary rabbis today. In fact, the way Nephi describes his vision actually encourages his readers to apply several of the more prominent and enduring principles of this approach to the Book of Mormon—principles which open the Book of Mormon up in extraordinary, even revolutionary, ways.

The Scriptures Require Sustained Mental Effort in Order to Be Understood

For instance, Nephi does not begin his visionary experience by having it suddenly thrust upon him without any personal preparation or effort, as it apparently did with Lehi. Instead, he actually initiates this process himself by seemingly going off somewhere private where he can sit, "pondering in [his] heart" his father's dream. Only then, after expending a certain amount of mental effort, is Nephi "caught away in the Spirit of the Lord, [to] an exceedingly high mountain," where he experiences his own vision (1 Ne. 11:1).

Nephi's deliberative approach to his father's vision is similar to the way that later rabbis advised their students to come to the Torah. Faced with the destruction of the Second Temple in 70 c.e., Jewish sages such as Johanan ben Zakkai, Gamaliel the Elder, and Eliezer ben Hyrcanus retreated to outlying towns to found not new temples, places where animal sacrifices could again be offered, but academies, schools where prayer and intense scripture study replaced those sacrifices as the preferred form of Jewish worship.[4] There, in a *yeshivah,* (pl. *yeshivot*)—a Hebrew word meaning "seated"[5]—generations of students were taught that they must "turn" the Torah over and over, like fertile soil, because everything is in the Torah, and therefore they should "grow old and gray with [the Torah]" and never leave off its study (Pirke Avot 5:25).[6] In addition, these students were given the literary tools and techniques that enabled them to follow these admonitions and continue their studies, with others, in their homes and in their synagogues.[7] In other words, at the very beginning of rabbinic Judaism, at a time when the role of the rabbi was just being established and the movement was just starting to spread, pondering the scriptures, as Nephi did—deeply, thoughtfully, and continually—was not only set up as one of rabbinic Judaism's most central values, but it was supported and reinforced by the establishment of an institution that would ensure its centrality for generations to come.

And this deliberative approach to the scriptures was extremely productive. Here in these early rabbinic academies, the scriptural discussions occurred that formed the Mishnah, the "Constitution" of the rabbinic

---

4. Paul Johnson, *A History of the Jews,* 149.

5. Moshe Beer, "Academies in Babylonia and Erez Israel," 1:347.

6. See George Robinson, *Essential Judaism: A Complete Guide to Beliefs, Customs, and Rituals,* 156–57.

7. Jacob Neusner, *The Way of Torah: An Introduction to Judaism,* 86.

movement, and, later as the rabbinic movement spread to Babylon, Europe, and elsewhere, the institutional descendants of these first *yeshivot* generated the Gemara, the classic exposition and elaboration of that constitution, as well as the classic commentaries of Rashi, the Tosafists, Maimonides (through his father),[8] and virtually every other important rabbinic writer.[9] As a result, Nephi-like pondering of the scriptures spread throughout the Jewish world, producing at least one Nephi-like vision. The Talmud, for instance, recounts, somewhat imaginatively, how Moses was once mystically conveyed like Nephi forward in time, not to an unknown mountain, but to Rabbi Akiva's first-century classroom. There Moses took a seat on the back, "at the end of the eighth row," and waited to hear what Akiva had to say. Moses was convinced that even this legendary teacher had nothing to teach him. But Moses was wrong. As Akiva lectured on the significance of the tiny decorative flourishes, called "crowns," atop certain Hebrew letters in the Torah, Moses became depressed. He knew nothing about these flourishes and, according to the story, began to feel small and weak in Akiva's presence. However, when a student asked Akiva how he knew what he was saying was true, Akiva, without hesitation, declared, "This is a teaching which was delivered to Moses on Sinai." Much as Nephi undoubtedly was when he heard how his writings would help the seed of his brethren despite the fact that he did "not know the meaning of all things" (1 Ne. 11:17; 13:35–37), Moses drew strength from Akiva's statement and "was quieted" (BT Menachot 29b).

The Scriptures Should Be Read Closely and Everything about Them Should Be Pondered and Thoroughly Considered

Granted, visions and visitations were rare in these early academies, even as imaginary events. However, the idea that intense scripture study yielded additional divine information was not. One of the reasons intense scripture study was so fruitful was that it was applied to every aspect of the Torah, not just to certain topics or special areas of interest. As suggested by the previous story, the Talmudic rabbis, as well as their medieval descendants, wholeheartedly accepted the biblical statement that God—not Moses or Ezra or some unknown "Redactor"—wrote the entire Torah (Ex. 34:1). Consequently, they believed that the Torah was "omnisignificant,"

---

8. Joel L. Kraemer, *Maimonides: The Life and World of One of Civilization's Greatest Minds*, 59–60.

9. Mordechai Breuer, Simha Assaf, and Adin Steinsaltz, "Yeshivot," 315–21.

as Michael L. Satlow writes, meaning that the Torah even "at its very finest detail encapsulated the divine message."[10] As Rabbi Noson Gurary, a modern Orthodox inheritor of this tradition, explains, not only are the Torah's basic ideas or "inner content" God's, but "every letter and every word is God's" as well.[11] Even Rabbi Norman J. Cohen, who, as a Reform Jew, does not ascribe the totality of the Torah to God, similarly stresses that each "element of [its] text—every word and action, even gaps in the text—possesses potential significance for the reader."[12] In other words, for these rabbis nothing about the Torah is insignificant or trivial. Everything about it is brimming with important information, but it is available only to those readers diligent enough to discover it.

Nephi, like these rabbis, similarly approaches Lehi's vision holistically, as a complete package. He believes "*all* the words of [his] father" and is therefore not content merely to taste the fruit his father spoke of. He instead desires to "see, and hear, and know" everything, all "the things which [his] father saw" (1 Ne. 10:17; 11:3). Consequently, at his request he is shown not just the fruit but the tree that bore the fruit (11:7), the rod of iron that led to it (v. 25), the spacious building that opposed it (v. 35), and the river of water that protected it (12:16). Furthermore, Nephi sees these things in detail, including some items, such as the "filthiness" of the river's water, that Lehi missed because his mind was "swallowed up in other things" (15:27). For Nephi, everything about his father's vision, like the Rabbis' Torah, is meaningful and full of divine significance.

The Scriptures Should Be Read Deeply on Several Levels and from Many Perspectives

However, despite the breadth of his vision, Nephi is not content to superficially view the many elements of his father's vision, without acquiring a full understanding and appreciation of them. He desires "to know the interpretation thereof" (1 Ne. 11:11). Thus, the Spirit guiding Nephi through his vision grants Nephi's wish and explains that the Tree of Life represents "the love of God," the rod of iron "the word of God," the great and spacious building "the pride of the world" (vv. 25, 36), and so forth. Nonetheless, despite the seeming finality of these explanations, the Spirit continues, augmenting many of these "one-to-one" interpretations with

---

10. Michael L. Satlow, *How the Bible Became Holy*, 268.

11. Noson Gurary, *The Thirteen Principles of Faith: A Chasidic Viewpoint*, 131.

12. Norman J. Cohen, *The Way Into Torah*, 74.

others on different, complementary levels. The Spirit, for instance, also connects the tree with the birth of "the Son of God, after the manner of the flesh" (v. 18) and expands the meaning of the rod of iron christologically to include the ministry and death of "the Redeemer of the world" (vv. 27–33). The Spirit similarly sees other visionary elements as prefiguring the fate of Lehi's descendants—their ascendancy, their near destruction, and finally their reclamation and resurgence—as well as the future of the House of Israel and its relation to the Gentiles.

In other words, Nephi gets much more out of this vision than he bargained for. He receives not just a simple equating of dream symbols to abstract ideas or interpretations related to his family and their immediate situation. He instead experiences an additional elucidation so vast and multi-leveled that in the end he could only write "a small part of the things which [he] saw" (1 Ne. 14:28). Nephi, as a result, is left to ponder his experience and trust that others will come along later who will appreciate it more fully and describe the meanings of the things he saw "in their purity" (vv. 24–26).

The Talmudic rabbis and their descendants similarly got much more than they bargained for from their scriptural studies, and the rabbinic tradition, as it developed and grew, is consequently awash with interpretive currents ebbing and flowing and intermingling with each other. Pre-talmudic Jewish sages, such a Philo, emphasized the allegorical meaning of the Torah. Talmudic rabbis, on the other hand, frequently stressed its homiletic meaning and attempted to solve textual concerns using imaginative stories that connect the details of the Torah to everyday life. Early medieval commentators, perhaps in response to Christian typological readings of the Old Testament, often concentrated on the plain, or simple, meaning of the text,[13] while Kabbalists focused on the Torah's mystical meaning and advocated an approach where readers experience the divine directly, through visions and ecstatic feelings. However, despite the differences of these approaches, never were they used exclusively, by themselves, without connection to the others, and never were the other approaches condemned, ignored, or presented as invalid.

Because these early rabbis believed that the Torah was written by God and not by human beings, they considered it capable of responding to an unlimited number of approaches at once and could therefore yield an infinite number of valid, divinely inspired meanings all at the same

---

13. See Esra Shereshevsky, *Rashi: The Man and His World*, 61–64.

time. Consequently, although historically there has frequently been in rabbinic Judaism a greater emphasis on one interpretative approach over others during certain eras, there has never been an effort to censor or otherwise restrict the other approaches. Even today, when the "historical-critical" approach espoused by university-trained professors and biblical scholars has gained ground even within Orthodox Judaism,[14] these other approaches remain in the Jewish exegetical "toolbox," as it were, providing handy mechanisms that continue to be helpful in prying out meaning from the Torah and exposing its treasures.

For instance, early rabbis frequently pondered why the Torah begins with the letter ב, the second letter in the Hebrew alphabet, and not א, the first. One Talmudic sage focused on the letter's shape, specifically how it is closed on all sides except for the left (Hebrew reads from right to left). He suggested, as Rabbi Wilfred Shuchat writes, that this letter showed that humans should not speculate as to what is "above or below, what is before or after and what is behind, but only on the day of creation and onwards." Another took a different approach and concentrated on this letter's numerical value and opined that since ב had a numerical value of 2, its usage here was to "teach that there are two worlds—this world and the world to come." A third rabbi, while not disagreeing with the first two, looked at the problem holistically, by connecting it with other words in the Torah that started with ב. He suggested that because the Hebrew word for blessing also begins with this letter, starting with ב therefore "connotes blessing"; while starting with א, the first letter in the word for cursing, would have connected the Creation with cursing. A fourth rabbi built upon this idea and added to it a contemporary context. For him, the blessedness associated with ב counters heretical Christian ideas concerning the fall of Adam and Eve and preemptively demonstrated that the world was not "created with the language of cursing." Finally, a fifth rabbi took a more folksy approach and told a story about how א was saddened by its position in the Torah. It complained to God and asserted that it was not right that it, the first letter, was not used to create the world. To this complaint, God responded, "The world and its fullness were created for the sake of the Torah alone. Tomorrow, when I come to give My Torah at Sinai, I will commence with none but you," a reference to the first word in Exodus 20:2, which begins with א.[15]

---

14. Marc Zvi Brettler, *How to Read the Bible*, 3–5.
15. Wilfred Shuchat, *The Creation According to the Midrash Rabbah*, 46–49.

These rabbis could have gone on, and in fact these rabbinical successors did, suggesting additional answers to this and other questions from perspectives not previously considered. However, although some of their answers may seem more satisfying than others, it is important to note that there was no effort on the part of these rabbis to pronounce one scriptural suggestion superior to another or to expunge it from the literature. These rabbis simply required each interpretation to be securely rooted in the text and in so doing set up an exegetical tradition of *inclusion*, an approach that embraces many later efforts to allegorize, sermonize, rationalize, and even mystify the Torah. Again, since the Torah is God's direct creation, these rabbis believed that it participates in God's power and therefore conveys an unlimited number of divine messages. As Rabbi Ishmael taught anciently: "Like a hammer that breaketh the rock in pieces . . . so also may one Biblical verse convey many teachings (BT Sanhedrin 34a).

For this reason, the Talmudic rabbis described the Torah as having at least seventy "faces" or facets (Numbers Rabbah 13:15), an idea that continues to be promoted by many rabbis today. Rabbi Stephen M. Wylen, a modern Reform rabbi, explains:

> The image of the seventy faces may be taken from the imagery of a jeweler's art. Each side of a cut gem is called a facet, a little face. A light sparkles within every fine gemstone. We know that this light is a reflection, but the ancients thought of the light in a gemstone as originating from within the stone. The beauty and fascination of a fine gem is that the one stone sparkled in so many different ways. We know that there is a single light within the stone, but we see that light differently depending upon which face we gaze upon. One diamond is like seventy different diamonds as we turn it, but of course it is one. In the same way there is only one God, whose light shines forth from every verse in the Torah. We see that light differently depending upon how we interpret the verse. The unitary light of God's Holy Spirit is fully revealed in many sparkles and flashes, as we seek God through a multitude of interpretations on every single verse of Scripture.[16]

Within rabbinic Judaism, each interpretative approach has value in and of itself. It in no way competes with or negates other approaches. In this way, the rabbinic tradition is indeed a *tradition*, a collection of inheritances from the past, and not an evolution where one approach is supplanted by the latest, most fashionable approach. Certainly, modifications and refinements were made, but for the most part, all these different forms of scriptural interpretation exist together, complementing each other,

---

16. Stephen M. Wylen, *Seventy Faces: The Jewish Way of Reading Sacred Scripture*, 63.

uniting together to provide a broader, fuller, ever-expanding understanding of God and his purposes. In other words, within rabbinic Judaism there is no one single "approved" approach—something the Spirit showed Nephi as well.

The Scriptures Should Be Read with Others and in Connection with Other Books

Given the endless possibilities that the "seventy faces" of the Torah allow, one has to wonder if such an approach is not an invitation to frustration as well as to confusion. After all, with so many ways of interpreting scripture to choose from, where does one begin? And how does one do this appropriately, without losing all connection to the text? These are real concerns. However, just as Nephi had the Spirit to instruct him and lead him forward in his understanding of his father's dream, so the Talmudic rabbis and their successors put into place guides, personal as well as literary, that must be consulted in order to interpret scripture legitimately.

Certainly, the early *yeshivot* went far in directing their students toward valid and valuable interpretations. In addition to supplying their students with rigorous curricula and experienced teachers, people who could pass down important scriptural discoveries to the next generation, they paired their students with other students of comparable ability and encouraged them to question each other's interpretations. As Rabbi Joshua ben Perachiah anciently advised his Torah students, "Choose for yourself a mentor, acquire for yourself a *friend*; and judge every person in a favorable light" (Pirke Avot 1:6). This "study buddy" arrangement combined with effective teaching consequently virtually guaranteed a close reading of the Torah text as well as interpretations based on sound principles.

In addition, the Talmudic rabbis sought to limit the heights scriptural speculation could go by grounding their studies in the firm soil of real life. As they saw it, one of the main purposes of Torah study was to comprehend God's laws so thoroughly and so completely that one could implement them accurately and appropriately on a daily basis. They therefore approached the Torah, at least initially, as a set of instructions (what the word *torah*, actually means in Hebrew) providing practical, down-to-earth advice. This may sound simple. However, it is not. One cannot just compile all of the laws in the Torah into a kind of commandment "crib sheet," which one can follow line by line as one would a set of answers to a test. Several of the Torah's commandments are quite sweeping and somewhat vague. The commandment to "love thy neighbour as thyself" (Lev. 19:18), for instance, does not explain exactly how that love is to be expressed or who precisely one's neighbor is. In addition, other laws that may seem fairly specific—laws concerning diet, ritual washings, contracts, marriages, sacrificial offerings, and the like—but are in fact not specific at all. For instance, although the Torah is very clear that the Sabbath is to be a day of rest, it is not nearly so forthcoming as to how one actually accomplishes this. For this reason, the Talmudic rabbis developed over time an "oral law," a compilation of traditions (including "minority opinions") that they inherited, discussed, added to, mostly concerning everyday matters—the sowing of seeds, for instance, as well as the observance of new moons and festivals, the proper way to conduct marriages, deal with divorce, repair damages inflicted on others, take care of the poor, and the like. This oral law contains frequent references to the Torah and was believed to be equivalent in authority to the written Law of Moses. The Oral Law was eventually written down—first as the Mishnah and then, in an expanded version, as the Talmud—in order to preserve it, and its study is still thought to be indispensable, to varying degrees, as Jews attempt to understand and implement the Torah.

Rabbi Wylen, again from the Reform movement, illustrates the need for these additional books with a parable from the twelfth-century Spanish sage Judah Halevi: "In the hands of a trained pharmacist, the drugs in a pharmacy provide healing. If an ignorant person were to pose as a pharmacist and dispense drugs, he would provide death rather than healing. A person who has learned Torah serves God properly and brings healing into the world. A person who attempts to serve God without learning is likely to do more harm than good."[17] For this reason, the Talmudic rabbis not only analyzed with great care the practical directions in the Torah, but they also scrutinized the stories found in the Torah as well as in the prophetic writings. Extending Halevi's analogy, studying these stories was for these rabbis akin to "shadowing" God, much as budding pharmacy students shadow their professors. By analyzing God's actions closely, these rabbis saw how he worked in the context of real life, how he speaks to real people, how he addresses their problems, and how he corrects their mistakes and praises their progress. Studying the stories in the Torah and the Prophets gave them a kind of virtual practical experience that better enabled them to follow the Torah and to help others do so as well.

---

17. Stephen M. Wylen, *Settings of Silver: An Introduction to Judaism*, 20.

For these reasons, the prophetic books, although deemed somewhat inferior to the Torah by some rabbis because they were only "inspired" by God and not written by him directly, were also considered indispensable. They too, like the Talmud, were "required reading" for rabbinic Jews. In this way, they hoped to acquire a better sense of who God was and what he expected them to do. As Michael Fishbane explains, the fact that the prophets' revelation was "more mediated"—that is, given indirectly through human beings—than that of the Torah did not diminish their authority, especially since their primary purpose was "to exhort the people to return in faithfulness to the covenant or to announce the consequences of sin and the future fate of the people."[18] In fact, the Talmudic sages saw themselves very much as "the heirs of prophecy"[19] and traced their authority back through the prophets to Moses (Pirke Avot 1:1–12). The linkage therefore with the Rabbis and the Prophets is close, and to this day reading the Prophets as well as the rabbinic writings in consultation with others and under the helpful eye of a teacher keeps rabbinic Jews on track interpretively and helps them better understand and implement the Torah's commandments.

Scripture Study Ultimately Is Not about Information;
It Is an Experience with God

However, for many Talmudic and post-Talmudic rabbis the acquisition of information for practical purposes though vital was still mainly a starting point, a way of getting one's "sea legs," as it were, as one begins one's Torah voyage. Such knowledge was never the final goal. God for these rabbis not only gave the Torah but followed it—studying its words, wearing a prayer shawl,[20] donning tefillin (phylacteries), and praying in the "rabbinic mode."[21] They therefore studied Torah ultimately in order to worship God through imitation and, by so doing, to come closer to him—learning more about him and his motivations, growing in love and appreciation for him, and seeing the world, at least partially, through his eyes. As Cohen explains, as the Rabbis saw it, "when the individual is occupied with the words of the Torah, the vehicles of divine expression,

---

18. Michael Fishbane, *The JPS Bible Commentary: Haftarot*, xix.
19. Ibid., xx.
20. C.G. Montefiore and H. Loewe, *A Rabbinic Anthology*, 167, 324.
21. Jacob Neusner, *The Way of Torah: An Introduction to Judaism*, 81.

he or she experiences God's presence."[22] In a very real way, serious Torah students touch the divine.

To be sure, the acquisition of practical instructional information remains important, even vital to such an effort. One cannot connect with God in a deep way without knowing and following his commandments. However, as Neusner explains, at some point "the act of [Torah] study itself becomes holy, so that its original purpose, which was mastery of particular information, ceases to matter much. What matters is piety—piety expressed through the rites of studying."[23] Readers must eventually turn away from themselves to God; they must ask not simply "What does God want me to do?" but instead "How does God himself act?" or even better "What does God think and feel and how can I be like him?" To this end, the Talmudic and later rabbis revered a practice called *Torah lishmah*, or "Torah study for its own sake." As Rabbi Michael Strassfeld describes it, *Torah lishmah* is an "intellectual endeavor with a spiritual purpose." It is extremely rigorous; however, it leads one "to contemplate or even encounter the Divine."[24] As Rabbi Meir, an early Talmudic sage, explains:

> Everyone who occupies himself with Torah for its own sake merits many things; not only that, but he makes the entire world worthwhile. He is called beloved friend, a lover of God, a lover of humanity, one who gladdens God, and gladdens humanity. His Torah study clothes him in humility and reverence, and leads him to be righteous, pious, upright, and faithful. It distances him from sin, and draws him near goodness. From him come the benefits of counsel and resourcefulness, of understanding and courage. . . . It gives him sovereignty and dominion and discerning judgment. It reveals the secrets of Torah. He becomes an ever flowing fountain, a stream that never runs dry. He becomes modest, patient, and forgiving of affronts. It magnifies and exalts him over all creation. (Pirke Avot 6:1)

As Wylen writes, *torah lishmah* often involves "studying only the sections of the law that were no longer current, such as those governing agricultural offerings that apply only in the land of Israel."[25] Jews who study this way do so in order to avoid distractions from current issues or politics and instead concentrate on God himself. As Wylen explains, "Although *Torah lishmah* is without pragmatic application, it is not without consequence. By

---

22. Cohen, *The Way Into Torah*, 13.

23. Neusner, *The Way of Torah*, 83.

24. Michael Strassfeld, *A Book of Life: Embracing Judaism as a Spiritual Practice*, 139–40.

25. Wylen, *The Seventy Faces of Torah*, 88.

learning *Torah lishmah,* one enters into intimate communion with God."[26] Cohen again agrees with Wylen and commends *Torah lishmah* to his readers as a most worthy approach. As he writes, "From the rabbinic point of view, the study of Torah is its own reward. It is not merely a means to achieving an end."[27] To Cohen, Torah study certainly provides its readers with knowledge and skills that can be used in daily life and advancement. However, "when Torah study is not used for personal gain, in the end it nevertheless will lead to tremendous reward: spiritual riches and reward, which we cannot even fathom when we first taste of the water of Torah. We, like all those who thirst, will be replenished and blessed."[28]

Nephi's vision, too, extends beyond the acquisition of practical knowledge—questions concerning his family and their immediate circumstances—to a closer, more worshipful connection with God. The word he uses throughout his vision to describe what he has experienced is not "saw" or even "observed," but "beheld": he *beheld* "a tree . . . like unto the tree which [his] father had seen," he "*beheld* . . . [a] rod of iron," he "*beheld* . . . a large and spacious building," he "*beheld* multitudes of people," and he was told to "*behold* the fountain of filthy water" (1 Ne. 11:8, 25, 35; 12:1, 16). This use of such a highly charged biblical word connects this vision to the Hebrew Scriptures and implies more than a superficial glimpse of a thing. It connotes a profound understanding, a spiritually heightened awareness, a kind of cosmic comprehension combined with a prophetic-aesthetic appreciation. Jeremiah, for instance, "*beheld* the earth . . . and the heavens," the preacher of Ecclesiastes "*beheld* all the work of God," and Ezekiel *beheld* the Lord God himself, whose likeness was "as the appearance of fire" and whose form was "as the appearance of brightness" (Jer. 4:23; Eccl. 8:17; Ezek. 8:2). God too after the creation, "saw every thing that he had made, and, *behold,* it was very good" (Gen. 1:31). Little wonder that Nephi, unlike Lehi, praises the beauty of the tree he beheld, claiming that it surpassed "all beauty; and the whiteness thereof did exceed the whiteness of the driven snow" (1 Ne. 11:8).

It is as if the boundaries of Nephi's spiritual sight are being stretched to the breaking point and his soul expanded beyond what he can express. He is not simply receiving images sent to his brain via optic nerves; he is viewing all things momentarily from God's eyes, and, in so doing, his perspective is changed forever. After his vision, Nephi returns to his father's

---

26. Ibid.

27. Cohen, *The Way Into Torah,* 102.

28. Ibid., 106.

tent where he finds his brothers "disputing one with another concerning the things which [his] father had spoken unto them." Nephi is "grieved because of the hardness of their hearts but also because of the things which [he] had seen." From Nephi's mortal point of view, the fate of his people is heart-wrenching. However, from God's point of view, it is much worse. As Nephi continues, "And it came to pass that I was overcome because of my afflictions, for I considered that mine afflictions were great above all, because of the destruction of my people, for I had *beheld* their fall" (1 Ne. 15:5). Nonetheless, such an exalted viewpoint brings greater insight and comfort as well as increased pain. After Nephi has received strength from some unmentioned, mystical source, he rejoins his family and joins in on the discussion. However, he does not argue with them, as he might have before his vision. Instead, he speaks to the heart of the matter, as he sees it, and pointedly asks them, "Have ye inquired of the Lord?" They respond in the negative, and he encourages them to ask God, as he did, "in faith, believing that [they] shall receive," and he promises them, that if they keep God's commandments, including studying the scriptures intensely, that the answers they seek "shall be made known unto [them]" (vv. 8, 11).

A close relationship with God, based on ongoing, deep communication, is Nephi's only lasting solace, and he therefore points his brothers to this as the ultimate solution to their conflicts. Later on, when he recounts his visionary experience in poetic form, Nephi praises God for hearing his daytime cry and for giving him "knowledge by visions in the night-time" (2 Ne. 4:23). He also rhapsodizes about how he was carried away "upon the wings of [God's] Spirit . . . upon exceedingly high mountains" and there "beheld great things, yea, even too great for man" (v. 25). However, in the end it is this *connection* with God, not *information* from God, that comforts him: "Yea, I know that God will give liberally to him that asketh. Yea, my God will give me, if I ask not amiss; therefore I will lift up my voice unto thee; yea, I will cry unto thee, my God, the rock of my righteousness. Behold, my voice shall forever ascend up unto thee, my rock and mine everlasting God" (v. 35). As a result of this vision, Nephi not only describes God as "*my* God," implying a close relationship to him, but calls him "my rock and mine *everlasting* God," an expression that pushes that relationship beyond time and space to eternal realms. Such is the sort of relationship rabbinic scripture study is ultimately all about. As Cohen writes, "The study of the words of the Torah is a holy act, one that lies at the basis of [the Jewish] covenantal relationship with God."[29]

The Book of Mormon and the Tree of Life

Nephi's use of the word *behold* in the final line of his poetic praise of God is significant. Not only does it seem to sum up his visionary experience, ultimately allowing him to see God more clearly and comprehend his ways more accurately, but it also connects Nephi's experience with scripture study. Before his vision, Nephi clearly only "partakes" of the Scriptures, the way his father partook of the fruit of the Tree of Life. After Nephi and his brothers initially fail to obtain the plates of brass, he preaches to them, reminding them of the Exodus story, but the retelling of this story is somewhat superficial. He admonishes them simply to be "strong like unto Moses" (1 Ne. 4:2) and quotes a few key words and phrases from Exodus 14:21. However after his vision, after his spiritual viewpoint has been expanded, Nephi approaches the Scriptures in a much more intense, deep, and personal way. As he later describes himself, he has become someone who "pondereth" the Scriptures in his heart continually (2 Ne. 4:15), and, almost as proof of his dedication, he includes large portions from the book of Isaiah in his writings, not just vague allusions or snippets. Furthermore, he "likens" these portions unto his people and to all people everywhere, interprets them for their "profit and learning," and offers "these words [that they] may lift up their hearts and rejoice" (2 Ne. 11:8) and "have hope" (1 Ne. 19:23–24).

Furthermore, the way Nephi describes his feelings for the Scriptures after his vision makes it plain that he considers the ultimate goal of scripture study to be more relational than informational. It is the encounter with God, and the joy that he receives from such an experience that now matters most to Nephi. He therefore uses the same verb, "delighteth," to describe both his feelings about the Scriptures as well as his feelings about God's grace, justice, power, and mercy (2 Ne. 4:15; 11:2, 5). It therefore comes as no surprise then that Nephi presses his brothers to inquire of the Lord concerning the meaning of their father's dream and urges them "to give heed unto the word of the Lord" (1 Ne. 15:25). The two activities, interpreting visions and understanding scriptures, seem to be linked in Nephi's mind.

---

29. Ibid., 5.

Just as he learned to "behold" the Tree of Life in his vision, so he also attempts to *behold* the Scriptures and commends the approach to others.

This book consequently is an attempt to do just that—to "behold" the Book of Mormon using the same classic rabbinic principles embodied in Nephi's dream but applied more extensively and more rigorously according to the techniques and practices specified in the Talmud and other, later rabbinic sources. As the subsequent chapters show, this approach is well-suited to the Book of Mormon's literary nature and allows the Book of Mormon, much like the Tree of Life in Nephi's vision, to continually blossom in beauty, extending its branches to new heights with life-giving significance and meaning, deepening its roots in the rich soil of the Hebrew Scriptures, and becoming truly a marvelous work and a wonder to behold.

Chapter Two

Reading on Multiple Levels

And the angel said unto me: . . . Knowest thou the meaning of the tree which thy father saw? And I answered him, saying: Yea, it is the love of God, which sheddeth itself abroad in the hearts of the children of men; wherefore, it is the most desirable above all things. And he spake unto me, saying: Yea, and the most joyous to the soul. (1 Ne. 11:21–23)

The fact that the Tree of Life and the Scriptures seem to be closely connected in Nephi's mind is itself a powerful inducement to approach the Book of Mormon rabbinically. The Talmudic and post-Talmudic rabbis often wax poetic in their descriptions of the Torah. They liken it to a wife, because one must remember to devote a significant portion of one's time to it (Ecclesiastes Rabbah, 24a); to wine, because imbibing it, according to them, strengthens one's resolve and fortifies one's convictions; to a double-edged sword, because it gives life in this world and the world to come; (Pesiktah Kahana, 102a–102b); and to medicine, because it cures evil thoughts (Pesiktah Rabbah, 32b). However, the most compelling and most long-lasting metaphor they use is that of the Tree of Life. Clearly it is prominent in the liturgy of the Torah,[1] but it is also conspicuous in the rabbinic literature as well. The rabbis in Leviticus Rabbah, for instance, explicitly link the Torah to the Tree of Life mentioned in Proverbs 3:18 and implicitly commend all to "lay hold of her" and be happy (Leviticus Rabbah 25:1).[2] Rabbi Hanin similarly connects the Torah to this proverbial tree (BT Berakoth 32b), as does Rabbi Meir in Pirke Avot, who there explains that as such the Torah "gives life to those who practice it, both in this world and in the world to come" (Pirke Avot 6:7). And this connection is entirely appropriate. After all, to these rabbis the Torah was an inexhaustible source of life-sustaining wisdom, a continuously flowing

---

1. David L. Lieber, ed., *Etz Hayim: Torah and Commentary*, xxiv.

2. Jacob Neusner, *Judaism and Scripture: The Evidence of Leviticus Rabbah*, 439–43.

fountain of truth that can make happy and prosperous "every one that retaineth her" (Prov. 3:18).

Much like a tree, Torah knowledge, as the Talmudic and post-Talmudic rabbis saw it, grows steadily, over time, enfolding each new approach as the Torah's potential for divine communication becomes more apparent and its wisdom better understood. However, Torah knowledge also requires deep roots in order to stabilize it, and the way to it is not easy. It is guarded, not by sword-wielding cherubim as in Genesis (Gen. 3:24) but by other challenges that make reading Torah treacherous. The Tosefta contains an intriguing account of four sages—Rabbi ben Azzai, Rabbi ben Zoma, Elisha ben Abuya, and Rabbi Akiva—who are taken up, much as Lehi is, into an Eden-like orchard, presumably containing the Tree of Life (TO Hagigah 2:3). There, all four sages witness the beauty and power of the place, but only Rabbi Akiva is able to enjoy it without suffering personal harm or difficulty. Rabbi ben Azzai immediately dies, Rabbi ben Zoma is smitten with a disease, and Elisha ben Abuya goes mad and apostatizes. The key to Akiva's survival, according to later medieval mystics, was his efforts to cling so tightly to the words of the Torah—holding them close, mastering their every nuance, scrutinizing their every detail—that he was prepared, step-by-step, to enjoy this mystical place without being overwhelmed or put off by it.

In an effort to emulate Rabbi Akiva, these mystics built upon earlier interpretive traditions to formulate a progressive approach to the Torah and divided this approach into four stages of scriptural exegesis, which, like the four rivers that "went out of Eden" (Gen. 2:10) give life to those who study the Torah diligently.[3] The names of these four stages, appropriately enough, were said to form the acronym *PaRDeS*, a word historically connected with esoteric studies, meaning "orchard" but with possible linguistic connections to the Greek word *paradeisos* or "paradise."[4] This acronym and the approach it represented were subsequently adopted by later non-mystical rabbis and adapted to their less hierarchical, less stratified approach to scripture. To them, the four levels affirmed the four most prominent ways rabbis have historically interpreted the Torah, and they therefore presented each approach as equally valid and worthwhile. Since this time, *pardes* has been an extremely popular and effective way of encouraging rabbinic Jews to approach the Scriptures from several ways at

---

3. Gershom Scholem, *On the Kabbalah and Its Symbolism*, 57–58.

4. Amy Grossblat Pessah, Kenneth J. Meyers, and Christopher M. Leighton, "How Do Jews and Christians Read the Bible?" 62; Normon J. Cohen, *The Way Into Torah*, 80.

the same time.[5] Rabbi Wylen, for instance, very much recommends it to
his congregants and describes the four levels as follows:

- **Peshat:** the literal level of meaning, the simple level, what the
  scriptural text actually says.
- **Remez:** the allegorical level, what the text represents—ideas, scientific principles, philosophic truths, historical trends, and so forth.
- **Derash:** the sermonic level, what the text means to people in terms
  of bettering their daily lives and spiritual situation.
- **Sod:** the mystical level, what the text signifies to mystics and how
  it reveals God to them.[6]

These levels are inclusive, and therefore it is not uncommon to hear modern rabbis, even within the same sermon, cite Rashi (a champion of plain
meaning), refer to Philo (an adept of allegory), retell a midrashic story,
and add an interesting scriptural explanation based on mystical numerology. All of these approaches are part of modern rabbinic Judaism and are
used seamlessly in rabbinic teachings—the only criterion being the force
and power of the citation as well as its clear connection to the text.

While none of these Hebrew terms appears in the Book of Mormon
by name, the Book of Mormon seems to encourage a *pardes*-like approach
to itself through the words its authors use to describe scripture study as
well as by the way the text of the Book of Mormon responds to it.

Peshat

Peshat, the simple or plain sense of the text, corresponds closely with
what Nephi refers to as "plainness," an approach to scripture that he both
delights in and sees as essential (2 Ne. 25:4). As Rabbi Avigdor Bonchek
writes, *peshat* is a concentration on "what the text says" and constitutes
"the starting point for all interpretation";[7] *peshat* is therefore fundamental
to all of the other approaches, and although *simple*, it is not simplistic.
Indeed *peshat* is the foundation upon which all the other levels are built.
Cohen writes,

> The *peshat* can be considered the original meaning of the text. It focuses the
> reader on the words of the text themselves without any interpretation. The

---

5. A. Van der Heide, "PARDES: Methodological Reflections on the Theory of
the Four Senses," 148.

6. Stephen M. Wylen, *Settings of Silver: An Introduction to Judaism*, 17.

7. Avigdor Bonchek, *Studying the Torah: A Guide to In-Depth Interpretation*, 8.

words are all that is important and are to be taken seriously at the outset of study. The rabbis constantly emphasize the importance of understanding the *peshat*, the original meaning of any particular text, as shaped by its context. They underscore this in the famous dictum "No verse can be deprived of its *peshat*" [BT Shabbat 63a].This is a warning against the tendency to creative interpretation of the text of Torah without holding onto the *peshat*.[8]

Understanding *peshat* is not easy. It is much more than a cursory scanning of a text to get its general sense. *Peshat* involves the meticulous scrutiny of the particulars of each passage, and therefore, as Rabbi George Robinson writes, it "draws on the context of the passage, its grammar, philology, historical content."[9] In other words, *peshat* is both rigorous and wide-ranging, requiring almost microscopic attention to detail as well as a macroscopic view of the text as a whole. *Peshat* also requires a well-developed sensitivity to the nuances and quirks of biblical expression as well as a willingness to question previous assumptions and a reverence for actual words of the Hebrew Scriptures. All in all, despite the attractions of the other levels of interpretation, *peshat* is what rabbinic scholars have historically spent most of their time studying. It is, in a very real sense, the root of all of the other modes of interpretation, providing not only stability but intellectual and spiritual nourishment.

Again, the Book of Mormon does not use the word *peshat*. However, the way Jacob condemns the pre-exilic Jews for despising the "the words of plainness," for seeking "things that they could not understand," and for "looking beyond the mark" very much suggests that he is advocating a *peshat*-like approach to the Scriptures—as does Nephi's delighting and glorying "in plainness" (Jacob 4:14; 2 Ne. 31:3; 33:6). For Nephi, this "plainness" is never linked to simplicity—as in "plain and simple," a phrase he never uses. For him, the phrase is always "plain and precious," and he predicts serious problems once the "plain and precious" have been removed from the biblical text, both physically and through interpretation (1 Ne. 13:26, 28–29, 32). As Nephi sees it, God uses plainness to speak "unto men according to their language, unto their understanding" (2 Ne. 31:3), and therefore removing this quality from scriptural interpretation effectively thwarts God's efforts to communicate with humanity. It can "blind the eyes and harden the hearts of the children of men" and cause an exceedingly great many to "stumble" and allow Satan to have "great

---

8. Norman J. Cohen, *The Way Into Torah*, 81.

9. George Robinson, *Essential Judaism: A Complete Guide to Beliefs, Rituals, and Customs*, 303.

power" over them (1 Ne. 13:27, 29). It is for this reason, perhaps, that Nephi poetically prays that he "may walk in the path of the low valley, that [he] may be strict in the *plain* road!" (2 Ne. 4:32). Without the plain sense of Scripture, there is no spiritual progress.

This emphasis on what the Scriptures actually say is further reinforced by the way Nephi, Jacob, and other Book of Mormon writers include in their writings entire chapters from Malachi and Isaiah, chapters nearly identical to those found in the King James Version of the Bible. In this way, they ground their ideas solidly on the actual words of the Bible and invite—almost demand—that their readers reread these chapters and judge for themselves the accuracy of the ideas these writers derive from them. Here the plain sense of the Scriptures remains the standard. No creative editing or changing of the words is allowed.

This inclusion of biblical chapters in their entirety also helps preserve the larger context of the text and ensures that the simple meaning, the *peshat*, is not obscured—something Nephi, for one, seems to see as vital for understanding Isaiah. He writes that many things that Isaiah wrote were not "plain" to the people living around him at the time and "were hard for many of [his] people to understand." This is because, according to Nephi, "they know not concerning the manner of prophesying among the Jews," the geographical and political context ("the regions round about"), or the historical and spiritual context ("the judgments of God, which hath come to pass among the Jews") (2 Ne. 25:1, 6). However, with a *peshat*-based understanding of its context and "the spirit of prophecy," Nephi is confident that Isaiah, and by implication all the Hebrew Scriptures, will be "plain" to his other, future readers (2 Ne. 25:4). In other words, if his readers concentrate on the plain meaning of the Scriptures, the Scriptures will be plain to them.

In addition to stressing the importance of *peshat* in understanding the Hebrew Scriptures, the Book of Mormon also asserts the superiority of living a life consistent with the plain sense of the Scriptures. Toward the end of his book, Jacob wonders how the Jews of his time "after having rejected the sure foundation, can ever build upon it" (Jacob 4:17). He states that the Jews at the time his family left Jerusalem (around 600 B.C.E.) were "a stiffnecked people; and they despised the words of plainness, and killed the prophets, and sought for things that they could not understand" (v. 14). In rabbinic terms, this seems to imply that these Jews rejected, among other things, *peshat*, "the words of plainness," and therefore attempted to find ideas in the Scriptures that were not based on the simple meaning of

the text. They instead attempted to use other methods of scriptural interpretation, and, since all valid scriptural interpretation is based on *peshat*,
it is not surprising that "they could not understand." Because of this error,
these pre-exilic Jews became spiritually blind, "which blindness came by
looking beyond the mark"—missing the *peshat*.

In reaction, God consequently removed "his plainness from them,
and delivered unto them many things which they [could not] understand,
because they desired it." In other words, because these ancient Jews wanted to see more complex or more mysterious or more fashionable things in
the Scriptures, they found them. However, because they did not understand *peshat*, they could not appreciate the Scriptures or interpret them
correctly, and therefore they stumbled and fell. Thus, *peshat* is the "safe
foundation" of scripture study, "upon which they might build" valid interpretations (Jacob 4:14–15).

Given Jacob's position on *peshat*, it is significant that when he interprets the allegory found in "the words of the [nonbiblical] prophet Zenos"
(Jacob 5:1; possibly one of the things that the Lord delivered to Israel
that they could not understand), he bases his interpretation solidly on its
peshat. After reading the entire allegory to his people, Jacob says,

> And now, behold, my brethren, as I said unto you that I would prophesy, be-
> hold, this is my prophecy—that the things which this prophet Zenos spake,
> concerning the house of Israel, in the which he likened them unto a tame
> olive-tree, must surely come to pass. And the day that he shall set his hand
> again the second time to recover his people, is the day, yea, even the last
> time, that the servants of the Lord shall go forth in his power, to nourish and
> prune his vineyard; and after that the end soon cometh.
>
> And how blessed are they who have labored diligently in his vineyard;
> and how cursed are they who shall be cast out into their own place! And the
> world shall be burned with fire. And how merciful is our God unto us, for he
> remembereth the house of Israel, both roots and branches; and he stretches
> forth his hands unto them all the day long; and they are a stiffnecked and a
> gainsaying people; but as many as will not harden their hearts shall be saved
> in the kingdom of God. Wherefore, my beloved brethren, I beseech of you
> in words of soberness that ye would repent, and come with full purpose
> of heart, and cleave unto God as he cleaveth unto you. And while his arm
> of mercy is extended towards you in the light of the day, harden not your
> hearts. (Jacob 6:1–5)

Although Jacob is clearly prophesying, he is careful to quote pertinent
terms and phrases from the allegory itself—not just general words such
as "vineyard," "nourish," "prune," "branches," and "roots," but significant

phrases such as "last time," "the end soon cometh," "servants of the Lord," "labored diligently," "cast out into their own place," and "be burned with fire"(Jacob 5:71, 75, 77). In essence, after explaining how the pre-exilic Jews rejected *peshat* and therefore missed the meaning of the revelations God gave them, Jacob takes one of those revelations and shows his people its meaning—using *peshat*. In this way, Jacob shows his later as well as contemporary readers the value of this most fundamental of all Jewish hermeneutical approaches.

In addition to stressing the importance and primacy of *peshat*, the Book of Mormon also emphasizes the effort involved in this approach. Again, although the *peshat* or the "plain" meaning of the Scriptures is almost by definition accessible to all readers, it is not an easy or superficial task to access it. Therefore, Nephi and other Book of Mormon authors continually encourage their readers to *search* the Scriptures, a word implying rigor and devotion. Lehi searches the plates of brass "from the beginning" as soon as he receives them (1 Ne. 5:10). Nephi laments that people generally "will not search knowledge, nor understand great knowledge, when it is given unto them in plainness, even as plain as word can be" (2 Ne. 32:7). Jacob praises his people because they did "search the prophets" so much so that their "faith becometh unshaken" (Jacob 4:6). Moroni pleads with his future readers to "*search* the prophecies of Isaiah" and grieves that he "cannot write them" (Morm. 8:23). Even Jesus himself is quoted as commanding his listeners to "*search* these things diligently; for great are the words of Isaiah" (3 Ne. 23:1).

Finally, it is the "*words* of Isaiah" that these authors rehearse, read, and delight in (1 Ne. 15:20; 2 Ne. 6:4, 11:2)—not the "writings" or the "sayings" or the "prophecies." This in itself suggests in a very *peshat* way the value they place in attending to scriptural details, another fundamental concept of *peshat*. By calling attention to his *words*, these authors seem to advocate a very close scrutiny of Isaiah as well as other prophets, revealing how much the Book of Mormon authors value close reading.

Remez

According to Cohen, the second level of rabbinic interpretation, *remez*, means "hint" or "allusion"—a way of interpreting the biblical text that preserves the "surface meaning" while adding to it significantly.[10] As Robinson

---

10. Cohen, *The Way Into Torah*, 82.

explains, *remez* "seeks the allegorical meaning of the text, focusing on the philosophical implications contained therein."[11] The classic biblical example of this approach, the one cited most often, is the Song of Songs, also known as Canticles or the Song of Solomon. Although seemingly simply a series of erotic love poems, the Song of Songs is traditionally interpreted allegorically, describing instead "the relationship between the people Israel and Adonai."[12] As Elsie Stern, in her introduction to the Song of Songs in the *Jewish Study Bible*, writes: "In rabbinic tradition, the Song narrates the words which God and Israel spoke to each other at the Red Sea, at Sinai, or in the Tent of Meeting. The descriptions of the male lover are understood as allegorical descriptions of God while the descriptions of the female lover are understood as divine praise of Israel. The statements of desire and love are read as expressions of love and intimacy between God and Israel."[13]

Once again, although the Book of Mormon does not make use of the word *remez* any more than it did *peshat*, it endorses this approach by including an elaborate example of an allegory in the book of Jacob. Toward the end of that book, Jacob reads to his people "the words of the prophet Zenos" in which he likens the house of Israel "unto a tame olive tree, which a man took and nourished in his vineyard; and it grew, and waxed old, and began to decay" (Jacob 5:1, 3). Clearly referring to the kingdoms of Israel and Judah immediately before their respective captivities—kingdoms that Jacob's family had fled and he himself previously stated "must needs fall"—this allegory portrays the "master of the vineyard" as pruning, digging about, and nourishing a tree to little avail (v. 4). Some "little, young and tender branches" appear but "the main top" nevertheless begins to perish (v. 6). Almost as an act of desperation, the master then hacks off "those main branches which are beginning to wither away" and casts them into the fire "that they may be burned" (v. 7)—just as God allows Assyria and Babylon to capture the kingdoms of Israel and Judah respectively, killing many of Israelites, and sending the remainder into exile.

In an effort to save the roots, the master then grafts in branches from a healthy wild olive tree into the tame olive tree, an action consonant with the way non-Jews were joined into Israel in various ways during the exile. At the same time, he also takes a few "young and tender" branches from the tame olive tree and plants them in the "nethermost parts" of his vineyard. This last action is a reference to Lehi and his family as well as

---

11. Robinson, *Essential Judaism*, 305.
12. Ibid., 5.
13. Adele Berlin and Marc Zvi Brettler, eds., *The Jewish Study Bible*, 1565.

to other members of "lost" tribes who were led out of the land of Israel. Two of the transported branches bring forth "much fruit," despite being planted in the "poorest spot in all the land" and a "spot of ground [that] was poorer than the first" (vv. 20–21, 23). The last, the one representing the Lamanites and the Nephites, is planted in a "good spot of ground" but brings forth "wild fruit" as well as "tame fruit" (v. 25).

Zenos continues prophetically with his allegory showing that the entire vineyard eventually becomes completely corrupted, with both the transplanted branches as well as the original tree producing nothing but wild fruit. At this point, the master decides to destroy the vineyard. However, one of the master's servants intervenes and convinces him to instead try to salvage the tree by regrafting the transplanted tame branches back into the original tree and by lopping off the grafted wild branches that have become "corrupt." Given the connections to Israel and its scattering that have been consistently developed throughout this allegory, it seems clear that this last action refers to the final gathering of Israel—when the messianic era will be established and all Israel, like the tame olive tree will "became like unto one body." At this time, the Israelites will be "equal," "the Lord of the vineyard [will have] preserved unto himself the natural fruit, which was most precious unto him from the beginning" and the "bad will [be] cast away into its own place" (vv. 74, 77).

Zenos's allegory is quite involved and proceeds for seventy-seven verses. It includes descriptions of the quality of the ground in which the branches grew as well as other significant details that reward close reading and supply additional information in a concentrated way: the fact that the initial problem with the tame olive tree was limited to its main top area, the idea that the master "hid" the transplanted branches in the vineyard (v. 14), the suggestion that despite the wildness of its fruit the root of the tame olive tree retained "much strength" from which the wild branches drew strength (v. 18), the notion that there were "all kinds of bad fruit" on the trees not just one (v. 32), the claim that the "loftiness" of the branches was a main problem, the assertion that the servants did "not clear away the bad [branches] thereof all at once" (v. 65), and so forth.

The richness of Zenos's allegory by itself goes far in encouraging a *remez* approach. However, there are other allegories in the Book of Mormon that similarly promote this approach. As he did in the New Testament, Jesus likens those who hear his sayings and follow them unto "a wise man, who built his house upon a rock—and the rain descended, and the floods came, and the winds blew, and beat upon that house; and it fell not, for it was founded upon a rock" (3 Ne. 14:24–25). Alma makes clear that the Lehites' journey to a "land of promise" (1 Ne. 2:20) is emblematic of humanity's path to God, a trek that requires divine intervention and guidance. Pointing to the Liahona, a mystical compass that showed Lehi and his family where to travel, he says, "For just as surely as this director did bring our fathers, by following its course, to the Promised Land, shall the words of Christ, if we follow their course, carry us beyond this vale of sorrow into a far better land of promise" (Alma 37:45). Lehi's dream, which has already been described, is saturated with allegorical meanings and hints. It is a dream like Joseph's in Genesis 37 and Nebuchadnezzar's in Daniel 2. It has some realistic elements, but it is presented in a suggestive, surreal manner, the details of which an angel later explains to Nephi in allegorical terms. According to him, the rod of iron is "the word of God," the tree is "a representation of the love of God," "the great and spacious building was the pride of the world," and the water, which was filthy, represents "an awful gulf, which separated the wicked from the tree of life, and also from the saints of God" (1 Ne. 11:25, 36; 15:28).

Lehi's vision not only encourages a *remez* approach to itself, but it shows how *remez* is dependent upon *peshat*. In this dream, many of the literal elements of Lehi's flight from Jerusalem are allegorized into a spiritual journey. Before he leaves his home, Lehi preaches to the people and is mocked just as those on the right path in his dream were mocked by the inhabitants of the great and spacious building (1 Ne. 8:26–27). After he and his family leave Jerusalem, Lehi actually wanders in a "wilderness" (2:4) just as he did in his dream (8:4). In that real wilderness, Lehi pitches his tent "by the side of a river of water" (2:6) in a fertile place, where there is "all manner of seeds of every kind, both of grain . . . and also of the seeds of fruit" (8:1)—again, just as a river flowed beside trees and fruit in his dream. Similarly, Laman and Lemuel actually refuse to heed their father and murmur against him (2:12), in a sense wandering off the right path, while Nephi and Sam and Sariah remain on the strait and narrow. And the pattern continues. When Nephi and his brothers fail to obtain the plates of brass for the second time, Laman and Lemuel "smite [Nephi and Sam] even with a rod" (3:28), a real angel appears to them and directs them just as a man "dressed in a white robe" showed Lehi the way in his dream (8:5). After the visit from the angel, Nephi enters Jerusalem "by night" (4:5), spiritually feeling his way through the darkness, "not knowing beforehand the things which [he] should do," just as the masses in Lehi's dream "did press forward through the mist of darkness, clinging to the rod of iron, even until they did come forth and partake of the fruit of the tree" (8:24).

All of these elements—the mocking, the wilderness, the river, the fruit, and so forth—appear in Lehi's dream much as they did in reality, but they are reconstituted into an allegory that synopsizes spiritually the point of his journey and the events that he and his family have experienced. In this way, Lehi's actual experience forms a symbiotic relationship with his dream—by placing it firmly in reality, concretizing its abstractions, and reinforcing its points with actual details—just as *peshat* does with *remez*.

Derash

According to Cohen, *derash*, the third level of rabbinic interpretation, means "to seek" or "to search out," in the sense of actively discovering a "contemporary meaning from the close study of the Bible."[14] It is the sermonic level, the level most often used in homilies and similar "lessons for our time." Ancient stories based on *derash* are called *midrashim* (sing. *midrash*), a word formed from the same root as *derash*, and they were compiled into a collection known as the Midrash. These stories, according to Rabbi Strassfeld, "enlarge upon the biblical narrative and draw lessons from the text," and although many of them were produced during the medieval period, *midrash*, according to Strassfeld, remains a living art form and continues to generate contemporary *midrashim* today.[15]

And this is only appropriate. After all, *derash* is more timely than timeless. As Rabbi Jacob Neusner writes, its basic thrust involves "transforming the genres of Scripture into patterns that apply to the acutely contemporary world as much as to times past."[16] Each of these universal patterns, what Neusner also calls scripture's "enduring truths,"[17] transcends time but applies to the present;[18] the traditional goal of *derash* in every era is for readers of that current era "to read Scripture as a letter posted that very morning from God to them."[19]

---

14. Cohen, *The Way Into Torah*, 15.

15. Michael Strassfeld, *A Book of Life: Embracing Judaism as a Spritiaul Practice*, 146.

16. Jacob Neusner, *Judaism and the Interpretation of Scripture: Introduction to the Rabbinic Midrash*, 3.

17. Ibid., 1.

18. Ibid., 5.

19. Ibid., ix.

Although based on the *peshat* of the scriptural text, *derash* goes beyond it, finding in the text a meaning outside its original setting. Robinson says that this approach exposes the text's "latent meaning, as opposed to its 'plain' meaning."[20] According to Cohen, *derash* attempts to interpret the text's

> structural and thematic elements in creative ways. It can at times juxtapose different biblical verses based on key theme words in order to convey meaning. Also, the words of the text can illumine the reader's life experience, while the reader, in bringing his or her life to bear on a text, can penetrate the human issues implicit in it. *Derash* essentially involves the 'reading in' of a meaning different from the text's *peshat*.[21]

The Book of Mormon encourages this kind of "reading in" by admonishing its readers on several occasions to "liken the scriptures unto themselves" as well as by providing several examples of this approach and ample opportunity to use it. Before Nephi includes his first block of Isaiah chapters, he explains that he is doing this to "fully persuade [his people] to believe in the Lord their Redeemer"—his point being that the Lord redeems *them*, his readers, not just their distant ancestors or theoretical descendants. To accomplish this very personal purpose, Nephi reads to his people the "books of Moses" as well as Isaiah and does "liken all scriptures unto [them], that it might be for [their] profit and learning" (1 Ne. 19:23). He then reminds them that they, as "a remnant of the house of Israel, a branch who have been broken off," may find hope in Isaiah's words. He consequently admonishes them to "liken [his words] unto yourselves" (v. 24). Nephi, again, returns to this theme before including his second, much larger block of chapters from Isaiah into his own record: "And now I write some of the words of Isaiah, that whoso of my people shall see these words may lift up their hearts and rejoice for all men. Now these are the words, and ye may liken them unto you and unto all men" (2 Ne. 11:8).

In addition to these admonitions, Nephi includes in his writings at least one specific example of likening. After he and his brothers twice fail to procure the brass plates from Laban, Laman and Lemuel are discouraged and begin to take their frustrations out on Nephi and Sam, beating them with a rod. An angel appears to the four brothers and instructs them to "go up to Jerusalem again, and the Lord will deliver Laban into your hands" (1 Ne. 3:29). Although Laman and Lemuel stop beating Sam and Nephi, they are not totally convinced that things will go as the angel

---

20. Robinson, *Essential Judaism*, 304.
21. Cohen, *The Way Into Torah*, 83–84.

said. They ask, "How is it possible that the Lord will deliver Laban into our hands? Behold, he is a mighty man, and he can command fifty, yea, even he can slay fifty; then why not us?" (v. 31). Possibly recognizing the similarity between their questions and Moses's when the Lord first commissions him to "deliver [Israel] out of the hand of the Egyptians" (Ex. 3:8), Nephi responds to Laman and Lemuel by likening Moses's eventual response to what theirs should be:

> Let us go up again unto Jerusalem, and let us be faithful in keeping the commandments of the Lord; for behold he is mightier than all the earth, then why not mightier than Laban and his fifty, yea, or even than his tens of thousands? Therefore let us go up; *let us be strong like unto Moses*; for he truly spake unto the waters of the Red Sea and they divided hither and thither, and our fathers came through, out of captivity, on dry ground, and the armies of Pharaoh did follow and were drowned in the waters of the Red Sea. Now behold ye know that this is true; and ye also know that an angel hath spoken unto you; wherefore can ye doubt? Let us go up; the Lord is able to deliver us, even as our fathers, and to destroy Laban, even as the Egyptians. (1 Ne. 4:1–3)

This short sermon of Nephi's is not a classical *midrash*. *Midrashim* tend to be more imaginative, conveying their meaning in story form, much like a legend or even a fairy tale, in order to better make their point more memorable. Nonetheless, Nephi's words attempt to draw an "enduring truth" from Moses's experience and apply it to his "acutely contemporary world." By likening himself and his brothers as they face Laban's soldiers in Jerusalem to Moses and the children of Israel just before they were delivered by the Lord from the Egyptian army, Nephi provides a vivid example of finding a relevant "latent meaning" of a passage in the Hebrew Scriptures. Although Nephi again likens himself and his brothers to Moses and the children of Israel when he is commanded to build a ship, and his brothers, again, murmur against him (1 Ne. 17:23–51), *derashic* interpretations of events that occur in the Hebrew Scriptures are not common in the Book of Mormon. However, such interpretations of events that occur in the Book of Mormon are common. When Alma, for instance, speaks to his son Helaman, he advises him to "counsel with the Lord in all thy doings" and then interprets Lehi's experience with the Liahona *derashically*. He explains how "it was prepared [by the Lord] to show unto [their] fathers the course which they should travel in the wilderness," how it "did work [mighty miracles] for them according to their faith in God," and how because it "worked by small means" Lehi and his family were sometimes "slothful, and forgot to exercise their faith and diligence and then those marvelous works ceased, and they did not progress in their journey" (Alma 37:37, 39–41).

Alma then asks rhetorically, "Is there not a type in this thing?" This is clearly a *remez*-like question, pointing out the allegorical significance of their experience with the Liahona. However, Alma pushes this point *derashically*, finding within it a contemporary application:

> For just as surely as this director did bring our fathers, by following its course, to the Promised Land, shall the words of Christ, if we follow their course, carry us beyond this vale of sorrow into a far better land of promise. O my son, do not let us be slothful because of the easiness of the way; for so was it with our fathers; for so was it prepared for them, that if they would look they might live; even so it is with us. The way is prepared, and if we will look we may live forever. And now, my son, see that ye take care of these sacred things, yea, see that ye look to God and live. (Alma 37:45–47)

Once again, these interpretive levels build upon one another. Just as Alma formed a *derashic* interpretation ("look to God and live") from a *remez* understanding (the Liahona represents the words of Christ) of a *peshat* experience (Lehi and family being guided to the Promised Land by the Liahona), so Nephi interprets Lehi's dream sermonically. After Lehi has told his family of his dream and after Nephi has experienced his own version of the same, his brothers ask Nephi to explain the meaning of several elements of their father's dream. Nephi responds by explaining the allegorical meaning of the main elements of Lehi's dream. For instance, he tells them that the rod of iron represents the "word of God," which will protect those who "would hold fast unto it" (1 Ne. 15:24). However, he also gives them the *derashic* meaning of holding fast to the rod: "I, Nephi, did exhort them to give heed unto the word of the Lord; yea, I did exhort them with all the energies of my soul, and with all the faculty which I possessed, that they would give heed to the word of God and remember to keep his commandments always in all things" (v. 25). In this way, Nephi too forms a *derashic* interpretation from a *remez* understanding of a *peshat* experience.

In addition to these "likenings," there are all sorts of principles put forth in *derashic* terms as lessons in the text of the Book of Mormon itself. Many of these lessons include the phrase "and thus we see" to include readers implicitly in the lesson and to indicate that readers should apply the principle in their lives. For example, Nephi finds meaning in the Liahona much as Alma did:

And there was also written upon them a new writing, which was plain to be read, which did give us understanding concerning the ways of the Lord; and it was written and changed from time to time, according to the faith and diligence which we gave unto it. And thus we see that by small means the Lord can bring about great things. (1 Ne. 16:29)

Nephi also finds other similar lessons in the journey he and his family make in the wilderness. There the women in his family are said to "give plenty of suck for their children," and despite a divine prohibition against making fires to cook with, "were strong, yea, even like unto the men" (1 Ne. 17:2). This leads Nephi to conclude that "if it so be that the children of men keep the commandments of God, he doth nourish them, and strengthen them, and provide means whereby they can accomplish the thing which he has commanded them" (v. 3).

Mormon too uses this pattern. In Alma 30, he relates the story of Korihor—a man who claimed that there was no God because people "cannot know of things which [they] do not see" and who advocated a philosophy by which "every man prospered according to his genius, and that every man conquered according to his strength; and whatsoever a man did was no crime" (Alma 30:15, 17). Korihor debates with Alma and was eventually "struck dumb . . . according to the words of Alma" when he demanded a sign (v. 50). Immediately afterwards, Mormon relates the following moral: "And thus we see the end of him who perverteth the ways of the Lord; and thus we see that the devil will not support his children at the last day, but doth speedily drag them down to hell" (v. 60).

Mormon similarly sees a pattern in the way, after a period of prosperity, the Nephites of his time "began again to forget the Lord their God" and "began to wax strong in iniquity" (Hel. 11:36). He says: "And thus we see that except the Lord doth chasten his people with many afflictions, yea, except he doth visit them with death and with terror, and with famine and with all manner of pestilence, they will not remember him" (12:3). This pattern is part of what has been called the "pride cycle" in the Book of Mormon—a larger, universal pattern where pride follows prosperity and precedes divine chastisement and humility. This pride cycle forms one of the major themes of the Book of Mormon and helps show how the entire Book of Mormon invites a *derash*-based interpretation. In other words the entire Book of Mormon serves as a story that reveals eternal principles, which readers are invited to apply to themselves and their situation.

As Moroni writes in the book of Ether, addressing his modern readers, whose "doing" has been shown to him in vision (Morm. 8:35), the Book of

Mormon comes to them "that ye may know the decrees of God—that ye may repent, and not continue in your iniquities until the fulness come, that ye may not bring down the fulness of the wrath of God upon you as the inhabitants of the land have hitherto done" (Ether 2:11). These lessons—often shown negatively as the people in the Book of Mormon do *not* follow them and therefore suffer the consequences—are then meant for modern readers to see and apply to themselves. In the end, readers are not so much to condemn the Nephites for their follies to "give thanks unto God that he hath made manifest unto [them, his people's,] imperfections, that [they] may learn to be more wise than [his people] have been" (Morm. 9:31).

Sod

Sod (pronounced *sōd*), or "mystery," is the fourth level of traditional rabbinic interpretation. According to George Robinson, it is "the method of biblical interpretation that search[es] for mystical significance."[22] In a sense, *sod* is the ultimate expression of the belief that God is the author of the Torah and has imbued everything about it with divinity. At the heart of this approach is the idea that the letters of the Torah themselves contain divine significance that extends beyond the words they form and therefore constitute keys to the mystery of God. As Gershom Scholem writes: "The acceptance of the Torah, in the strictest and most precise understanding of the concept of the word of God, in other words . . . Torah from heaven . . . [is the] basic assumption upon which all traditional Jewish mysticism in Kabbalah and Hasidism is based."[23]

Sod is the special province of Kabbalists and other mystics. They tend to view the stories in the Torah as its "mantle" or "outer garments" and not as its essence. They seek what lies under this mantle,[24] and therefore, according to Robinson, "read the Bible as a sort of codebook, a dictionary of symbols to be deciphered by methods such as *gematria* and *notarikon*."[25] *Gematria* focuses on the numerical value of words and phrases, and it attempts to find meaning or significance in these numbers. This approach is possible because each Hebrew letter also has a numerical value. Therefore, a group of letters can be read as both as a number as well as a word. The

---

22. Robinson, *Essential Judaism*, 305.

23. Gershom Scholem, *On the Possibility of Jewish Mysticism in Our Time*, 14.

24. Michael Berg, ed. and comp., *The Zohar: by Rav Shimon bar Yochai: from the book of Avraham: with Sulam commentary by Rav Ashlag*, 17:415.

25. Robinson, *Essential Judaism*, 305.

Hebrew letters ׳ ח, for instance, can mean both the Hebrew word *chai* (or "life") as well as 18, since this grouping consists of the eighth and tenth letters in the Hebrew alphabet. *Notarikon*, in contrast, still views the Hebrew letters as forming words, but these words can also be acronyms or multiple words, each hiding a secret or mystical meaning. As one mystical text puts it, "Many lights shine forth from each word and each letter."[26]

Because the Book of Mormon was neither written in Hebrew nor originally translated into Hebrew, any interpretation using *sod* in this way is naturally limited. Nonetheless, the Book of Mormon not only commends seeking after mysteries, but it also provides at least one mystical experience consistent with Jewish tradition. For instance, Nephi seems very interested in mysteries. In his introduction, he claims that he has had "a great knowledge of the goodness and the mysteries of God" (1 Ne. 1:1). Later he mentions that he had "great desires to know of the mysteries of God" as a youth and this is what motivated him to "cry unto the Lord" regarding his father's initial prophecies. Given his experience where "the Lord did visit [him]," Nephi commends seeking such mysteries for all, saying, "For he that diligently seeketh shall find; and the mysteries of God shall be unfolded unto them, by the power of the Holy Ghost, as well in these times as in times of old" (2:16; 10:19).

Jacob too praises the mysteries of God, especially their limitlessness, calling them "unsearchable" because of their depth and claiming that "it is impossible that man should find out all [God's] ways. And no man knoweth of his ways save it be revealed unto him; wherefore, brethren, despise not the revelations of God" (Jacob 4:8). King Benjamin further teaches that the plates of brass, his version of the Hebrew Scriptures, contain the "mysteries of God" and serve an irreplaceable function in allowing people to "read and understand of [God's] mysteries" (Mosiah 1:3, 5). King Limhi extends this function to the Book of Mormon by saying that "Doubtless a great mystery is contained within these plates [from which the book of Ether came], and these interpreters were doubtless prepared for the purpose of unfolding all such mysteries to the children of men" (Mosiah 8:19).

Knowing the mysteries of God, especially those contained in the Scriptures, seems vital to these and other writers of the Book of Mormon. In addition, the Book of Mormon recounts a protracted mystical experience that demonstrates how these mysteries of God can be revealed. As Robinson points out, in traditional Judaism "mystical truth is derived

---

26. Ibid.

from an esoteric symbol system embedded in the sacred text, but mystical truth can also come from dreams, visions, and revelations vouchsafed to a fortunate few"—prophets such as Ezekiel who saw God on his Chariot Throne or others who attempted to "re-create Ezekiel's experience and ascend in the Chariot to explore the heavens."[27] It is from the latter that Nephi learns mystical truth. Soon after he learns of his father's vision of the tree of life (mentioned earlier as an example of *remez)* but before he explains that vision to his brothers (an example of *derash*), Nephi desires a similar vision for himself. As Nephi writes: "For it came to pass after I had desired to know the things that my father had seen, and believing that the Lord was able to make them known unto me, as I sat pondering in mine heart I was caught away in the Spirit of the Lord, yea, into an exceedingly high mountain, which I never had before seen, and upon which I never had before set my foot" (1 Ne. 11:1).

The fact that Nephi is "caught away" into this mountain connects close-ly with the prototypical mystical experience of Ezekiel's, which, although, according to Rabbi Lawrence Kushner, "remained central to Jewish mysti-cism through history," has detractors.[28] According to Robinson, the later kabbalistic mystics shunned the Ezekiel tradition and attempted more "to understand the sacred texts, to see meaning *behind* the words, to explore the nature of God rather than to pay a house call."[29] Nephi's vision, in a sense, does both. Not only does he ascend to a temple-like mountain, but there he asks questions concerning his father's words and receives explana-tions. Similar to the way *gematria* and *notarikon* extend the significance of the Torah's words far beyond their usual meaning, these answers that Nephi receives go far beyond the actual words of Lehi's dream. In the true mystical spirit, Nephi hears much that is behind or beyond mere words.

When Nephi asks for an interpretation of the tree that his father saw, he is given an extended vision of the birth and life of the Lamb of God. When he sees the rod of iron, the vision continues showing how the Lamb performed miracles—how many were "healed by the power of the Lamb of God; and the devils and the unclean spirits were cast out" (1 Ne. 11:31). When he sees the "large and spacious building," he is told that it is the "the pride of the world." However, he also experiences an extended vision that includes the rise, fall, and eventual dispersion of his people, the

27. Ibid., 364–65.
28. Lawrence Kushner, *The Way Into Jewish Mystical Tradition*, 91.
29. Robinson, *Essential Judaism*, 370.

formation of a great and abominable church, the rise and problems of the Gentiles, as well as the final destruction of the earth.

In addition to retelling this significant mystical experience, the Book of Mormon encourages its readers to seek similar experiences. After his dream, Nephi returns "to the tent of [his] father" and there finds his brothers "disputing one with another concerning the things which [their] father had spoken unto them" (1 Ne. 15:2). Rather than beginning with his own explanations, recently received, Nephi pleads with them to seek the same experience he had, asking them "Have ye inquired of the Lord?" (v. 8). He then recites to them, as well as to his future readers, God's own words, saying: "If ye will not harden your hearts, and ask me in faith, believing that ye shall receive, with diligence in keeping my commandments, surely these things shall be made known unto you" (v. 11). In context, Nephi's "these things" means much more than the answer to their questions; it means Nephi's full vision.

In many ways, this statement of Nephi's is a foretaste of what he explains more expansively later on. In 2 Nephi 31, Nephi discourses at length on "the tongue of angels." By this he does not seem to mean glossolalia or the speaking in an unknown language but rather a way of conversing with the divine—both asking questions and receiving answers. He continues:

> Do ye not remember that I said unto you that after ye had received the Holy Ghost ye could speak with the tongue of angels? And now, how could ye speak with the tongue of angels save it were by the Holy Ghost?
>
> Angels speak by the power of the Holy Ghost; wherefore, they speak the words of Christ. Wherefore, I said unto you, feast upon the words of Christ; for behold, the words of Christ will tell you all things what ye should do. (2 Ne. 32:2–3)

Nephi never totally explains what this tongue of angels is. Like all mystical experiences, it seems beyond words. He instead attributes any lack of understanding on the part of his readers to the fact that they "ask not, neither do [they] knock" (2 Ne. 32:4). Moroni also takes up this theme at the end of the Book of Mormon when he encourages his readers to have mystical experience with God by engaging the scriptural text:

> Behold, I would exhort you that when ye shall read these things, if it be wisdom in God that ye should read them, that ye would remember how merciful the Lord hath been unto the children of men, from the creation of Adam even down unto the time that ye shall receive these things, and ponder it in your hearts. And when ye shall receive these things, I would exhort you that ye would ask God, the Eternal Father, in the name of Christ, if these

things are not true; and if ye shall ask with a sincere heart, with real intent, having faith in Christ, he will manifest the truth of it unto you, by the power of the Holy Ghost. And by the power of the Holy Ghost ye may know the truth of all things. (Moro. 10:3–5)

In this way, both Nephi and Moroni encourage their readers to have a *sod* experience with the text of the Book of Mormon as well as understand its plain sense, its allegorical meaning, and its sermonic significance. *Peshat, remez, derash*, and *sod* function together in the Book of Mormon much as they do in the Torah—by connecting its text with God, a never-ending source of enlightenment.

Chapter Three

Reading Closely

And he said unto me: Knowest thou the condescension of God? And I said unto him: I know that he loveth his children; nevertheless, I do not know the meaning of all things. (1 Ne. 11:16–17)

And they said unto me: What meaneth the river of water which our father saw? And I said unto them that the water which my father saw was filthiness; and so much was his mind swallowed up in other things that he beheld not the filthiness of the water. (1 Ne. 15:26–27)

Approaching the Torah, like approaching the Edenic Tree of Life, may indeed be treacherous. Textual problems—odd constructions, inconsistencies, and redundancies—can block the way into it just as effectively as cherubim wielding flaming swords. However, according to several Talmudic and post-Talmudic rabbis, such problems exist not so much to prevent readers from finding a way into the Torah as they encourage them to find its true path. As an orator in the Talmud states, "A man does not fully understand the words of the Torah until he has come to grief over them" (BT Gittin 43a). Called *kotzim* or "thorns," seemingly growing naturally out of the Tree of Life itself, these encouragements, as Cohen explains, are "small irritants in the Torah text that demand resolution," problems that prick their readers' attention, snagging it, sometimes painfully, holding on to their thoughts until they come to a deeper understanding of the text.[1] Much like Nephi's vision, where the Spirit shows Nephi an event and then waits expectantly for Nephi to ask about it, these problems are seen more as invitations to thoughtful inquiry than impediments to comprehension. They too patiently but persistently wait, spurring readers to move forward and to ponder everything about the scriptural text. For this reason, *peshat* was championed by Rashi, Ibn Ezra, and other classic

---

1. Norman J. Cohen, *The Way Into Torah*, 62.

rabbinic commentators as the most fundamental and most fruitful level of *pardes*. Close reading for them was the best way to solve these puzzles and unearth the text's hidden treasures.

Although *sod* could be considered the highest level of rabbinic interpretation (and indeed it was for the kabbalists), *peshat* is generally thought to be the foundation of all scriptural interpretation. Regardless of the approach—whether it is allegorical, sermonic, or mystical—the plain sense of a verse must be understood correctly or the validity of an interpretation falls to dust. Consequently, as Bonchek writes, "early and later rabbinic commentators of the Torah made use of rules of interpretation to probe [its plain] meaning and discover its message."[2] For instance, as Wylen writes, to prevent unfounded interpretations, the Rabbis taught that although "they did not believe that the message of Scripture was fully revealed in the literal sense of the words[, it] was generally agreed that 'the Torah speaks in the language of humans' [Sifre, Numbers 112] and 'the Torah never departs from its simple meaning' [BT Shabbat 63a]." In other words, the literal meaning is always part of the message of the Torah. But the literal meaning is not the only message, and it may not even be the most important message."[3]

Hillel, long before the Talmud was compiled, offered some rules that are helpful in interpreting the Torah, as did Rabbi Ishmael and others. However, as Rabbi Avigdor Bonchek, a gifted Torah teacher and lecturer at Hebrew University, explains, most of the rules that Talmudic Rabbis and the classic medieval commentators used "have remained implicit, never having been formally spelled out."[4] Nonetheless, these rabbis did supply copious examples of how to approach scripture productively and left a fairly clear idea of what that involved. As a result, it is clear that *peshat* is more than an unstructured effort to approach scripture in a careful, word-for-word way. According to Rabbi Bonchek, there is within rabbinic writings—especially in the later, medieval works—a well-developed discipline of *peshat*, which focuses on certain "keys" or aspects of the Scriptures that are particularly fruitful when it comes to discovering their deeper meanings. His book *Studying the Torah* conveniently attempts "to abstract, specify, and categorize" several of these keys possibly for the first time.[5] These keys include the following:

---

2. Avigdor Bonchek, *Studying the Torah: A Guide to In-Depth Interpretation*, 3.
3. Stephen M. Wylen, *Settings of Silver: An Introduction to Judaism*, 16.
4. Bonchek, *Studying the Torah*, 3.
5. Ibid., 6.

- **Opening sentences**—"Sentences that introduce sections often convey more information than is apparent at first glance. These sentences can set the tone for the ensuing section."
- **The contiguity principle**—"Meaning is always derived from its context. We can no more understand the meaning of a word isolated from its sentence than we can appreciate a musical note torn from its melody. . . . What [Bonchek calls] the contiguity principle [means] deriving interpretive clues from the neighboring text."
- **Similarities between different texts**—"Rare words or phrases which appear in different sections of the Torah, no matter how far separated, may be used as connecting links between the two sections. By tying together two apparently unrelated and separated by means of verbal association, the Torah creates an opportunity for us to become aware of a deeper message."
- **Differences between similar texts**—"Unexpected inconsistencies in the Torah can be as revealing as are subtle similarities. Often we find an event or statement repeated twice in the Torah yet, while the details are basically the same, there are glaring differences between the two accounts. These ostensible discrepancies cry out for interpretation."
- **Repetitions and redundancies**—"Repetitions and Redundancies are grist for the mill of classical biblical exegesis. Understanding the purpose of seemingly gratuitous Repetitions and apparent Redundancies is one of the most frequently used interpretive Keys of both the early midrashic Sages and the medieval Torah commentators."
- **Word order**—"One of the most obvious, and at the same time, most subtle, means by which we communicate nuances in meaning is by the way we choose to order our words. . . . The significance of word order is also apparent in the Torah's skillful use of literary allusion. An analysis of the Torah's language reveals an exquisitely sensitive use of Word Order to convey intended emphasis. By training our ear to notice these subtleties, we become conscious of the omnipresence of the phenomenon and become attuned to deeper meanings in the text."[6]

---

6. Ibid., 37, 49, 60, 71, 83, 95. Bonchek includes two additional keys—the psychological dimension and the seven code—which although part of a rabbinic approach to the Torah does not strictly deal with *peshat* and is therefore excluded from this study.

As Bonchek explains, following these rabbinic keys prevents interpretations that are "glaringly wrong."[7] They yield instead what he calls
"In-Depth Interpretation" or, more simply, valid Torah readings based on
peshat. They similarly produce rewarding readings when applied to the
Book of Mormon.

Hebrew Roots

Although not one of Bonchek's keys, reading the Torah in Hebrew
is implicit in all of them. As he writes, "all translations are necessarily interpretations and all interpretations are open to dispute."[8] Consequently,
he strongly advocates reading the Torah in Hebrew in order to interpret
the Torah more correctly and to see the nuances of words and relationships between words that a translation cannot show. Since the Book of
Mormon was neither originally written in Hebrew nor initially translated
into Hebrew, this presents its readers with a problem, one that the Book of
Mormon's original writers seem to bemoan. Moroni, for instance, pleads
with his future readers to "condemn me not because of mine imperfection, neither my father, because of his imperfection, neither them who
have written before him." He then adds that "if our plates had been sufficiently large we should have written in Hebrew; but the Hebrew hath
been altered by us also; and if we could have written in Hebrew, behold, ye
would have had no imperfection in our record" (Morm. 9:31, 33).

Moroni and the other writers of the Book of Mormon, like many
traditional Jews, seem to honor and revere Hebrew as a holy tongue, a
language vital to any clear communication with God. This is one of the
major reasons Nephi, a Jerusalemite, is grateful to have the brass plates,
that "we may preserve unto our children the *language* of our fathers" (1
Ne. 3:19)—he wanted his descendants to know Hebrew. Enos blesses
God that his father, Jacob, a "just man," taught him in "his language,"
also Hebrew (Enos 1:1), and one of King Mosiah's most notable achieve-
ments is that he "caused that [the Mulekites] should be taught in his language," most probably a dialect of Hebrew, since his people, the Nephites,
had brought an early version of the Hebrew Scriptures with them from
Jerusalem and their language had not "become corrupted" (Omni 1:17–
18). King Benjamin similarly caused that his sons "should be taught in
all the language of his fathers," undoubtedly Hebrew, so that "they might

---

7. Ibid., 12.
8. Ibid., 8.

become men of understanding" and read "the prophecies which had been spoken by the mouths of their fathers" (Mosiah 1:2) —another reference to the Hebrew Scriptures.

Nonetheless, the only Hebrew that remains in the Book of Mormon is preserved in the names of some of its major figures. However, as if to reinforce Bonchek's point, the meanings of many of these Hebrew names can greatly enhance a reader's understanding of these figures and their actions. The name *Benjamin*, for instance, means "son of the right hand" in Hebrew, and one of the main desires expressed in King Benjamin's final address is that those who shall take upon themselves the name of Christ "shall be found at the *right hand* of God" (Mosiah 5:9). Similarly *Noah* means "rest" and one of the most significant and vivid descriptions of King Noah involves the creation of a breastwork in front of the golden seats in which he and his priests sat, which was constructed so "that they might *rest* their bodies and their arms upon while they should speak lying and vain words to his people" (Mosiah 11:11).

However, kings are not the only figures in the Book of Mormon with Hebraically significant names. Gideon also, whose name means "hewer" or a person who "cuts off" something, is "a strong man and an enemy to the king, therefore he drew his sword, and swore in his wrath that he would slay the king" (Mosiah 19:4). Enos, "man or mankind," lays claim to no special attribute or quality that sets him above other men. He simply goes out "to hunt beasts in the forests" but soon hungers for eternal life, praying first for himself and then widening his concern to embrace all mankind, his enemies as well as his friends (Enos 1:3, 9, 11). Jared too, whose name means "to go down" in Hebrew, descends the Tower of Babel and goes "down into the valley which was northward." There his brother, known only as the "brother of Jared," speaks with the Lord, falls "down" before Him, comes "down out of the mount from the presence of the Lord," and upon reaching his Promised Land prompts his people to bow "down upon the face of the land, and did humble themselves before the Lord" (Ether 2:1; 3:6; 4:1; 6:2, 12).

These and other Hebraic names in the Book of Mormon reinforce many of its plots and portrayals, deepening the book and encouraging its readers to approach it with the kind of in-depth analysis that is the hallmark of traditional Jewish scripture study and is presented in all of Bonchek's keys.

Opening Sentences

To facilitate a yearly cycle of reading the entire Torah, the Rabbis divided the year into sections or *parashot* (also known as a *sidrot*—singular forms: *parashah* and *sidra*), which served as a kind of weekly reading assignment. The opening sentences of these *parashot*, according to Bonchek, are particularly meaningful and reward close reading. The Book of Mormon obviously is not similarly divided. However, it is divided into books, and the opening sentences of these books seem to function in the same way. According to Bonchek,

> Sentences that introduce sections in the Torah often convey more information than is apparent at first glance. These sentences can set the tone for the ensuing section, whether it be of a narrative or halachic character. The sensitive reader will pay close attention to the nuances in these sentences for clues which reveal either a motif, an important emphasis, or the main message of the passage.[9]

As an example of this approach, Bonchek cites Numbers 32:1, which in Hebrew begins with the word *miknei* or "cattle," the object the Reubenites and Gadites possessed, rather than "the children of Reuben" as the King James Version renders it. Therefore, in Hebrew the verse reads something like this: "Now a very great multitude of cattle the children of Reuben and the children of Gad had and when they saw the land of Jazer, and the land of Gilead, that, behold, the place [was] a place for cattle." Phrased this way, this sentence is extremely awkward, which is why most English versions rearrange it. However, to Bonchek the Hebrew phrasing is more appropriate and more meaningful. Not only does the odd word order signify that something is wrong—out of synch, so to speak—but it specifies what the problem is: the Reubenite and Gadite obsession with cattle. In this sentence, the word "cattle" appears twice, at the end as well as at the beginning. In this way, the word *cattle* "both opens and closes the sentence" and grammatically underlines how the lives of the Reubenites and Gadites begin and end with their livestock.[10] As the rest of the chapter shows, these two tribes decline to enter into the Promised Land with the other tribes, largely because of the cattle they found in the land of Gilead and Jazer.

The first sentence in the Book of Mormon functions in a similar way, revealing the major events as well as the thematic structure of 1 Nephi: "I, Nephi, having been born of goodly parents, therefore I was taught some-

---

9. Ibid., 37.
10. Ibid., 39.

what in all the learning of my father; and having seen many afflictions in the course of my days, nevertheless, having been highly favored of the Lord in all my days; yea, having had a great knowledge of the goodness and the mysteries of God, therefore I make a record of my proceedings in my days."

As with Numbers 32:1, this sentence has certain oddities that call attention to itself—especially the fact that it goes on and on, piling clause upon clause, in a meandering, almost undirected, haphazard way, until it reaches an almost too neat conclusion. Odd as this may seem, the structure of this sentence, however, fits in perfectly with the journey this book describes—a journey that similarly piles on event after event, goes on much longer than the travelers involved expect, and, although the journey involves many unexpected twists and turns, it all resolves in the end, landing them in a place that seems in retrospect to be the goal all along: the promised land.

In addition, although this opening sentence may seem somewhat random, showing little reason as to why one particular clause follows the other, the order of these clauses actually prefigures the stages of the journey described in 1 Nephi. In chapter 1, Nephi describes the situation of his "goodly parents," especially his father Lehi's prophetic call and work. In chapter 2, Nephi relates several experiences with Lehi, where he is taught "somewhat in all the learning of [his] father" both by precept (such as when Lehi speaks to his children in the valley of Lemuel) and by example (such as when Lehi builds an altar of stones and gives thanks unto God). In chapters 3 through 7, Nephi attempts to procure the brass plates and suffers "many afflictions in the course of [his] days." Here his brothers beat him after one failed attempt to get the plates and later, as they make their way back after retrieving Ishmael and his family, they bind him and consider killing him. In chapter 8 Lehi dreams a mysterious dream about a rod of iron leading to a tree of life. Nephi prays to "know the things that [his] father had seen," and in chapters 11 through 14 he receives a more expansive and explanatory version of his father's dream in which he gains a "great knowledge of the goodness and the mysteries of God." Finally, in chapter 19, Nephi is commanded to "make plates of ore that [he] might engraven upon them the record of [his] people" and record their "journeyings in the wilderness, and the prophecies of [his] father; and also many of [his] own prophecies" (v. 1). This effort continues through the rest of 1 Nephi and coincides with the last clause of his opening sentence: "therefore I make a record of my proceedings in my days."

The opening sentences in the Book of Jacob also prefigure two of the main topics of this book, although in different ways. As Jacob writes, "Wherefore Nephi gave me, *Jacob*, a commandment concerning the small plates upon which these things are written. And he gave me, *Jacob*, a commandment that I should write upon these plates a few of the things which I considered to be most *precious*" (Jacob 1:2). Here "Jacob" and "precious" signify the major topics Jacob treats in his book. In the next chapter, Jacob mentions how his people have "begun to search for gold, and for silver, and for all manner of *precious* ores" (2:12). He describes the problems that have arisen among them as they acquired such riches—namely, their being "lifted up in the pride of your hearts," having "stiff necks and high heads because of the costliness of your apparel," and persecuting "your brethren because ye suppose that ye are better than they" (v. 13). At this point, he enjoins them to seek "for the kingdom of God" before they "seek for riches" and then, if they obtain riches, to use them "to clothe the naked, and to feed the hungry, and to liberate the captive, and administer relief to the sick and the afflicted" (vv. 18–19). Finally he turns the topic completely on its head when, by explicitly using the word "precious," (the same word used to describe the things he was supposed to write about in Jacob 1:2), and by admonishing them to cease pridefully setting themselves above others and instead remember that "one being is as *precious* in his sight as the other" (2:21).

Later on in chapter 5, Jacob switches topics. As befits someone named after the father of the children of Israel, Jacob gathers his people together that he may similarly tell them "that which shall befall [them] in the last days" (Gen. 49:1). He does this by reading to them the words of Zenos, who spoke "unto the house of Israel" (Jacob 5:1), the original Jacob's other name, and unfolds the great saga of the scattering and gathering of Israel in the form of an allegory. This allegory, again as is appropriate to someone named Jacob, builds upon the patriarch's blessing of Joseph, from whom the Nephites are descended, but instead of a single "fruitful bough" (Gen. 49:22), Zenos likens all of the house of Israel "unto a tame olive-tree" (Jacob 5:3).

After recounting the allegory, Jacob prophecies that "the day that [the Lord] shall set his hand again the second time to recover his people, is the day, yea, even the last time, that the servants of the Lord shall go forth in his power, to nourish and prune his vineyard; and after that the end soon cometh" (Jacob 6:2). He pleads with them not to "bring forth evil fruit" but to instead repent "and enter in at the strait gate, and continue in the way which is narrow." He then bids them farewell as though he were about to die, or, as he says, "until I shall meet you before the pleasing bar of God" (vv. 11, 13). This also is similar to his forefather's final words, where he concludes his blessings with instructions as to his burial (Gen. 49:29). In this way, the opening sentences in both 1 Nephi and in Jacob fulfill Bonchek's *peshat* requirement that such sentences reveal "a motif, an important emphasis, or the main message of the passage."[11]

The Contiguity Principle

According to Bonchek, the Contiguity Principle involves "deriving interpretive clues from the neighboring text." It is a more focused application of the principle prominent in In-Depth Interpretation of "viewing the text within its larger context."[12] For example, a quick reading of Genesis 3 does not seem to justify its description of Eden's serpent as "more subtil than any beast of the field" (Gen. 3:1). As Bonchek writes: "We can take it as a given that the serpent's subtlety wouldn't have been mentioned were it not integral to the story. Yet what the serpent said was not particularly subtle or sly. What he said was quite to the point, that this was a Tree of Knowledge or Good and Evil and that knowledge would make man similar to God. He was just 'telling it as it is.'"[13]

However, by carefully noting Eve's inaccurate quotation of God's prohibition a few verses later, Bonchek shows that by "exaggerating the actual prohibition (from one tree to 'every tree of the garden'), the serpent created a new, but lopsided, frame of reference," a frame that catches Eve off guard and slyly manipulates her into ultimately deciding on a course of action she would not have agreed upon otherwise. Eve does not merely respond that God commanded her and Adam not to eat of the "tree of the knowledge of good and evil," as is quoted in Genesis 2:17. Instead she adds an additional prohibition: "neither shall [they] touch it" (3:3). This response is also an exaggeration and suggests that the serpent has tricked her into bargaining. Because he began the exchange with an offer far out of proportion with what he really wanted, she responded similarly, out of reflex. They ultimately "settle" then on an action the serpent wanted all

---

11. Ibid., 37.
12. Ibid., 49.
13. Ibid., 51.

along. As Bonchek concludes, in this way "the Torah is subtle about the serpent's subtleness," by revealing it quietly through its neighboring text.[14]

Nephi's description of the Liahona as being "of curious workmanship" (1 Ne. 16:10) similarly seems odd. Because of the near-King Jamesian language used in the Book of Mormon, some readers look to that version of the Bible for help and connect this object with Aaron's high-priestly "girdle," which is also described as "curious" (Ex. 28:8). These readers conclude that the Liahona must, like that girdle, be somehow ingeniously or cunningly made. This is, after all, what the Hebrew word translated as "curious" in the King James Version means.[15] The problem, however, is that there is nothing in the description of the Liahona itself that supports such an interpretation. Nowhere does Nephi even hint that the way this object is made is somehow ingenious or cunning. The description of "curious" in this way does not fit. However, a close look at the text that follows the introduction of the Liahona does fit the idea that the Liahona was curious in a different way—as an object of puzzlement whose "workmanship," meaning how it works rather than how it was *made*, remains a mystery for Lehi's family for a very long time.

From the moment it appears, the Liahona creates more questions than it answers. First of all, it simply shows up at the door of Lehi's tent without any explanation as to how it got there or who made it. It is assumed that it was formed by the Lord and placed there by Him. However, Nephi does not describe the Liahona in this way initially. Only much later, when they are at sea, does Nephi state that the Liahona was "prepared of the Lord" (1 Ne. 18:12). Secondly, Nephi's description of the Liahona could hardly be more vague. He calls it a "round ball" of "fine brass"—saying nothing about its size, weight, ornamentation, composition, or construction. It is not even clear if the Liahona is hollow or not. Nephi adds that it has two spindles, but he does not reveal how they are attached, how they move, or how they are visible (whether they can be seen outside the ball or require opening it somehow). He says only that one of the spindles "pointed the way whither [they] should go into the wilderness" (1 Ne. 16:10)—a statement that almost cries out for further clarification. What, after all, did the other spindle do and how did he know which one to trust? This description of the Liahona is about as helpful as calling a laptop computer a flat box made of plastic with buttons on it, one of which turns it on.

---

14. Ibid., 52.

15. See the definition of *cheshev* in Francis Brown, S.R. Driver, and Charles A. Briggs, *The Brown-Driver-Briggs Hebrew and English Lexicon*, 363.

In many ways, the appearance of the Liahona recalls the appearance of manna in the wilderness of Sinai. In the morning, "when the dew that lay was gone up," the Israelites wake up to find "a small round thing, as small as the hoar frost on the ground" (Ex. 16:14). This description is also extremely vague, and although it too appears to be a miracle, prepared in its own way by God, the Israelites do not know what to make of it—what it is or what it is for. In fact the word "manna" in Hebrew actually means "'what is it?" Judging by the succeeding verses, Lehi and his family react similarly to the Liahona. Although it is supposed to point the way in the wilderness, supplying an obviously miraculous and much needed function, the Liahona does not seem to be appreciated or even used at first. In the verse following the discovery of the Liahona, Lehi and his family do not explicitly gather around the Liahona, watch as it amazingly points to the direction they should go, or march off confident that God is directing them to the Promised Land. Instead they rather matter-of-factly "gather together whatsoever things [they] should carry into the wilderness," take their tents, and "depart into the wilderness, across the river Laman" (1 Ne. 16:11–12). They then travel for "the space of four days, nearly a south-southeast direction" and make camp at a place they called Shazar (v. 13).

Only after many days of traveling, "following the same direction," does Nephi mention, as an afterthought, that they "did follow the directions of the ball, which led [them] in the more fertile parts of the wilderness" (vv. 14, 16). The fact that the Liahona is not mentioned for six verses coupled with the statement that it led them to "fertile parts" long after they had found suitable places to camp gives the impression that they neither understood fully what the Liahona was, nor did they really know how to use it. Its "workmanship," in other words, remains a mystery to them.

This lack of understanding becomes even more apparent when Nephi breaks his bow, an act that severely limits the family's ability to find food. A crisis ensues, so serious that not only do "Laman and Lemuel and the sons of Ishmael . . . begin to murmur exceedingly," but so does Lehi. For the first time, he too starts "to murmur against the Lord his God" (v. 20). However, despite the seriousness of this situation, no one suggests consulting the Liahona or even mentions it. It is only when Nephi takes matters into his own hands, constructs a bow of his own, and asks Lehi for instructions on where to hunt that the idea of using the Liahona comes up—and then only by divine intervention.

After Lehi did "inquire of the Lord," the "voice of the Lord" comes to him and chastens him because of his murmuring" (vv. 24–25). This communication seems to come directly to Lehi and not through any means such as the Liahona. Instead, "the voice of the Lord said unto him: Look upon the ball, and behold the things which are written" (v. 26). This seems like a novel idea to Lehi, but not so shocking as what happens next. When he scrutinizes the Liahona, Lehi sees that there are "things which were written upon the ball." So unexpected is this that Lehi "did fear and tremble exceedingly, and also [Nephi's] brethren and the sons of Ishmael and [their] wives" (v. 27). Apparently, they all had no idea the Liahona worked this way.

Nephi, however, does not seem as surprised. Perhaps he has used the Liahona more while hunting and therefore knew more about it. Perhaps he is not recalling his reaction correctly. Still, this has to be somewhat of a shock to him because he too did not suggest using the Liahona previously. Furthermore, it is only at this point in the story that Nephi relates the basic operating principle of the Liahona—that "the pointers which were in the ball, . . . did work according to the faith and diligence and heed which we did give unto them" (v. 28). Expressed as it is, at the end of this experience, this principle comes off as an important discovery, an "aha" moment, if you will. At long last Nephi and the rest of the family understand how the Liahona works and how to use it, knowledge that they now use especially in crossing the sea. In other words, the workmanship of the Liahona is no longer "curious." The puzzle has finally been solved, the mystery revealed, and Nephi therefore offers a concluding moral to this lesson: "And thus we see that by small means the Lord can bring about great things" (v. 29). In this way, it is apparent that Bonchek's contiguity principle applies to the Book of Mormon as well as to the Torah—by enabling its readers to better understand its meaning by "deriving interpretive clues from the neighboring text."[16]

Similarities between Different Texts

Passages in one place in the Torah can also help readers interpret passages in another. Subtle similarities in word usage or sentence construction can connect otherwise very different and often distant passages in such a way as to amplify both and deepen their significance. Looking for meaningful similarities in distant passages is therefore another of Bonchek's keys to the Torah. As he writes: "The Torah is a unified document. At the

---

16. Bonchek, *Studying the Torah*, 49.

same time, it is a large variegated tapestry, an intricate masterpiece with different patterns woven in it. Yet, for all that, it remains a cohesive whole. This means, in effect, that to be able to fully understand any one section of the Torah, one must be familiar with all its sections."[17]

Studious, like-minded Jews therefore attempt to listen for faint echoes of one passage—an odd word, a strange phrase, an unusual way of framing a sentence, a notable name—in other places in the Torah, always looking for subtle connections that could shed additional light on or give more meaning to the first passage. One such passage that Bonchek provides as an example comes from Genesis 47:22, which reads: "Only the land of the priests bought he not; for the priests had a portion assigned them of Pharaoh, and did eat their portion which Pharaoh gave them: wherefore they sold not their lands."

This passage, which describes the situation of the Egyptian priests during the time of Joseph, shows how the priests by virtue of their calling—the word "wherefore" ("*al kain*" in Hebrew, signifying causality)—had land assigned to them and therefore Joseph did not buy it from them with grain he had stored in preparation for the seven-year famine. Although this passage may not seem terribly significant or meaningful on its own, according to Bonchek it becomes so when connected to a very different passage in Deuteronomy. This passage reads: "At that time the Lord separated the tribe of Levi, to bear the ark of the covenant of the Lord, to stand before the Lord to minister unto him, and to bless in his name, unto this day. Wherefore Levi hath no part nor inheritance with his brethren; the Lord is his inheritance, according as the Lord thy God promised him" (Deut. 10:8–9).

This passage in Deuteronomy like the one in Genesis also deals with the situation of priests—the tribe of Levi—and the land rights (or lack thereof) they have because of their position as priests. As Bonchek writes, "The contrast is striking. The precise reason justifying the holding of land by the Egyptian priests is the reason for the Jewish priests *not* to be landholders!" Bonchek notes that "this contrast is brought to our notice by the use of the similar term *Al Kain*," the "wherefore" in this passage from Deuteronomy, which serves as the "connecting phrase that makes us aware of the true difference between the two priestly cases." In other words, although these two passages are separated by many pages and describe very different peoples, the fact that they deal with a similar subject, display the same sort of cause-and-effect reasoning, and use identical phraseology

---

17. Ibid., 59.

unites them and highlights the uniqueness of Levitical priests. Unlike the Egyptian priests, they are called to be, as Bonchek writes, wholly "devoted to spiritual pursuits" as opposed to worldly concerns.[18]

In similar ways, the Book of Mormon uses a few words to connect an incident from its very beginning to one near its end. Although Nephi's agonized killing of Laban in 1 Nephi 4 is very different from Coriantumr's brutal decapitation of Shiz in Ether 15, the two are verbally connected in a way that helps readers understand and appreciate just what Nephi did. Few incidents from the Book of Mormon are more memorable and more troubling than Laban's death at the hands of Nephi. The very idea that the same God who commanded his people not to murder would also demand that one of his servants cut off the head of an unconscious man gives most sensitive readers pause—as it does Nephi. As Nephi writes, "I said in my heart: Never at any time have I shed the blood of man. And I shrunk and would that I might not slay him" (1 Ne. 4:10). The Spirit, however, persists and lays out several reasons why Nephi should kill Laban. The first reason the Spirit gives is that "Lord hath delivered him into [Nephi's] hands." This fact seems only too clear to Nephi as he contemplates the once powerful Laban lying defenseless in a drunken stupor in front of him. However, Nephi is not convinced he should kill Laban and considers its morality and legality. He recalls that Laban "had sought to take away [his] own life," "would not hearken unto the commandments of the Lord," "and he also had taken away [their] property" (v. 11). As Nephi considers these additional aspects, the Spirit seems to confirm his line of reasoning and again commands Nephi to "slay [Laban], for the Lord hath delivered him into thy hands" (v. 12). But, this time the Spirit adds an additional explanation. Building upon Nephi's reasoning, the Spirit says, "Behold the Lord slayeth the wicked to bring forth his righteous purposes. It is better that one man should perish than that a nation should dwindle and perish in unbelief" (v. 13). This explanation seems to convince the hitherto skeptical Nephi. He recalls the promise the Lord made to him concerning his posterity, how they would prosper in the land if they obey the Lord's commandments, and he realizes none of this will occur if he does not kill Laban and obtain the plates of brass:

> I also thought that they could not keep the commandments of the Lord according to the law of Moses, save they should have the law. And I also knew that the law was engraven upon the plates of brass. And again, I knew that

18. Ibid., 61.

the Lord had delivered Laban into my hands for this cause—that I might obtain the records according to his commandments. (1 Ne. 4:15–17)

It is at this point then, after fully considering the Spirit's points and weighing them in his mind, that Nephi finally obeys the voice of the Spirit, takes "Laban by the hair of the head," and smites "off his head with [Laban's] own sword" (v. 18). Nephi's action is certainly not rash or performed in the heat of the moment. He considers it carefully and lays out a rigorous rationale before actually killing Laban—a rationale that includes being certain the Spirit actually commands such a thing, demanding repetition to avoid mistakes in spiritual perception, considering Laban's moral situation as demonstrated by his actions, and requiring a greater good that affects multitudes. It is this "greater good" argument that, though powerful, concerns many modern readers. This argument has, after all, been misused and misappropriated by Nazis, Soviets, terrorists, and even, in the view of some, certain American politicians to one degree or another. Any invocation of this argument must, therefore, be checked and rechecked before it can be considered.

In this light, it is helpful that there is another incident in the Book of Mormon that verifies the truth of the Spirit's explanation to Nephi and shows in clear terms what the alternative is. In Ether another instance of decapitation uses the same verb and direct object as Nephi does to describe this event: "And it came to pass that when Coriantumr had leaned upon his sword, that he rested a little, he *smote off* the *head* of Shiz" (Ether 15:30). This passage and the one concerning Nephi and Laban are the only two places in the entire Book of Mormon where anyone kills someone using these three words. Nowhere else do they occur. However, despite these shared words, nothing else about these two events seems similar. Nephi's action, as we have seen, comes at the start of his story. He is a young man, somewhat unsure of himself. His family is struggling to figure out what the Lord wants them to do in the wilderness, and his killing of Laban seems very much out of character both for Nephi and for his family's situation. No one in the family seems to be trained to use a sword, they are not at war, and they have no history of conflict or, as far as we know, violence. The opposite is true of Coriantumr. His killing of Shiz comes at the very end of not only his story, but of the story of his people. Coriantumr is an older man, a soldier-king. He is trained in swordplay and skilled "in all the arts of war and all the cunning of the world" (13:16). His world seems to be in a continual state of war, and he has been involved in many battles, both receiving and giving severe wounds. The history of Coriantumr's people is, for the most part, identical to his own. They seem to be always at war, one side temporarily prevailing, while the other gathers strength and returns to power, until the first revives and retaliates, continuing the struggle, again and again and again, culminating with Coriantumr's final battle with his sworn enemy, Shiz. At that time

> so great and lasting had been the war, and so long had been the scene of bloodshed and carnage, that the whole face of the land was covered with the bodies of the dead. And so swift and speedy was the war that there was none left to bury the dead, but they did march forth from the shedding of blood to the shedding of blood, leaving the bodies of both men, women, and children strewed upon the face of the land, to become a prey to the worms of the flesh. (Ether 14:21–22)

In many ways, the situations of Nephi killing Laban and of Coriantumr killing Shiz could not be more different. But that is the point. By verbally connecting these two killings through the use of the words "smote off" and "head," the Book of Mormon brings these two situations together to highlight their differences. The contrast dramatically reveals just what it was that Nephi averted when he killed Laban: a violent, lawless civilization that could not follow the commandments of the Lord because it did not have them. Consequently, all the people in Ether "dwindle and perish in unbelief"—*all* of them—just as the Spirit predicted Nephi's descendants would if he had not killed Laban and taken the plates. Coriantumr's "smiting off of the head" of Shiz is then a poignant reminder, a kind of verbal flashback, showing that had Nephi not killed Laban as he did he would have condemned hundreds of thousands of his own descendants to a similar grisly death.

Obviously, things did not turn out well in the end for Nephi's descendants either. After a thousand years, many of them also became thoroughly evil and were similarly destroyed. However, their history is not nearly so bloody nor so wholly devoted to violence as is the Jaredite history. Armed with the plates of brass, the Nephites enjoy several long periods of peace and prosperity where they kept the Law of Moses (2 Ne. 25:24) and "the laws of the land were exceedingly strict" (Jarom 1:5). They also experience a blissful two hundred year period where "there was no contention in the land, because of the love of God which did dwell in the hearts of the people" (4 Ne. 1:15). In addition, theirs was not a complete destruction. Not only did the Lamanites survive to be reclaimed at a later time, but so did many Nephites who mixed with the Lamanites earlier or later "deserted over unto the Lamanites" near the end (Moro. 9:24).

The Jaredite history, as recorded in the book of Ether, however, shows almost no periods of peace or righteousness. Since they came to the Americas long before Moses and had no contact with him, they did not have the benefit of the Law of Moses and therefore could not follow its commandments. For the same reasons, they did not have anything close to the current body of Hebrew Scriptures. Abraham, Isaac, and Jacob lived long after they left the Near East. They also had no book detailing the Exodus or recounting the ever volatile history of the kingdoms of Israel and Judah or preserving the prophecies of Isaiah or Jeremiah or Ezekiel. The Jaredites had prophets among them, but there is no record of these prophets reading from the Scriptures or commanding the people to study them. At one point, a record of some sort is mentioned, writings that their "fathers brought across the great deep." However this does not seem to be anything like the Hebrew Scriptures. Instead of commandments and prophecies, it contains "secret plans [with which they] did obtain kingdoms and great glory" (Ether 8:9)—hardly biblical stuff.

The history of the Jaredites is a stark contrast with that of the Nephites on the very same land, and the verbal connection to Nephi's killing of Laban at the end shows it to be a vision of what the Nephite history could have been had not Nephi killed Laban. The Lamanites and the Nephites, like the two factions in Ether, would have been continually at each other's throats, swearing like Shiz to slay the other or "perish by the sword," and fighting with no respite until they "had all fallen by the sword" (Ether 15:28–29). Without the Scriptures to ground them Satan would have "had full power over the hearts of the people; for they were given up unto the hardness of their hearts, and the blindness of their minds that they might be destroyed" (v. 19). In this way, the Book of Mormon supports the idea that it is indeed "better that one man should perish than that a nation should dwindle and perish in unbelief" (1 Ne. 4:13).

Differences between Similar Texts

Not only are similarities between different scriptural texts illuminating, but so are differences between similar texts. As Bonchek writes, "Unexpected inconsistencies in the Torah can be as revealing as are subtle similarities. Often we find an event or statement repeated twice in the Torah yet, while the details are basically the same, there are glaring differences between the two accounts."[19] Such differences have given rise to the multiple source approach to the Torah. The reason these inconsistencies exist, so say these scholars (and many liberal Jews), is that they come from different sources and different times and therefore are dealing with similar events but in significantly different ways, which reflect their different backgrounds, political situations, and viewpoints.

Traditional Jews, however, seek instead to reconcile these inconsistencies and find meaning in them. They consider approaches such as source criticism to be an insult to the integrity of the Torah, even a kind of blasphemy. To them these approaches represent a kind of "bailing out," where readers fail to put in the necessary effort required to patiently plumb the Scriptures for hidden messages from God. For this reason Bonchek essentially lectures his readers, writing that "too often academic biblical scholars consider [small differences between similar texts] to be evidence of several oral traditions, 'editorial oversights,' inadvertent inconsistencies, signifying nothing. Glossing over inconsistencies in this way reflects a gross underestimation of the Torah's narrative precision and its literary sophistication. It also deprives one of retrieving valuable insights that the Torah intended to convey."[20]

Bonchek cites two apparently conflicting texts as an example of his point. Both Exodus 20 and Deuteronomy 5 command Israel to keep the Sabbath and refrain from working on this day. However, they offer two very different reasons for doing so. Exodus 20 claims that the Sabbath points back to the pattern of Creation: "in six days the Lord made heaven and earth, the sea, and all that in them is, and rested the seventh day: *wherefore the Lord blessed the sabbath day, and hallowed it*" (v. 11). Deuteronomy 5, however, harkens back to the time when Israel was delivered from slavery in Egypt: "And remember that thou wast a servant in the land of Egypt, and that the Lord thy God brought thee out thence through a mighty hand and by a stretched out arm: *therefore the Lord thy God commanded thee to keep the sabbath day*" (v. 15).

Bonchek sees no conflict in these passages. To him these differences are merely the result of different emphases, which complement each other. As he writes, "The discrepancy disappears once we look closely at the full text in the Torah." As he continues, "In Exodus, we are told why the Sabbath is a special day, why the Lord blessed it. . . . [In Deuteronomy, we] are told why, of all nations, the Jews are commanded to observe the

---

19. Ibid., 71.
20. Ibid.

Sabbath. . . . The reason given in Deuteronomy is that since the Jews were slaves in Egypt and the Lord redeemed them, they are thus beholden to Him. They are commanded to proclaim His dominion in the world by keeping the Sabbath."[21] In other words, neither text is actually stating why the Sabbath exists in some sort of general way; they are much more specific, giving reasons for more specific aspects of the Sabbath—Exodus explains why it is blessed and Deuteronomy offers a reason as to why Israel is to keep it. In this way the two complement or help complete each other and in no way are contradictory.

The Book of Mormon bridges these two scholarly traditions. Although it openly and frequently states that many authors penned its original source text—a good bit of which was later edited or abridged by Mormon and his son, Moroni—it also responds well to efforts to reconcile and find truths in apparent differences in similar texts. For instance, although Mosiah 27 and Alma 36 deal with the same incident—the conversion of Alma the Younger—they come from different authors and tell the story in significantly different ways. In Mosiah 27, Alma is an evil menace to his community. He is a "very wicked and idolatrous man." He flatters many and leads them away "after the manner of his iniquities." He is consequently a "great hinderment to the prosperity of the church of God" and causes "much dissension among the people" in general (vv. 8–9). In Alma 36, however, although Alma claims to have "many sins," he only mentions seeking "to destroy the church of God" and does so briefly (vv. 9, 17). In Mosiah, an angel appears to Alma and his companions, chastises them at length, and causes "Alma and those that were with him [to fall] again to the earth" (27:18), but in Alma, it is only he that falls, and the angelic sermon is much shorter. In Mosiah, the fallen Alma is carried to his father where he is prayed over for two days and nights until he recovers. In Alma, he is paralyzed for three days and three nights, and there is no mention of anyone praying. In other words, there would seem to be major fundamental differences between these accounts. However, despite these differences, a close reading of the two stories explains the reasons for their differences and shows them to be complementary, offering a more complete view of Alma's experience.

Mosiah 27 is Mormon's edited account of Alma's conversion. It is told in the third person and is, in general, a larger, more external view of the incident, based on the account of his companions, the sons of

21. Ibid., 74.

Mosiah. Here the context is the general prosperity in the land and how the Nephites had "became a large and wealthy people" (v. 7), always an indication in the Book of Mormon that the people are about to become prideful and forget God. The account of Alma's being "numbered among the unbelievers" (v. 8) along with the sons of Mosiah, who are the sons of the king just as Alma is the son of the high priest, very much falls in line with this pattern. In many ways this is a story about the "rich and powerful" and therefore serves as an emblem of the spiritual situation of the people as a whole. In keeping with this approach, Mormon dwells on Alma the Younger's unbelief from a societal point of view, describing at length his iniquities and how his behavior and that of Mosiah's sons impacted his society as a whole.

At some point an angel appears to Alma and the sons of Mosiah, descending spectacularly "as it were in a cloud" and speaking to them "as it were with a voice of thunder, which caused the earth to shake upon which they stood" (Mosiah 27:11). They all fall to the earth, and Alma is told to stand. The angel then asks him why he is persecuting the church, affirms that it is the Lord's church, and then states it is because of the prayers of the people in that church that he has come: "Behold, the Lord hath heard the prayers of his people, and also the prayers of his servant, Alma, who is thy father; for he has prayed with much faith concerning thee that thou mightest be brought to the knowledge of the truth; therefore, for this purpose have I come to convince thee of the power and authority of God, that the prayers of his servants might be answered according to their faith" (v. 14). The angel consequently commands Alma to remember the captivity of his fathers in Helam, a place where Alma's father and his people had been enslaved by the Lamanites and had escaped only after the people "did pour out their hearts" to the Lord their God and the Lord promised to "deliver them out of bondage" (24:12–13). Alma is also admonished to "seek to destroy the church no more, that their prayers may be answered, and this even if thou wilt of thyself be cast off (27:16).

After the angel departs, Alma and "those that were with him," a sweeping description that seems to include not just the sons of Mosiah but others, fall again to the earth, and Alma is struck dumb. Alma becomes "weak, even that he could not move his hands; therefore he was taken by those that were with him, and carried helpless, even until he was laid before his father" (Mosiah 27:18–19). Alma's father invites "a multitude . . . that they might witness what the Lord had done for his son," and, seemingly as a communal act of penance, this multitude begins "to fast, and to pray to the Lord their God that he would open the mouth of Alma, that he might speak, and also that his limbs might receive their strength—that the eyes of the people might be opened to see and know of the goodness and glory of God" (vv. 21–22). The people continue fasting and praying for "two days and two nights" at which time "the limbs of Alma received their strength, and he stood up and told all present that he had repented of his sins, was "redeemed of the Lord," and had been "born of the Spirit" (vv. 23–24). The remainder of the chapter concerns Alma's explanation as to how "after wading through much tribulation, repenting nigh unto death, the Lord in mercy hath seen fit to snatch [him] out of an everlasting burning" and allowed him to be "born of God" (v. 28). The chapter also describes Alma's effort from that "time forward to teach the people, . . . traveling round about through all the land, publishing to all the people the things which they had heard and seen, and preaching the word of God in much tribulation" (v. 32). Considering the context and the emphasis on prayer, this incident seems to stress as its main point the power of prayer and its effect in counteracting both internal and external evil as well as keeping the people humble and spiritually prosperous.

Alma 36, on the other hand, deals with the same incident but from an entirely different point of view and purpose. This version is presented in the first person, presumably written by Alma the Younger himself. It is an internal account, concentrating on what happens to Alma without making much mention of anything that happens to others. The context of this account is therefore much more intimate. Here Alma and his family are gathered in a Passover-like setting, commemorating Israel's deliverance from slavery in Egypt. Consistent with a Passover Seder, Alma begins advising his sons, each in a way that is appropriate to him, "to do as [he has] done, in remembering the captivity of [their] fathers." He has already discussed how the children of Israel "were in bondage, and none could deliver them except it was the God of Abraham, and the God of Isaac, and the God of Jacob," and he now explains in personal terms how God continues to "deliver them in their afflictions" (v. 2).

Appropriate to this setting, Alma avoids the larger, more impersonal, society-wide perspective and focuses instead on the present state of his sons' lives. Here he attempts instead to make the point that if Helaman and his brothers "shall put their trust in God [they] shall be supported in their trials, and their troubles, and their afflictions, and shall be lifted up at the last day" (v. 3). Consequently, Alma says nothing about the state of Nephite society at the time of his experience and almost nothing about his problems with the church. He also avoids any lengthy discussion about the sons of Mosiah, stating only that he "went about with the sons of Mosiah, seeking to destroy the church of God" (v. 6). His description of the encounter with the angel is also significantly shortened, saying only that "God sent his holy angel to stop us by the way" and that the angel spoke to them "as it were the voice of thunder, and the whole earth did tremble beneath our feet; and we all fell to the earth, for the fear of the Lord came upon us" (v. 7). Alma also does not mention that they were astonished or that they did not understand the angel at first.

The angel's speech is also severely truncated. In this account, the angel asks no questions and says nothing about the prayers of the people or Alma's father. There is no mention concerning Alma's disputing the power of God or failing to remember the captivity at Helam. Alma recounts only that the angel commanded him to "seek no more to destroy the church of God." This command is virtually identical to the one given in Mosiah. However, Alma prefaces it with a condition that is not found in Mosiah: "If thou wilt of thyself be destroyed" (v. 9). The singularity of the pronoun here seems to be significant. It is almost as if Alma goes off at this point to some psychological state by himself, alone, away from others and their concerns. He says that he subsequently fell to the earth without mentioning Mosiah's sons or elaborating on what the angel said next. As Alma explains, "the angel spake more things unto me, which were heard by my brethren, but I did not hear them; for when I heard the words—If thou wilt be destroyed of thyself, seek no more to destroy the church of God—I was struck with such great fear and amazement lest perhaps I should be destroyed, that I fell to the earth and I did hear no more" (v. 11).

At this point, after Alma became paralyzed, he describes in great detail what went through his mind: not how the people prayed for him for two days, but how he was "racked with torment" for "three days and for three nights" as he "was harrowed up by the memory of [his] many sins"; how he remembered his father prophesying "the coming of one Jesus Christ, a Son of God, to atone for the sins of the world"; how he "cried within [his] heart: O Jesus, thou Son of God, have mercy on me"; and how his "soul was filled with joy as exceeding as was [his] pain" and he thought he saw "God sitting upon his throne, surrounded with numberless concourses of angels, in the attitude of singing and praising their God" (vv. 16–22).

When Alma recovers, he states, as in the Mosiah account, that he will now dedicate himself to the teaching of his people. However, here he does so in a manner that is much more expressive and in a way that is more sensory and personal. He says not only that "from that time even until now, I have labored without ceasing, that I might bring souls unto repentance" but that "I might bring them to *taste* of the exceeding joy of which I did *taste*; that they might also be born of God, and be filled with the Holy Ghost" (v. 24). This trend he continues as he goes on to relate his experience in internal, personal terms, using food imagery consistent with a Seder meal:

> Yea, and now behold, O my son, the Lord doth give me exceedingly great joy in the fruit of my labors; For because of the word which he has imparted unto me, behold, many have been born of God, and have *tasted* as I have *tasted*, and have *seen* eye to eye as I have *seen*; therefore they do *know* of these things of which I have spoken, as I do know; and the knowledge which I have is of God. (Alma 36:25–26)

Finally, Alma returns to his original Passover purpose and encourages his son Helaman to put his trust in the Lord's power to deliver him in times of difficulty:

> Yea, and now behold, O my son, the Lord doth give me exceedingly great joy in the fruit of my labors; For because of the word which he has imparted unto me, behold, many have been born of God, and have tasted as I have tasted, and have seen eye to eye as I have seen; therefore they do know of these things of which I have spoken, as I do know; and the knowledge which I have is of God. And I have been supported under trials and troubles of every kind, yea, and in all manner of afflictions; yea, God has delivered me from prison, and from bonds, and from death; yea, and I do put my trust in him, and he will still deliver me. And I know that he will raise me up at the last day, to dwell with him in glory; yea, and I will praise him forever, for he has brought our fathers out of Egypt, and he has swallowed up the Egyptians in the Red Sea; and he led them by his power into the promised land; yea, and he has delivered them out of bondage and captivity from time to time. (Alma 36:25–28)

In this way, the accounts the Mosiah and Alma though different are not contradictory or inconsistent. They instead work together to show the personal as well as the societal side of sin, repentance, and forgiveness.

Redundancies and Repetitions

Redundancies and repetitions are also frequent sources of hidden meaning for traditional Jewish interpreters of the Torah. Although, as Bonchek points out, there is "no essential difference" between repetitions and redundancies in that both appear to be superfluous and therefore demand interpretation, they each present slightly different challenges, and therefore, it is helpful to treat the two types separately.[22]

Redundancies

Resolving redundancies frequently means looking more closely at what seems to be a redundancy to ascertain if it truly is one. For example, Bonchek, following the French rabbis ben Manoah and David Kimchi,[23] cites Genesis 11:30, "But Sarai was barren; she had no child," as a false redundancy. Here, the two statements seem to say the same thing—if Sarai was barren, of course, she would have no children. However, a more careful reading reveals that this is not so. Not only does "she had no child" clarify Sarai's situation—meaning, she could possibly be barren at the present time but have had a child earlier in her life—but, as Bonchek points out, it also sets up what is to come. As he writes, "The Torah is telling us that Sarai was barren and had no child at this time, whereas later she would be barren and nevertheless have a child! Meaning that her giving birth would be a true miracle—she would have a child yet even then she would remain biologically barren!" In other words, this apparently redundant phrase is actually setting the stage, so to speak, for the miracle of Sarai's giving birth: two conditions that naturally go together will be separated because of the intervention of God. This phrase is then a kind of foreshadowing of what is to come and underlines what Bonchek calls "the supernatural significance of the birth."[24]

The Book of Mormon contains a similar example of a false redundancy in the story just discussed. In the Mosiah 27 account it states that Alma "became dumb" and then immediately adds "that he could not open his mouth" (v. 19). This addition, like "she had no child," seems redundant. However, upon closer analysis, this phrase not only explains more precisely the cause of Alma's inability to speak, but it sets up the miracle in this story. In this same verse, it is apparent that Alma's muteness was not the only problem his body was experiencing. As verse 19 continues, Alma "became weak, even that he could not move his hands; therefore he

---

22. Ibid., 84.

23. Eliyaho Munk, trans., *Hachut Hameshulash: Commentaries on the Torah by Rabbeinu Chananel, Rabbi Shmuel be Meir (Rash'bam). Rabbi David Kimchi (R'dak), Rabbi Ovadiah Seforno*, 267.

24. Bonchek, *Studying the Torah*, 88.

was taken by those that were with him, and carried helpless, even until he was laid before his father." Although the text here mentions only his inability to use his hands, later on priests assemble to pray that "his limbs might receive their strength" (v. 22). From these passages, it seems clear that Alma's entire body was paralyzed.

This general paralysis explains why Alma's father would immediately assume that the cause of his son's condition was "the power of God" and why, rather than calling for a physician to treat a possibly minor throat problem, he caused the priests to pray and fast for his son (v. 22). When Alma the Elder was a priest in the court of King Noah, the prophet Abinadi was brought into that court and tried for prophesying against the king. Abinadi defended himself and spoke with "power and authority from God" so much so that his face "shone with exceeding luster" and King Noah's guards "durst not lay their *hands* on him" and had "not the *power* to slay [him]" (13:5–7). The text does not explicitly state that everyone in the room was paralyzed, but since Abinadi speaks to them, uninterrupted, for four chapters, and since only after he is finished could King Noah's priests take him (17:1), it seems highly likely that they were.

Alma's father therefore sees in his son's paralysis a repeat of his own experience with Abinadi—and hopes for a similar result. So affected was Alma the Elder by the power that held him bound, as a priest in King Noah's service, that he immediately left that service, "repented of his sins and iniquities, and went about privately among the people, and began to teach the words of Abinadi" (Mosiah 18:1). Consequently, the miracle of Alma the Younger, at least for his father, is not so much that "the limbs of Alma received their strength," but that his son "stood up and began to speak unto [the people], bidding them to be of good comfort" and announcing that he had repented of his sins (27:23–24)—just as Alma the Elder had long ago.

It is also significant that Alma the Younger immediately announces that he has been "born of the Spirit" (Mosiah 27:24). Not only is this phrase consistent with the baptism his father underwent after leaving King Noah, but it is consistent with what happened during and after his paralysis. Like a fetus in the womb, Alma was "helpless," "weak," and unable to use his limbs. Consistent with the etymological meaning of the word *infant*, he could not speak. Like a baby going through the birth process, he then experiences "much tribulation," leaves "the darkest abyss," beholds "the marvelous light of God," and his "soul is pained no more" (vv. 28–29). In this way, the fact that Alma "could not open his mouth" foreshadows the miracle he is about to experience as well as explains why his father prayed for him. Alma is to be born a second time and emerge from a helpless state to one where he can function as a spiritually mature person, traveling "round about through all the land" and "preaching the word of God" (v. 32), much as his father did years before.

Repetitions

Understanding the reasons for repetition often involves looking closely at the context of the repeated phrase. For instance, to explain why the phrase "they went both of them together" is used to describe Abraham and Isaac in Genesis 22:6 and then again just two verses later, Bonchek notes what happens between these two verses: Isaac asks Abraham where the lamb for the offering is, and Abraham responds that God will provide one. This exchange changes everything. Isaac is a different man in verse 8. There he knows that he will be the offering, and yet he "continues with the same innocence as before."[25] The repetition of "they went both of them together" therefore shows his continued faith in his father and in God despite his new understanding of what this journey is all about. The repetition of this phrase then is a necessary and powerful reaffirmation under different circumstances.

Repetitions and redundancies are also an area that fascinates not just traditional religious Jews but nontraditional secular ones as well. Although these Jews may not believe that God wrote the Torah or that everything about it is meaningful, some of them similarly emphasize the folly of assuming that apparent redundancies and seeming repetitions serve no literary purpose. Robert Alter, for instance, writing as a secular literary scholar, stresses that "the repetition of single words or brief phrases [in the Hebrew Scriptures] often exhibits a frequency, a saliency, and a thematic significance quite unlike what we may be accustomed to from other narrative traditions."[26] Alter notes that many seemingly insignificant variations in a repeated phrase or description signal important changes, highlighting "many of the psychological, moral, and dramatic complications of biblical narrative."[27]

Alter cites the story of Bathsheba appearing before King David as an example. In 1 Kings 1, Nathan gives her a question to recite: "Didst not thou, my lord, O king, swear unto thine handmaid, saying, Assuredly

---

25. Ibid., 86.
26. Robert Alter, *The Art of Biblical Narrative*, 179.
27. Ibid., 97.

Solomon thy son shall reign after me, and he shall sit upon my throne?" Bathsheba dutifully repeats this question to the king but adds "by the Lord thy God." The addition of these few words reveals a great deal about Bathsheba's feelings about David's oath as well as the love she has for her son and the import of promises made by the king of Israel.

In like manner, the subtle changes introduced by Nephi, Lehi, and others to what might be called the "motto" of the Book of Mormon—that "inasmuch as ye shall keep my commandments, ye shall prosper, and shall be led to a land of promise" (1 Ne. 2:20)—also highlight important aspects of those who repeat this motto as well as the motto itself. This motto first appears in the Book of Mormon very early on, soon after the Lord visits Nephi and softens his heart so that he "did believe all the words which had been spoken by [his] father" (v. 16). At this point, Nephi attempts to tell his brothers Laman and Lemuel about his experience, but they do not listen to him, and Nephi is so grieved "because of the hardness of their hearts" that he prays for them (v. 18). It is at this point that the Lord gives Nephi the motto as a pledge of sorts to him and his family, that "inasmuch as ye shall keep my commandments, ye shall prosper, and shall be led to a land of promise; yea, even a land which I have prepared for you; yea, a land which is choice above all other lands" (v. 20).

In this initial form, the pledge directly answers Nephi's concern about his brothers and helps him understand that the ultimate goal of his family's stay in the wilderness is not simply to thwart plots against Lehi's life but to travel to a uniquely blessed land. It does this first by virtue of the pronouns it employs, second-person plural pronouns, "ye" and "you," which include *all* of Nephi's family as recipients of this pledge; and secondly, it describes the land they are being led to as "a land of promise," a land prepared for them, and a land "which is choice above all other lands." This pledge, especially because it is given directly by the Lord, prepares Nephi for what is to come. It sets him up to be faithful to his father during the arduous journey that is before him and especially to remain emotionally connected to his brothers and be tolerant of their behavior despite the difficulty that they cause him. Coupled with the warnings that the Lord adds concerning the result of any rebellion on the part of Nephi's brothers, this pledge also forms the foundational principle of the Lehite civilization as a whole as well as a central message and warning of the entire Book of Mormon itself, a statement that as the book progresses is expanded and explained.

The next version of this motto occurs when Nephi returns to Jerusalem and comes upon the unconscious body of Laban. When the Spirit of God tells Nephi to kill him, Nephi balks at such a prospect. However, as Nephi ponders the points the Spirit makes, he recalls his prayer concerning his brothers' indifference to him and remembers in particular that the Lord spoke to him "in the wilderness, saying that: Inasmuch as *thy* seed shall keep my commandments, they shall prosper in the land of promise" (1 Ne. 4:14). In other words, the motto again appears as a pledge to Nephi. However, this version is slightly different than the one Nephi himself quoted in 1 Nephi 2:20. There, the recipients of these blessings were "ye," his immediate family, while here in chapter 4 they are "*thy* seed," all of Nephi's offspring extending for generations. This change from a second-person plural in the nominative case to a second-person singular in the genitive or possessive case shows the development of the pledge in Nephi's mind and reflects a deeper understanding of what traveling to any distant land, much less a promised land, means over time. He is coming to understand, with the aid of divine inspiration, that this is not just a journey that affects him or his family; it changes the situation of tens of thousands of his descendants. Simply by changing a few words, the Book of Mormon speaks volumes about Nephi, his inner workings and motivations, as well as the scope and power of the pledge itself.

There is no record of Lehi receiving a similar pledge from the Lord in 1 Nephi or of Nephi discussing it with his father. Nevertheless, in 2 Nephi, after they arrive at the "land of promise," Lehi speaks to his sons about that land and says that he too has "obtained a promise, that inasmuch as those whom the Lord God shall bring out of the land of Jerusalem shall keep his commandments, they shall prosper upon the face of this land" (1:9). Here differences in this version again offer insights into the mind of the speaker as well as uncovering additional implications of the original pledge. Unlike Nephi's two versions, Lehi's is more general, specifying the recipients of the pledge to be *anyone* led out of Jerusalem, not just members of Lehi's family. However, it is more specific as to what "prospering" entails. Lehi says that such people, provided they "keep [the Lord's] commandments" shall "be blessed upon the face of this land, and there shall be none to molest them, nor to take away the land of their inheritance; and they shall dwell safely forever" (v. 9).

This version reflects a larger vision of the Lehite mission as well as that of the promised land that Lehi had obtained earlier. Just a few verses before, Lehi mentions that "the Lord hath covenanted this land unto me, and to my children forever, and also all those who should be led out of other countries by the hand of the Lord" (2 Ne. 1:5). This view reflects a change in their traveling party since Nephi's quotation of the pledge. After Nephi and his brothers obtained the plates, they were sent back to retrieve Ishmael's family in order to produce "seed" in the promise land. Obviously, since they were sent for and came along, Ishmael's family must also enjoy the benefits of this pledge, especially since they too came from Jerusalem. In addition, Lehi says that "according to the workings of the Spirit which is in me, that there shall none come into this land save they shall be brought by the hand of the Lord" (v. 6). Given what Lehi and his family went through to get to the promised land—traveling across deserts, avoiding bandits, living on raw meat, and completing a long and difficult voyage across the ocean—the impossibility of anyone arriving without such divine help has to have been impressed upon him. He calls the things the Lord did for them in bringing them out of the land of Jerusalem "great" and praises his God for "sparing their lives, that they were not swallowed up in the sea" (vv. 1–2). Lehi, in other words, understands the bright side of their ordeal: that these same trials that afflicted them in a negative way, in a positive way protect them from other, stronger nations.

However, although the seas and the deserts may protect those brought to the promised land from foreign invasions, these natural impediments will not protect them from the evils they may bring with them or eventually fall into. This concern is also reflected in Lehi's version of the pledge. After reciting the pledge, Lehi makes it plain that if his sons or their descendants "dwindle in unbelief," other nations will be brought to afflict them, despite the difficulties of getting to them, and the Lord will "take away from [his son's descendants] the lands of their possessions, and he will cause them to be scattered and smitten" (2 Ne. 1:11) just as he did with the inhabitants of Jerusalem at the time of the Babylonian captivity. Thus, Lehi adds a punishment to the pledge, a natural consequence should its conditions be unfulfilled. In 2 Nephi 1:20, Lehi quotes a new version of the pledge where the Lord states that "Inasmuch as ye shall keep my commandments ye shall prosper in the land; but inasmuch as ye will not keep my commandments ye shall be cut off from my presence." This version not only makes plain what was implicit in Lehi's earlier version but reflects Lehi's very real concern about his two sons Laman and Lemuel, who have already shown a penchant for rebellion and murderous mutiny. Again, these changes are not fundamental. They do not alter the substance of this pledge as it was initially given or modify its original intent. They do, however, reflect the concerns of Lehi at that time as well as reveal more of the meaning and significance of that pledge to him and to his people.

This pattern continues throughout the Book of Mormon. Three chapters later, after more time has passed and more children are born, Lehi again speaks of this pledge to the children of Laman and of Lemuel, and although he recites word for word his most recent version, including the punishment clause, he tells them that "if ye are cursed, behold, I leave my blessing upon you, that the cursing may be taken from you and be answered upon the heads of your parents" (2 Ne. 4:6). This makes sense since culture and history must be considered when meting out justice, and it is consistent with Lehi's position as a grandfather and parent who, like many parents, feels partially to blame for the errors of his children. Even Lehi's rationale for removing the curse from his posterity—that they were brought up in a way contrary to the commandments and, because such training is so fundamental, "will not depart from it" (v. 5)—implies that Laman and Lemuel's actions are similarly influenced by him since, if they had been reared properly, they would not have departed from that way either.

Word Order

Variations in the order and presentation of words in an otherwise similar description can reinforce major points in a story as well as reveal subtle nuances of character. As an example, Bonchek cites two verses from Genesis 18, which in the Hebrew read: "Behold, a son will be born to Sarah your wife" (v. 10) and "to Sarah [will be born] a son" (v. 14). According to Bonchek, the movement of the phrase "to Sarah" from the end of the clause in verse 10 to the beginning of the clause in verse 14 shows a shift in the intended recipient. In the first instance, Abraham learns he is to have a son; in the second, Sarah is assured that that son will indeed be born to her, despite her advanced age.[28]

The Book of Mormon uses this technique as well. For instance, immediately before Captain Moroni presents his "Title of Liberty" to his people, he fastens on "his head-plate, and his breastplate, and his shields" (Alma 46:13) in a different order than these pieces of Nephite armor are usually presented. In all other instances, breastplates are mentioned first, followed by shields, and then, if they are included at all, come head-plates (Alma 43:19, 21, 38; 44:9; 49:24). The prominence of head-plates here is consistent with Moroni's appeal to his peoples' minds, as he gives reasons for going to war on his title. However, it also reinforces the necessity of

---

28. Bonchek, *Studying the Torah*, 98.

God *being* their head—their leader, their guide—as well as the need to protect their belief in God, the first item on Moroni's title, if they are going to be successful. This is a point Captain Moroni makes in his prayers to God as well as through his words to others (Alma 46:13, 18). It is also a point his Lamanite enemies do not understand—the same people who fail to list head-plates among the Nephites' assets (Alma 43:19; 44:9).

In addition, omitting or adding a word to a commonly used series or changing the way the items in a series are described can also bolster a main idea or point. In the second chapter of 1 Nephi, for instance, Lehi departs from Jerusalem leaving behind three kinds of valuables: "his gold, and his silver, and his precious things" (v. 4). The use of "precious things" seems particularly notable since the items are not listed, only his valuation of them, an esteem he felt at the time. However, since Lehi leaves these valuables behind and "took nothing with him, save it were his family, and provisions, and tents" in an effort to follow God's will (1 Ne. 2:4), it is likely that his opinion regarding their value has changed. This likelihood is reinforced by Nephi's substitution of the more objective "all manner of riches" for the more personal "precious things" when he later describes what his father abandoned, as well as his omission of the possessive pronoun *his*. As Nephi writes, "for behold [my father] left gold and silver, and all manner of riches. And all this he hath done because of the commandments of the Lord" (3:16). According to Nephi at least, Lehi is an obedient servant of God, and although the valuables he left behind may still have some intrinsic worth to others, Lehi no longer considers them his property or feels that they are "precious" to him.

Laman and Lemuel, however, very much do treasure these valuables. In 1 Nephi 2, just a few verses after the first description of the left-behind property, not only are the original three components firmly in place (including "precious things"), but they are now Laman and Lemuel's property. When these two brothers murmur against their father, they complain about leaving "the land of *their* inheritance," and they moan about forsaking "*their* gold, and *their* silver, and *their* precious things" (v. 11). In other words, unlike faithful Lehi, Laman and Lemuel very much prize these valuables and even consider them to be their own.

Nephi's own view regarding this wealth is somewhat ambiguous. On the one hand, he seems to be united with his father in his desire to follow the Lord's commandments without regard to riches. However, in the same chapter where Laman and Lemuel lay claim to these valuables, Nephi unites with his brothers calling them "*our* gold, and *our* silver, and *our* precious things," and he does so twice (1 Ne. 3:22, 24). Perhaps Nephi is simply justifying his plan to trade these items for the brass plates—after all, if he and his brothers own them, they can do with them as they will—or perhaps he is setting up Laban's later confiscation of these items as a theft and therefore a partial justification for Laban death. Three times Nephi calls these items "our property" as he describes what Laban saw, what Laban desired, and what Nephi and his brothers left behind (vv. 25–26). It is as if he no longer thinks these valuables are valuable. Only the fact that they do not belong to Laban and that Laban took "our property" matters (4:11).

This particular hoard of gold, silver, and precious things is never mentioned again. However these same three varieties of valuables come up again later on in the Book of Mormon, and they do so with significant additions. When Nephi describes the corruption of the great and abominable church, he does so using terms that reveal a corruption that exceeds that of Laban. In his extended vision, Nephi sees, in addition to gold and silver, "scarlets, and fine-twined linen, and all manner of *precious* clothing" (1 Ne. 13:7–8). These items, his angel-guide announces, are the consuming desires of this abominable "church," as they are the focus of several other similarly wicked populations. The Nephites, early on in the book of Alma, "wax proud, because of their *exceeding* riches, and their fine silks, and their fine-twined linen" as well as "their *many* flocks and herds, and their gold and their silver, and all manner of precious things" (Alma 4:6). The Zoramites, several chapters later, are described as "a wicked and a perverse people; yea . . . their hearts *were set* upon gold, and upon silver, and upon all manner of fine goods" (31:24). And in Helaman, both the Lamanites and the Nephites "became *exceedingly* rich . . . and they did have an *exceeding* plenty of gold, and of silver, and of all manner of precious metals" (Hel. 6:9). The addition of other valuables as well as the use of intensifying modifiers clearly shows that the wickedness of these later people exceeds even that of Laban, opening them up to an even worse fate.

In this way, paying close attention to the subtle alterations in the order and presentation of words, like following Bonchek's other keys, deepens and enhances a reader's experience with the Book of Mormon. By scrutinizing opening sentences, considering a phrase's context, searching for similarities between different texts and differences between similar texts, as well as entertaining the reasons seemingly redundant words might be repeated, readers can uncover the richness of the Book of Mormon's extensive *peshat*.

Chapter Four

Reading with Others

And he said unto me: What desirest thou?

And I said unto him: To know the interpretation thereof—for I spake unto him as a man speaketh; for I beheld that he was in the form of a man; yet nevertheless, I knew that it was the Spirit of the Lord; and he spake unto me as a man speaketh with another. (1 Ne. 11:10–11)

As may now be apparent, approaching scripture rabbinically, although tremendously productive, requires a good deal of instruction and encouragement. Few readers, even the most literarily inclined, are acquainted with *pardes* or instinctively approach scripture in this close-reading, multi-leveled way. Most readers need guides—knowledgeable study partners and qualified teachers—who can support them as they approach scriptural texts and help them find their way when they get lost "in the woods," so to speak. As Rabbi Joshua ben Perachiah anciently advised his *yeshivah* students, "Choose for yourself a mentor; acquire for yourself a friend; and judge every person in a favorable light" (Pirke Avot 1:6).

It is therefore significant that Nephi, the Book of Mormon's most vocal champion of rigorous scripture study, not only has such a guide, the Spirit, in his vision of the Tree of Life, but that he and other writers of the Book of Mormon similarly serve as guides for their readers—and they do so in a very rabbinic way. Consistent with Jewish tradition, Nephi begins the Book of Mormon not with "mythic beginnings" or "anonymous narratives," as Terryl Givens describes Genesis and the Gospel of Matthew, but instead, "presses upon his audience the very human, very local, and very historical nature of his narrative."[1] In other words, Nephi as well as Jacob, Enos, Jarom, and the other writers of the Book of Mormon approach their readers not as superior, omniscient beings that speak with booming

---

1. Terryl L. Givens, *The Book of Mormon: A Very Short Introduction*, 7.

voices from on high, but more as peers, friends even, actual people who figuratively walk beside their readers, addressing them directly, relaying their inmost thoughts, and always coaxing their readers onward, as they discover and react to the events of their lives. Mormon too accompanies his readers. However, he does so more as a mentor, an "in-text" teacher, than as a peer. His is a voice between the lines, as it were, a presence temporally removed from the action at hand but still showing his readers by his real-life advice what they can learn from these events and how they can be better for having studied them. In this way, Mormon is like a rabbinical scriptural commentator. His goal is not so much to interpret text in any sort of final or absolute way as it is to educate his readers and inspire them so that they can find meaning in it for themselves.

Chavrutot

For some, the idea of mixing friendship with intense scripture study may seem incompatible. After all, scrutinizing the Bible closely often conjures up images of solitary monks sequestered in dark rooms, laboring over massive tomes, all by themselves, in silence. However, for rabbinic Jews it is not. For them, scripture study is actually quite social. Again, the Talmud is not simply a list of laws, arranged in a cold, impersonal way as best suits information retrieval. In fact it is an almost maddening compendium of ancient rabbinic discussions complete with digressions, personal comments, temporary positions, off-hand musings, and even the occasional joke. Furthermore, the sages the Talmud cites are frequently set up as pairs (*zugot*, in Hebrew), partners who, for the most part, respectfully argue back and forth, explaining, refining, emending, and exploring their different views, all in order to engage the Torah more effectively and delve more deeply into it. The Talmud describes this process as "sharpening" and states that when two Torah scholars participate in it, treating each other courteously, actually listening to each other, "the Holy One, blessed be He, gives them success . . . , gives heed to them . . . , [and] listens to their voice" in turn (BT Shabbat 63a).

Consequently, when Jewish boys begin their formal study of the Torah (scripture study was limited to Jewish boys until fairly recently), they are immediately paired with study partners of comparable age and ability. These partnerships are called *chavrutot* (sing. *chavrutah*), an Aramaic word derived "from the word *chaver*, meaning 'friend.'"[2] The teacher may give these pairs some introductory instruction at first to get them started, but very soon he turns the newly formed "friends" loose to learn on their own—assigning them to read a certain section out loud and discuss it, one presenting his interpretation of the section while the other asks questions and requests clarifications. Rabbi Robinson likens this exchange to "batting ideas back and forth like a badminton birdie," a kind of game that continues until "every nuance of every word has been explored."[3] The discussion is often noisy and vigorous, creating what Rabbi Emil L. Fackenheim diplomatically calls "a gentle, reverent humming sound."[4] However, whether the discussion is reverential or not is beside the point. The point is that two people get more out of a sacred text when they read it together than they would if they simply read it by themselves—even under the supervision of a trained teacher. As Cohen explains:

> Each one of us also needs someone with whom to study continually, from whom we can learn in a variety of ways. Therefore [after "Get yourself a teacher"] the text adds, "Acquire (*k'nei*) for yourself a friend," using the verb *kanah*, also meaning "possess [in perpetuity]." The same verb is used by the Rabbis when a man marries a woman. This, then, indicates to the perceptive reader not only the sense of the enormity of the task but also that one must strive to establish a lifelong relationship with a companion from whom and with whom one can learn Torah.[5]

Studying with a *chavrutah* consequently is not simply a useful pedagogical technique; it represents an ancient pattern and is believed to be the most appropriate way of studying God's words. Studying with such a partner helps both students experience God within a relationship. As Cohen continues, the Talmudic sages stressed "that when two individuals are engaged in Torah, the *Shechinah*, God's immanent presence, is between them" (Pirke Avot 3:3).[6] If, for instance, one's *chavrutah* is sometimes demanding, God can also be demanding. If one's *chavrutah* is occasionally blunt, God can also be blunt. If one's *chavrutah* is at one time or another seemingly silent or talkative, hard to understand or easy, repetitive or amazingly brilliant, God can be that way as well—or at least can appear to

---

2. Norman J. Cohen, *The Way Into Torah*, 96.

3. George Robinson, *Essential Judaism: A Complete Guide to Beliefs, Rituals, and Customs*, 354.

4. Emil L. Fackenheim, *What Is Judaism?* 162.

5. Cohen, *The Way Into Torah*, 96–97.

6. Ibid., 98.

be. Such a set-up shows how God can work through other people to reach his children and also helps a student see other people in a new and more understanding way. In addition, this sort of approach reveals something about God's love and commitment to his children. Just as a true *chavrutot* stay committed to their partners through all the ups and downs of their relationship, so the true God remains committed to Israel. Students may occasionally argue like Abraham, be blind to the obvious like Isaac, use deceptive words like Jacob, feel weak and complain like Moses, or even openly rebel like Miriam and Aaron; yet their *chavrutot* remain by their sides, continually urging them on without letting them be content with superficial thought. True *chavrutot*, like God, are always optimistic, full of faith and confidence in their partner and in the Torah.

For these and other reasons the Talmudic rabbis and their followers have historically discouraged solitary scripture study. For instance, according to Cohen, Rabbi Meir "suggests that the Torah that we drink can be supplied only by a person with whom we are close, a soulmate if you will, who can serve as a perpetual source of nourishment."[7] Such a feast is simply not possible alone—or in a large group. Again, it is much like a marriage, the foremost image of the relationship God has with his people. As Rabbi Fackenheim writes, "Just as it is not good for man to be alone, so it is not good for a student to study Torah alone."[8]

Nephi as *Chavrutah*

Like students in a *yeshivah*, or rabbinic academy, readers of the Book of Mormon are also never alone. Right from the beginning, Nephi is there in the text, encouraging them to "search the Scriptures," delighting in "plainness," and providing examples of *pardes*-based interpretations. In this way, he not only provides a kind of literary *chavrutah* for his readers, but he promotes a *chavrutah*-style approach by attempting to befriend his readers, by speaking to them directly and personally and by exemplifying the kind of person this approach is designed to produce.

Nephi Befriends His Readers

Nephi begins his writings not with a bang, as does Genesis, or with a list of his heroic ancestors, as does the Gospel of Matthew, but sim-

---

7. Ibid., 99.
8. Fackenheim, *What Is Judaism?* 163.

ply by introducing himself, in humble, unpretentious terms: "I, Nephi," he writes, "having been born of goodly parents, therefore I was taught somewhat in all the learning of my father" (1 Ne. 1:1). Such a modest beginning understates his solid familial and educational background and carries no hint of his accomplishments—fashioning tools from raw ore, building a ship, traversing oceans, colonizing a new world, writing his society's history, and the like. If overawing his readers is Nephi's desired result, he has failed utterly. Rather than setting himself above and apart from ordinary people, he seems to be deliberately doing his best to join them on common ground. Admittedly, Nephi does state that he has been "highly favored of the Lord in all [his] days" and that he has received "great knowledge of the goodness and the mysteries of God"—statements which could seem to present him as exceptional—but, in this context, they sound more like self-effacing expressions of appreciation than arrogance, comments detailing more the greatness of the giver than the size of his gift. And his admission that he has "seen many afflictions in the course of [those same] days" further reinforces such an impression. Nephi has suffered and struggled just like everybody else.

Much like a newly assigned *chavrutah*, Nephi seems to be trying to make friends with his readers by avoiding any pretense of superiority and by establishing some basic commonalities. He then continues his friend-making efforts by revealing other facts about himself, personal aspects that anyone who grew up with siblings can sympathize with. He describes himself as "exceedingly young" (2:16) with older brothers who disparage him, a mother who worries about him (5:2), and a father who makes challenging requests of him (2:16)—including moving him to a new place far away from his friends and familiar surroundings (2:2–3). As Nephi's story unfolds, this initial impression of him as just another well-intentioned, but awkward adolescent deepens. He blurts out dramatic declarations that seem disproportionate to the tone of the discussion going on around him (3:7), and he delivers strident speeches using words and phrases that show little awareness of how others might react to them. One cannot help but cringe, for instance, when he bluntly attempts to persuade his older, more experienced brothers to be faithful in "keeping the commandments of God" (3:21) or urges them to be "be strong like unto Moses" (4:2) or interrogates them like children, asking them such personally challenging questions as "How is it that ye have not hearkened unto the word of the Lord?" and "How is it that ye have forgotten that the Lord is able to do all things according to his will?" (7:9, 12). Certainly, the violent way Nephi's brothers react cannot be excused, but given the tone of Nephi's words, it seems neither unexpected nor, according to the code of adolescent boys, unjustified.

Nonetheless, despite these incidents, few readers fail to feel sympathy for Nephi. Some may notice, or sense in him, a similarity to certain heroes in the Hebrew Scriptures. After all, young Joseph, the son of Jacob, also said awkward things to his older brothers and was similarly persecuted by them. David too, as a youth, undiplomatically chastised all Israel (1 Sam. 17:29) and, for the good of his people, decapitated their now unconscious enemy with his own sword (1 Sam. 17:51; 1 Ne. 4:18). And Samson, also like Nephi, was bound with "cords" by his enemies (1 Ne. 7:16; Judg. 15:13), prayed to the Lord and watched as "the bands were loosed from off [his] hands and feet" (1 Ne. 7:18; Judg. 15:14). These heroes turned out all right despite these early foibles. Perhaps Nephi's problems too are simply excesses of a promising youth.

Nephi Speaks to His Readers Directly

These similarities to famous biblical figures may indeed persuade many readers to think of Nephi kindly. However, the fact that Nephi tells his story personally, even intimately, using first-person singular pronouns, is also compelling. In this way, Nephi nurtures the relationship he initiated with his readers and creates a bond of trust that is not easily broken or challenged. Not only does he begin with "I, Nephi," but he continues: "*I* did cry unto the Lord; and behold he did visit *me*, and did soften *my* heart that *I* did believe all the words which had been spoken by *my* father; wherefore, *I* did not rebel against him like unto *my* brothers" (1 Ne. 2:16). Through these personal statements "I, Nephi" makes it clear that he is speaking from his heart, that he has mixed feelings and doubts, just like other people. However, he is still a good person, the kind of person that makes a helpful *chavrutah*. Nephi loves his brothers and, despite their accusations to the contrary, in no way wants to lord over them. He simply wants to help. As Nephi says, "I cried unto the Lord for [Laman and Lemuel]" (2:18), and "grieved for the hardness of their hearts" (7:8). He appears shocked that his brothers became "wroth" with him after "I had spoken these words" (4:4). He is uncomfortable that "I, your younger brother, should speak unto you, yea, and set an example for you" (7:8). And he does not chastise them willingly. As he explains, it was "the Spirit of the Lord [that] constraineth me that I should speak" in this manner (7:15). Later when his brothers apologize, Nephi says, "I did frankly forgive them" (7:21); in fact he was so impressed with their humility that he states that "I had joy and great hopes of them, that they would walk in the paths of righteousness" (16:5).

Given these personal insights into Nephi's heart, it also seems clear that his occasional abrasiveness is unintentional, that they are the clumsy efforts of a young boy unable to adequately express his feelings. Nephi is in no way cruel or ambitious but is kind and even sensitive. Despite the fact that his brothers' humility is short-lived and that they continually seek his life, Nephi never retaliates or disconnects himself emotionally from them. Instead "I, Nephi, did cry much unto the Lord my God, because of the anger of my brethren" (2 Ne. 5:1). It is only when the Lord finally warns him of his brothers' murderous plans, possibly in a dream, that "I, Nephi did take my family, and also Zoram and his family, and Sam, mine elder brother and his family, and Jacob and Joseph, my younger brethren, and also my sisters, and all those who would go with me" and escape into the wilderness (vv. 6–7).

Furthermore, and perhaps most convincingly, Nephi seems to be aware of his mistakes—and is sorry for them. In what is often called "Nephi's Psalm," Nephi confirms, again using first-person pronouns, his goodness. As he writes, "My soul delighteth in the things of the Lord; and my heart pondereth continually upon the things which I have seen and heard." However, he also exclaims, "O wretched man that I am!" and grieves because of his "iniquities." "I am encompassed about, because of the temptations and the sins which do so easily beset me," he writes, and "my heart groaneth because of my sins" (2 Ne. 4:18–19). Nephi says that his heart weeps and his soul lingers "in the valley of sorrow," his flesh wasting away "because of mine afflictions" (v. 26). In addition, in a kind of poetic justice, Nephi also asks himself blunt questions similar to the ones he put to his brothers: "And why should I yield to sin, because of my flesh? Yea, why should I give way to temptations, that the evil one have place in my heart to destroy my peace and afflict my soul? Why am I angry because of mine enemy?" (v. 27).

Finally, Nephi is not easy on himself nor does he come up with easy answers for his behavior. He does not fall back on his accomplishments or on some vague claim of general goodness. Instead he pleads for God to encircle him "around in the robe of [God's] righteousness," to "make a way for [his] escape before [his] enemies," and to "hedge not up [his] way, but the ways of [his] enemy" (v. 33). Nephi knows that he needs help just as his brothers require assistance and asks for that aid openly. In this way

Nephi seems to feel a kinship with his brothers, despite the differences in their actions, and is still united with them in his heart.

All in all, Nephi comes across as a fine example of a *chavrutah*, a helpful model of the kind of study companion all readers of the Book of Mormon should aspire to be. In addition to being approachable and friendly toward his readers, he is sincere, loyal, humble, and open about himself and his feelings. Furthermore, as has already been shown, he is also knowledgeable of the Scriptures, has a passion for them, and is adept at applying the Scriptures to himself and those around him.

Nephi Serves as an Example

Indeed Nephi is not only an suitable *chavrutah*; he is an excellent one, exemplifying, in specific ways, the kind of person a rabbinic education is meant to foster. As Rabbi Hayim Halevy Donin writes, the Jewish goal of education is more than just an academic concern. It involves *living* certain principles as well as *knowing* them:

> That Judaism places great stress upon education is well known. But what Judaism means by education is not as well known. The Hebrew word for education is *hinukh*. It does not mean only formal schooling. It literally means "consecration" and refers to training a child for living, not only for a livelihood. The primary aims in the education of Jewish children are to (1) instill the moral and ethical values of the Jewish heritage; (2) encourage active observance of the Torah's commandments (mitzvot); (3) transmit knowledge of the Torah, the Talmud, and the major Jewish sources; (4) create a strong sense of identification with and concern for all Jewish people.[9]

Even though Nephi lived long before Rabbi Donin and the rabbinic tradition he represents, Nephi excels in each of the aims he sets for Jewish education.

Appreciating the Moral and Ethical Values of the Jewish Heritage. Consistent with the first of Rabbi Donin's goals, Nephi is continually concerned about the morals and the ethics of each situation in which he finds himself. Nowhere is this more evident than when he is "constrained by the Spirit" (1 Ne. 4:10) to kill Laban. As mentioned previously, Nephi is repelled by the idea and agonizes over it at length. The Spirit must repeatedly command him to proceed. Nevertheless, Nephi cannot obey blindly. He must make sure that what he is asked to do is just and true. Consequently,

---

9. Hayim Halevy Donin, *To Be a Jew: A Guide to Jewish Observance in Contemporary Life*, 129–30.

Nephi holds a trial of sorts—not so much to decide Laban's fate as to determine if an execution is indeed justifiable. On his own, without being prompted by the Spirit, Nephi considers the "charges" against Laban: how Laban attempted to murder him, how Laban disobeyed God's commandments, and finally how he stole his property from him. However, despite the fact that two of these charges are potentially justifiable reasons for capital punishment under the Law of Moses (see Lev. 24:16–17), he hesitates. Legal arguments do not seem to be enough for Nephi. He seems to require a larger context, one that reveals the full ramification of this action. It is only when the Spirit once more commands Nephi to slay Laban, this time explaining that "the Lord slayeth the wicked to bring forth his righteous purposes," and that "it is better that one man should perish than that a nation should dwindle and perish in unbelief" (1 Ne. 4:13), that Nephi seems ready to proceed.

Nonetheless, even these justifications, as powerful as they are, are not enough to make Nephi jump into action. He must think through their implications carefully and determine if they actually apply in this particular situation. He therefore falls back upon two vital Jewish ideas, the requirement to obey God's commandments (*mitzvot*) and the necessity of preserving the Scriptures:

> And now, when I, Nephi, had heard these words, I remembered the words of the Lord which he spake unto me in the wilderness, saying that: Inasmuch as thy seed shall keep my commandments, they shall prosper in the land of promise. Yea, and I also thought that they could not keep the commandments of the Lord according to the law of Moses, save they should have the law. And I also knew that the law was engraven upon the plates of brass. And again, I knew that the Lord had delivered Laban into my hands for this cause—that I might obtain the records according to his commandments. Therefore I did obey the voice of the Spirit, and took Laban by the hair of the head, and I smote off his head with his own sword. (1 Ne. 4:14–18)

Only after Nephi has carefully considered the legality, ethics, morals, and theology of the situation, does he execute Laban. Nephi is no murderer. He is not even much of a soldier. Later his brother Jacob says that Nephi had "wielded the sword of Laban" in the defense of his people (Jacob 1:10), but Nephi does not make such a claim. He states only that he "did take the sword of Laban, and after the manner of it did make many swords, lest by any means the people who were now called Lamanites should come upon us and destroy us" (2 Ne. 5:14). Nephi does not kill lightly. He does not brag about his exploits or even point to them with pride. To him killing is only justified when it is done in self-defense, as a last resort, and even then it is regrettable. This quality of Nephi's is further demonstrated by the many times his brothers attempted to kill him, and how he not only refused to exact revenge but frankly forgave them. Nephi, it is clear, very much wants to do the moral and ethical thing.

Observing the Torah's Commandments (Mitzvot). Throughout his experience with Laban, Nephi's commitment to Rabbi Donin's second educational goal is clear—as it is both before and after it. Even before Nephi leaves Jerusalem the Lord himself urges Nephi to keep his commandments and explains to him their benefits: "Inasmuch as ye shall keep my commandments, ye shall prosper, and shall be led to a land of promise," he says, adding that such obedience will also make Nephi "a ruler and a teacher over [his] brethren" (1 Ne. 2:20, 22). His father too emphasizes obedience to the commandments when he responds to Laman and Lemuel's complaints about returning to Jerusalem to obtain the brass plates. As he tells Nephi, "thy brothers murmur, saying it is a hard thing which I have required of them; but behold I have not required it of them, but it is a commandment of the Lord" (3:5). Such lessons must have sunk deeply into the soul of Nephi and transformed him. Although he too has questions about their departure from their home, he tells his father that he will "go and do the things which the Lord hath commanded, for," as he affirms, he knows "that the Lord giveth no commandments unto the children of men, save he shall prepare a way for them that they may accomplish the thing which he commandeth them" (v. 7).

This classic statement consequently becomes Nephi's motto, the basis for nearly everything he does and says. Despite their murmuring, Nephi's brothers return with him to Jerusalem as they were commanded. However, they fail on their first try to obtain the plates. They are discouraged and are about to return to their father. However, Nephi persuades them to try again by presenting them with a new plan and by reminding them that their mission was commanded by God: "Wherefore, let us be faithful in keeping the commandments of the Lord; therefore let us go down to the land of our father's inheritance, for behold he left gold and silver, and all manner of riches. And all this he hath done because of the commandments of the Lord" (v. 16). Unfortunately, this attempt fails as well. Laban, seeing their valuables, covets them and sends Nephi and his brothers running for their lives. Nephi's brothers are furious at the loss of their precious things and beat Nephi and his brother Sam with a rod. Nonetheless, Nephi's devotion to keeping the commandments is not diminished. An angel appears, stops his brothers from hitting him, and departs, after promising that Laban will be delivered unto their hands (v. 29). Nephi picks up where the angel left off, urging his brothers to press on. However, Nephi barely mentions the angel and instead returns again to the fact that they were commanded by God to obtain the plates as the most compelling reason they should continue. As he tells his brothers: "Let us go up again unto Jerusalem, and let us be faithful in keeping the commandments of the Lord; for behold he is mightier than all the earth, then why not mightier than Laban and his fifty, yea, or even than his tens of thousands?" (v. 4:1).

And this pattern continues. Frequently, when Nephi attempts to persuade others to act more righteously or more generously, he exhorts them first and foremost to follow God's commandments. For instance, when he tries to enlist his brothers in building a ship to cross the ocean, he exhorts them "with all the energies of [his] soul, and with all the faculty which [he] possessed, that they would give heed to the word of God and remember to keep *his commandments* always in all things" (1 Ne. 15:25). Additionally, when Nephi explains to his brothers the scattering and gathering of Israel, as put forth in Isaiah, he concludes his exegesis with "Wherefore, my brethren, I would that ye should consider that the things which have been written upon the plates of brass are true; and they testify that a man must be obedient to *the commandments of God*" (22:30). And also when Nephi, in his last testament, seeks to dissuade his descendants from practicing priestcraft and other economically parasitical practices bent on obtaining the "gain and praise of the world," he reasons for "the Lord hath forbidden this thing; wherefore, the Lord God hath given *a commandment* that all men should have charity, which charity is love. And except they should have charity they were nothing. Wherefore, if they should have charity they would not suffer the laborer in Zion to perish" (2 Ne. 26:29–30).

For Nephi, there is great virtue in obedience to God's commandments, in this world as well as in the world to come. After he and his family are preserved despite years of traveling in the wilderness, Nephi remarks: "And thus we see that the commandments of God must be fulfilled. And if it so be that the children of men keep the commandments of God he doth nourish them, and strengthen them, and provide means whereby they can accomplish the thing which he has commanded them; wherefore, he did provide means for us while we did sojourn in the wilderness" (1 Ne. 17:3). However, Nephi's confidence in God's commandments extends beyond those whose fulfillments he can see. His record, for instance, the account that eventually becomes 1 and 2 Nephi, serves for the "instruction of [his] people," but it also has "other wise purposes, which purposes are known unto the Lord" (1 Ne. 19:3). Nephi has no idea what those other purposes are, and yet it is enough for him to know that God knows them and that God has commanded him to keep these plates so that those purposes can be accomplished. Indeed, "Obey the commandments" seems to be the main message he puts into those plates as well as what he gets out of the Hebrew Scriptures. As he writes, "Wherefore, my brethren, I would that ye should consider that the things which have been written upon the plates of brass are true; and they testify that a man must be obedient to the commandments of God" (1 Ne. 22:30). Consequently, it is with great pleasure that he describes his people as keeping "the judgments, and the statutes, and the commandments of the Lord in all things, according to the law of Moses" (2 Ne. 5:10). For Nephi, obedience to God's commandments is everything.

Possessing Knowledge of the Torah. Consistent with Nephi's commitment to obey the commandments of the Torah are his devotion to and knowledge of the Torah, Rabbi Donin's third aim. Even before he procures the brass plates—which contain the five books of Moses (1 Ne. 5:11)—Nephi must have had some exposure to the Torah. Certainly, he is familiar with the story of the Exodus. When he and his brothers fail twice to obtain the plates and are threatened by Laban, Nephi immediately connects their efforts to those of Moses. "Let us be strong like unto Moses," he says, "for he truly spake unto the waters of the Red Sea and they divided hither and thither, and our fathers came through, out of captivity, on dry ground, and the armies of Pharaoh did follow and were drowned in the waters of the Red Sea. . . . [Therefore] Let us go up; the Lord is able to deliver us, even as our fathers, and to destroy Laban, even as the Egyptians" (4:2–3).

Perhaps Nephi had been educated somewhat in the Torah by his father or some other relative. Deuteronomy requires fathers to teach their sons Torah (Deut. 11:18–19), but the Rabbis obligated grandfathers to do this duty as well (BT Kiddushin 30a). Nevertheless regardless of how much scriptural education Nephi had received before this incident or who gave it to him, the process of procuring the brass plates for his father provided Nephi with three key lessons about the Torah that appear to have changed his life forever. For one, the mere fact that Lehi sent Nephi and his brothers back to obtain these plates, a dangerous assignment since they had so recently fled Jerusalem for their lives, certainly showed Nephi the value his father escribed to the Scriptures and explains why Nephi would later suggest that he and his brothers offer Laban all of their gold and silver and precious things in exchange for the plates that contained the Scriptures (1 Ne. 3:22–24). Second, Nephi's inspired realization that he and his family "could not keep the commandments of the Lord according to the law of Moses, save they should have the law" (4:15) not only justified his killing of Laban for the plates but revealed that the Scriptures are worth more than his or any other single person's life since without them entire nations would dwindle and perish in unbelief (vv. 12–15). Third, the way Lehi later receives the plates when Nephi and his brothers finally bring them to him—offering "sacrifice and burnt offerings unto the Lord" and then searching "them from the beginning" (5:9–10)—taught Nephi not just how good the Torah is but what it is good for: studying, deeply and frequently and continually.

And Nephi learns these lessons well. Not much later Nephi's brothers again need encouragement (this time to help Nephi build a ship), and he again turns to the story of Exodus to motivate them. However, this time his examples are much more numerous, more wide-ranging, and more cutting—revealing a greater familiarity with the Scriptures, their issues and import. This time he begins by pointedly asking his brothers if the Israelites "would have been led away out of the hands of the Egyptians if they had not hearkened unto the words of the Lord?" and if the "Lord had not commanded Moses that he should lead them out of bondage?" (1 Ne. 17:24). He then lists the many miracles the Israelites experienced—beginning again with their being led out of bondage, seeing the Red Sea divide, and watching the Egyptian army drown, just as he did before; he continues, though, adding receiving manna in the wilderness, witnessing Moses produce water from a rock, being led day and night through the wilderness, crossing the river Jordan, and becoming "mighty unto the driving out of the children of the land" (vv. 22–32). Nephi then asks an intriguing question, one that has challenged many Torah scholars: "do ye suppose that the children of this land, who were in the land of promise, who were driven out by our fathers, do ye suppose that they were righteous?" (v. 33). Nephi then answers his own question in the negative, explaining it and defending it at length, much as *chavrutot* do their interpretations, until he finally comes to his answer's real-life application and tells his brothers plainly that they should not be like the ancient Canaanites, who were destroyed because of their wickedness, or like the complaining Israelites, who wandered, but "they should murmur no more against their father; neither should they withhold their labor from [him], for God had commanded me that I should build a ship" (vv. 35–49). Granted, Nephi could have been less verbose and perhaps more diplomatic in speaking to his brothers. However, his increased knowledge and love of the Torah is plainly on display here.

Later on, Nephi also refers to a prophet like unto Moses in Deuteronomy 18:18 (1 Ne. 22:20). Nonetheless, his increasing scriptural knowledge is not limited to the five books of Moses. Clearly, he has also studied the book of Isaiah extensively. In fact, so impressed is he with the *peshat* of that book that he includes several complete chapters from it in his own work. However, he is also delighted with his *derash*. As Grant Hardy writes, "Nephi gives the impression of someone who has read and reread Isaiah, trying to discern precedents for his experiences, eager to literally connect his own prophecies with those of his predecessor." So thoroughly has Nephi scrutinized the Book of Isaiah and connected it with himself and his ideas that his words seem to have become inextricably intertwined with those of Israel's most literary prophet. As Hardy continues, "We sometimes speak of 'reading between the lines,' but [especially in 2 Nephi 26–27] Nephi is 'writing between the lines,'" blending his own words with words from Isaiah 29 until they virtually become one, a composite creation.[10]

Given how Nephi delights in the words of Isaiah and those of the other prophets in the Hebrew Scriptures (2 Ne. 11:2), it seems clear that Nephi has studied them extensively and is therefore eminently qualified as a knowledgeable *chavrutah*. Not only does he "read many things unto [his people] which were written in the books of Moses" and the book of Isaiah, but he finds relevance in them by likening the scriptures unto himself, his readers, and his people, "that it might be for [their] profit and learning" (1 Ne. 19:23).

Identifying with and Being Concerned for All Jewish People. Nephi's background may seem to conflict with Rabbi Donin's final educational aim, that of identifying with and being concerned for all Jewish people. After all, when Nephi's father preached to the inhabitants of Jerusalem and warned them of the coming catastrophe, "the Jews did mock him because of the things which he testified of them" and "sought his life" (1 Ne. 1:19–20). Considering Nephi's love for his father and the respect he has for Lehi's message, it is understandable that he would have bad feelings about those who attempted to murder him. For instance, Nephi describes his mur-

---

10. Grant Hardy, *Understanding the Book of Mormon: A Reader's Guide*, 64.

muring brothers as being "like unto the Jews who were at Jerusalem, who sought to take away the life of my father" (2:13). And later, when Laman and Lemuel attempt to kill Lehi, Nephi tells them, "ye are murderers in your hearts and ye are like unto" the Jews they left in Jerusalem (17:44). However, Nephi has a vision that explains to him the larger picture of the scattering and gathering of Israel, and he speaks to his brothers in positive terms "concerning the restoration of the Jews" (15:20).

Nephi appears to have complicated feelings toward "the Jews," sometimes denouncing them, sometimes defending them. As his people grow in number and begin to be established, he does not teach them "many things concerning the manner of the Jews," reasoning that "their works were works of darkness, and their doings were doings of abominations" (2 Ne. 25:2). Nevertheless, he says that "there is none other people that understand the things which were spoken unto the Jews like unto them" (v. 5). Despite this apparent double-mindedness, paying close attention to the tense of the verbs Nephi uses shows that he is actually referring to different groups of people. When Nephi refers to those Jews "from whence [he] came" (33:8), often describing them in very negative terms, he uses the past tense. He uses other tenses to refer to future Jews, people whom he describes in more positive terms. The time of Nephi's writing is therefore a marker that helps identify which group of Jews he is talking about.

Scholars often use the term *Judahites* to differentiate the members of the ancient Kingdom of Judah, the people whom Nephi and Lehi left behind in Jerusalem, from the Jews who lived during Jesus's time and later. This term is useful here to further highlight the distinction Nephi makes. Therefore, when Nephi says that "their works *were* works of darkness, and their doings *were* doings of abominations" (2 Ne. 25:2), he is talking about the Judahites, and when he says that "I know that the Jews *do* understand the things of the prophets, and there *is* none other people that *understand* the things which were spoken unto the Jews like unto them" (v. 5), he is talking about future Jews.

Viewing Nephi's writing this way, one can clearly see that, excepting the Judahites of his time, Nephi thinks positively about Jews in general. The Scriptures, as he says, "go forth from the Jews in purity unto the Gentiles" (1 Ne. 13:25). He pleads for "all ye ends of the earth" to "respect the words of the Jews" (2 Ne. 33:13–14). He quotes the Holy One of Israel asking rhetorically if the Gentiles who persecute the Jews "remember the travails, and the labors, and the pains of the Jews, and their diligence unto me, in bringing forth salvation unto the Gentiles?" (2 Ne. 29:4). And he records the Lord's answer—an affirmation that the Jews continue to be his "ancient covenant people," that he has not forgotten his people, and that he will "return [the cursings and hatred of the Gentiles] upon the heads of the Gentile nations" (v. 5).

Furthermore, Nephi concludes his writings by confirming that he has "charity for the Jew"—including those Judahites "from whence [he] came" (2 Ne. 33:8). His Jewish heritage is clearly very important to him as is the future of the Jews in general. He takes pleasure in knowing that through his writings and those of his successors, the remnant of his seed after generations of not knowing who they are will find out "that they are descendants of the Jews," and the Jews "shall be restored unto the knowledge of their fathers," and "they shall be a pure and a delightsome people" (2 Ne. 30:4–6).

Other *Chavrutot*

Nephi may be the most extensive example of a literary *chavrutah* in the Book of Mormon, but there are others. Jacob, Enos, Jarom, and Omni all similarly introduce themselves to their readers and speak to their readers directly, in friendly terms, often explaining why they are writing and what they are going to write about. In addition, all of these writers offer enough information about themselves to present their ideas from a very personal, even intimate point of view. Jacob, for instance, the writer who immediately follows Nephi, is described as Lehi's "firstborn in the wilderness" (2 Ne. 2:2). It is therefore significant that he spends considerable time recounting the "words of the prophet Zenos" (Jacob 5:1), an allegory concerning the future gathering of the dispersed House of Israel from their figurative wilderness (6:1–2). Jacob is also said to have "suffered afflictions and much sorrow, because of the rudeness of [his] brethren" (2 Ne. 2:1) and, consequently, it is personally understandable—and compelling—that he prophetically criticizes "those of *you* which have afflicted *your* neighbor, and persecuted him because *ye* were proud in your hearts" (Jacob 2:20).

Enos, Jacob's son and his inheritor of the plates, was apparently an ordinary, fallible human being who struggled to follow in his "just" father's impressive footsteps. He therefore introduces himself to his readers as a peer, without fanfare, and speaks to them directly, announcing his purpose plainly: "I will tell *you* of the wrestle which I had before God, before I received a remission of my sins" (Enos 1:2). So great is Enos's identification with ordinary people that after he receives forgiveness for his own sins, he feels "a desire for the welfare of [his] brethren"—all of the Nephites—and similarly pours "out [his] whole soul unto God for them" (v. 9). And when this prayer is answered, his faith begins to be "unshaken in the Lord," and his concern for people transcends political and ethnic boundaries. He then prays for the Lamanites, his people's long-time enemy, and, after his "many long strugglings," the Lord grants unto Enos "according to [his] desires, because of [his] faith" (vv. 11–12).

Mormon, too, in his smaller, autobiographical book, recounts how he, as an eleven-year-old boy, was taken from his home in the north by his father "into the land southward, even to the land of Zarahemla" (Morm. 1:6). There he is continually on the move—fighting battles in the city of Angola, marching forth to the land of Joshua, fleeing to the land of Jashon, moving northward to "the land which was called Shem," finally retreating to the land of Desolation and to the city Boaz, close to the place where he is eventually killed (2:4, 6, 16, 20; 3:5; 4:20; 6:2). Given the transience of his life, it is little wonder that Mormon devotes himself so completely to documenting the wanderings of his people and speaks directly "unto you, house of Israel" in order that they may "prepare to return to the land of [their] inheritance" (3:17). Mormon's own peregrinations infuse his writings with personal pathos and cause his anguish over how his people "*departed* from the ways of the Lord!" (6:17) to be both intellectually and emotionally understandable to his readers.

Nevertheless, this infusion occurs retrospectively, working its way backwards in readers' minds after they have read Mormon's earlier non-autobiographical books. In these books—Mosiah, Alma, Helaman, 3 Nephi, and 4 Nephi—Mormon comes across as too superior to be a good *chavrutah*. In his prefatory Words of Mormon, for instance, he introduces himself, much as Nephi does—giving his name, describing himself as someone who has "witnessed almost all the destruction of [his] people," and explaining that he is writing "according to the knowledge and the understanding which God has given [him]" (W of M 1:1, 9). However unlike Nephi, Mormon does not quickly follow up this initial introduction with friendship-forming personal details—there is no description of his looks, activities, triumphs, failures, and other matters that present him as an equal to his readers. Instead, he seems more interested in relating information than in relating to his readers. Even the few personal tidbits he mentions—where he got his name and what his lineage is (3 Ne. 5:12, 20)—appear to pertain more to his credibility as a conveyer of information than to his likeability as a person.

This is not to say that Mormon does not care about his readers or wants no relationship with them. He does. Mormon, like Nephi, often speaks to them using personal pronouns and direct address. However, he does so from *above* his readers, not *beside* them. His frequent "and thus we see" summations, for instance, may be grammatically inclusive, but in actuality they are not. They do not include Mormon since he has not recently discovered these insights nor do they embrace his readers since he has no way of knowing if they actually understand his point or not. Instead they are reminiscent of how a kindly but awkward college professor might explain a fairly elementary point to a struggling freshman—a similarity reinforced by the way Mormon uses this phrase to make such basic points as "the Lord worketh in many ways to the salvation of his people" (Alma 24:27), "the children of men do [quickly] forget the Lord their God" (Alma 46:8), and unless "the Lord doth chasten his people with many afflictions . . . they will not remember him" (Hel. 12:3).

Rabbinic Commentators

In the books of Mosiah, Alma, Helaman, 3 Nephi, and 4 Nephi, Mormon may not be a very good *chavrutah*, but he is an excellent example of a scriptural commentator. As Rabbi Wylen writes, such commentators are vital to a rabbinical approach to the Scriptures:

> When an educated Jew reads the unadorned text of the Bible it seems "hollow" to him. The Jew does not share the belief of the Protestant that the voice of God speaks directly out of the scriptural text. God's voice is heard through tradition. Our learned Jew, when he reads the Bible, will wish to immediately run to the commentaries that summarize tradition in order to find out what the Bible is saying.[11]

Commentators Teach Interpretation

So crucial are these commentaries to the rabbinical approach that many Jewish editions of the Hebrew Scriptures contain so many explanatory notes from classic rabbinic commentators that, even in their abbreviated form, they often take up over half of the page. These notes from Rashi, Maimonides, Ibn Ezra, and others contain a wealth of information—explaining the significance of Hebrew names, clarifying obscure phrases, solving apparent problems with redundancy, and connecting odd word usages

---

11. Stephen M. Wylen, *Settings of Silver: An Introduction to Judaism*, 14.

with other scriptural books. In short, they apply many of the same techniques described in Chapter Three. However, despite the quality of these comments, their authors do not so much endeavor to provide their readers with *the* interpretation of a particular text as they attempt to provide *an* interpretation—a learned opinion that their readers can study, learn from, and ultimately eclipse. In other words, rabbinic commentators function primarily as teachers, along the lines Rabbi Joshua ben Perachiah advised, and not as authoritarian scriptural judges or theological arbitrators.

Their comments may be logical, well-supported, and cogently presented. They may even be brilliant and amazingly perceptive. However, they are not considered infallible or complete. These comments are simply examples offered by learned but still learning human beings, which should be taken seriously but are not to be equated with the Word of God itself. They are instead meant to be built upon and improved. Richard Elliott Friedman, for instance, justifies his very modern *Commentary on the Torah* by claiming that he is simply emulating the rabbinic commentators that went before:

> The purpose of Rashi's commentary and of Ibn Ezra's and Ramban's was to show the readers new things in the text, problems that they had not seen, or to address old problems that had not been solved—and to offer the commentator's solutions to those problems. In this commentary, I mean to return to the classical purpose. . . . to make new contributions to the understanding of the Torah . . . to try to offer explanations for old problems and to address new ones . . . to shed new light on the Torah and, more important, to open windows through which it sheds its light on us.[12]

Commentators Require Reader Interaction

In other words, rabbinic commentary is never complete. It is not "set in stone," as it were, permanent, unmoving, finished, complete. The discussion goes on. Rabbi Strassfeld, for instance, sees these commentaries as "a sort of giant 'chat room' of the Jewish people," where students of the Scriptures engage Rashi, Maimonides, and the rest as if they were present in a class setting in order to better learn from them.[13] Obviously, since these rabbinic commentators are dead, they cannot respond in real-time to contemporary comments or queries. However, rabbinic readers are often trained to have a lively "conversation" with these commentators nonetheless in their imaginations. They are taught to approach Rashi's commentaries as if these

---

12. Richard Elliott Friedman, *Commentary on the Torah*, viii.
13. Michael Strassfeld, *A Book of Life: Embracing Judaism as a Spiritual Practice*, 140.

commentaries represent the answer half of a question-and-answer dialogue. Consequently, it is the readers' task, with their *chavrutot*, to reconstruct the question half in order to participate in the dialogue. As Rabbi Bonchek points out, the key to understanding Rashi's commentaries has always been to ask, "What is bothering Rashi?" As he explains, Rashi's "commentary sparkles with brevity, clarity and fine-tuned precision. It is not only what he says, but how he says it, that conveys a maximum of meaning in a minimum of words. . . . Discovering the implicit question behind Rashi's comment is what the study of Rashi is all about."[14]

In fact, serious students of Rashi often become so proficient using this technique that they actually begin to "hear" his voice and relate to him as they would a beloved teacher. The Jewish educator Joel Lurie Grishaver writes:

> Obviously, I've never met Rashi, and little biographic material is available, but his personality comes through in his work. First, he is quiet and patient. He doesn't shout out—"You are going to learn three things from this passage." Rather, he sits waiting in the margins. As I am reading the text and something isn't clear, I turn to him. Usually, he is waiting with an answer which begins, "I thought you might have a problem with this verse." Then rather than giving a full answer, he begins with a few cryptic words—a hint and gentle sigh . . . "Now go work it out for yourself." Sometimes I scream in anger, "Why can't you just tell me what you're trying to teach me." But Rashi doesn't say anything. His commentary just echoes—"Look at the text again; think; you'll find it." And in the end, with satisfaction like that of the mountain-climber who has reached the top, my understanding of the text has brought me the satisfaction of owning this small piece of Torah. Rashi just smiles and says: "I knew you could figure it out." Rashi lived in the twelfth century, yet we talk regularly.[15]

This close relationship is evident even in the names of these great scholars. "Rashi," for instance, is not the actual given name of this great rabbinic commentator. It is an acronym, a kind of nickname made from the initials of Rabbi Sholmo ben Yitzchak. In like manner "Rambam" is a frequently used nickname for Rabbi Moses ben Maimon or Maimonides and "Ramban" for Rabbi Moses ben Nachmanides.

---

14. Avigdor Bonchek, *What's Bothering Rashi?: A Guide to In-Depth Analysis of His Torah Commentary*, 3.

15. Joel Lurie Grishaver, *Learning Torah: A Self-Guided Journey through the Layers of Jewish Learning*, 170.

Commentators Encourage Readers to Eclipse Them

Again, the purpose of such an approach is not to memorize Rashi's ideas or accept them without modification. It instead allows readers to get into Rashi's "mental shoes," to approach him as they would a living teacher, and to learn, as Bonchek explains, "an approach to Torah interpretation which can be applied throughout the [Hebrew Scriptures]."[16] Far from stifling individual involvement or in any way placing itself between the current reader and God, this large corpus of rabbinic commentary is meant to enhance a direct, living communication with the Divine through rigorous scripture study. The point of this tradition is to help Jews develop new insights into the Scriptures and share them. As Bonchek writes, "the student only begins to *understand* Rashi when he starts to *think* on his own."[17]

The rabbis even had a word for a new insight: *chiddush* (or *hiddush*), from the Hebrew word *chadash* or "new." According to Neusner,

> The chief glory of the commentator is his or her *hiddush* (novelty). The *hiddush* constitutes a scholastic disquisition upon a supposed contradiction between two earlier authorities chosen from any period, with no concern for how they might in fact relate historically, and upon a supposed harmonization of their "contradiction." Or a new distinction might be read into an ancient law, upon which basis ever more questions might be raised and solved.[18]

Discovering and even publishing a *chiddush* is encouraged as a spiritual as well as an intellectual contribution. As Cohen writes, "At every moment when a student of Torah discovers new meaning, the original experience of revelation is re-created."[19] In this way, as Ismar Schorsch writes in his forward to *Etz Hayim* (a *chumash* aptly named for the tree of life), not only does our understanding of the Scriptures grow, but, in sense, the Scriptures themselves grow as well:

> Judaism is above all a life of dialogue. Ever since Sinai, God and Israel have conversed and interacted through the medium of Torah. Revelation destined Israel to become a nation of readers and interpreters. Yet as the incarnation of the divine word, Scripture bore an infinite range of meanings. Jews learned to read deeply rather than quickly, disjunctively as well as contextually. Each generation and every Jew was bidden to pore over the text afresh to internalize its normative force and to garner another layer of undetected

---

16. Bonchek, *What's Bothering Rashi?* 1.
17. Ibid., 10.
18. Jacob Neusner, *The Way of Torah: An Introduction to Judaism*, 83.
19. Cohen, *The Way Into Torah*, 19.

meaning. Endlessly malleable because it was supremely venerated, Scripture functioned as a canon without closure.[20]

In this way, rabbinic commentators function very much as personal tutors, along the lines Rabbi Joshua ben Perachiah advised. They supply mountains of commentary but their comments are to be built upon, not buried under. These comments are provided to teach important principles and techniques and consequently function as examples of how readers *might* interpret the Scriptures. They are meant to be engaged as one might study the teachings put forth by an actual tutor—as part of an ongoing discussion where those ideas are questioned, analyzed, challenged, learned from and ultimately built upon as one forms interpretations of one's own. Far from stifling creativity and individual thought, rabbinic commentators encourage and even rejoice in it.

Mormon as Commentator

In many ways, Mormon, especially in the earlier books in the Book of Mormon, bears a marked resemblance to rabbinic commentators, especially to Rashi. Just as Rashi comments extensively on the Hebrew Scriptures, Mormon also offers a multitude of comments on the scriptural history he is writing. According to Grant Hardy, Mormon provides more than a hundred editorial interruptions in his narrative—explanations concerning historical omissions, promises of material yet to be presented, source notes, summaries, additional details, intensifying exclamations, and sermonettes.[21] Granted, Mormon does not comment on nearly every verse in the Book of Mormon as Rashi does the Hebrew Scriptures, but still his presence is hard to miss. Much as Chaim Pearl describes Rashi, Mormon too seems to have dedicated himself "to the single task of making [his text's] meaning clear" and therefore "injects himself into the text, identifying question and statement, explaining words and phrases, making sense of an argument or a point in the discussion."[22]

---

20. David L. Lieber, ed., *Etz Hayim: Torah and Commentary*, xvii.
21. Hardy, *Understanding the Book of Mormon*, 97–99.
22. Chaim Pearl, *Rashi*, 69.

Mormon Also Teaches Interpretation

In addition, although frequent and often helpful, Mormon's comments are, like Rashi's, not to be viewed as final or definitive. They also serve as examples of how Mormon's readers might productively approach his history. They also are meant to be questioned, analyzed, challenged, learned from, and ultimately built upon as Mormon's readers form interpretations of their own. This is true even with Mormon's famous "and thus we see" statements. Although these statements sound complete, they are not.

For instance, Mormon seems to sum up the Anti-Nephi-Lehi incident—where a number of Lamanites are converted to the Lord when their brother Lamanites, who have already been converted, refuse to fight them—by writing: "and thus we see that the Lord worketh in many ways to the salvation of his people" (Alma 24:27). This statement, although true as far as it goes, is much too general to cover every philosophical, political, much less theological implication associated with this event, especially since Mormon himself continues to discuss it for several pages afterwards. Similarly, Mormon seems to conclude "the account of the wars and contentions among the Nephites, and also the wars between the Nephites and the Lamanites" (28:9)—twenty-eight chapters—with just two lessons:

> And thus we see how great the inequality of man is because of sin and transgression, and the power of the devil, which comes by the cunning plans which he hath devised to ensnare the hearts of men. And thus we see the great call of diligence of men to labor in the vineyards of the Lord; and thus we see the great reason of sorrow, and also of rejoicing—sorrow because of death and destruction among men, and joy because of the light of Christ unto life. (Alma 28:13–14)

However, Mormon does not mention the dangers of priestcraft, the enticements of pride and position, the constant availability of repentance, the power of the atonement, the effectiveness of example, the sweep of the resurrection, the mercy of God, or any of the other important themes he has presented in these chapters.

Mormon Also Requires Reader Interaction

These "and thus we see" statements of Mormon's may sound like divine summations, perfect and complete, but they are not. As Mormon makes clear, he is "but a man" and has only the "strength of a man" (Moro. 9:18). The statements are therefore simply examples of the kinds of things

inspired human readers can and should see in the Book of Mormon as
they engage it fully. Faced with the daunting task of recounting a thousand years of history in a fairly small book, Mormon was forced to employ
an incredibly economic style, much like Rashi. He sounds fairly frustrated
when he complains, as he does several times, that he "cannot write the
hundredth part of the things of [his] people" (W of M 1:5; Hel. 3:14;
3 Ne. 5:8; 26:6). Mormon therefore had to choose his events and words
as best he could to represent the most important lessons of his people's
history and to pack them with meaning. As a result, these summation
statements serve as reminders that there is much to be seen in Mormon's
work as well as samples of what he saw in it at the time. Careful readers
therefore must, according to Hardy, approach everything about Mormon's
writings—much like Rashi's—with probing questions, asking "Why
would Mormon choose to include this? What might he have omitted?
Is there any significance in the way he arranges events or tells particular
stories?"[23] As a result, meaning in the books of Mosiah, Alma, Helaman,
3 Nephi, and 4 Nephi is not limited to Mormon's summations. Readers
must seek, as Mormon himself did, to find all the many meanings contained within their pages. Much as faithful students of Rashi must master
his approach in order to transcend him, faithful followers of Mormon
should similarly get to know Mormon, imaginatively hear his "sorrowful,
humane, moralistic, and precise" voice, as Hardy describes it,[24] and find
additional significance beyond what Mormon claims to see in his book.

This is particularly true since Mormon as well as his son, Moroni, the
final compiler of the Book of Mormon, both make it clear that God is
actually the author of their text. Despite their involvement in producing
it, they are still its students and therefore are still struggling to understand
its totality. For example, near the beginning of the Words of Mormon,
Mormon explains how he made "an abridgment from the plates of Nephi,
down to the reign of this king Benjamin." However, although his record
of this early period of Nephite history is seemingly complete, he feels
inspired to include with it other, unabridged plates from this era "which
contained this small account of the prophets . . . and also many of the
words of Nephi" (W of M 1:3). Mormon cannot really explain why he
does this. He says only that it is for "a wise purpose" and does so simply
because "the workings of the Spirit of the Lord which is in [him]" (v. 7).

---

23. Hardy, *Understanding the Book of Mormon*, 90.
24. Ibid., 97.

Additionally, Moroni at one point includes in the book of Ether the sweeping vision of the brother of Jared in which he saw "all the inhabitants of the earth which had been, and also all that would be" (Ether 3:25). Moroni is overwhelmed by the scope and profundity of this vision. As he says, "there never were greater things made manifest than those which were made manifest unto the brother of Jared" (4:4). Nevertheless, despite Moroni's eagerness to share the brother's vision, he is commanded to seal it up to come forth at some unknown time which he knew not of (v. 5). As a result, Moroni can only bewail the faithlessness of his future readers and plead with them to come unto the Lord so that they can receive "greater things" (v. 13). Again, God is the ultimate author of the Book of Mormon. He controls what information it contains and what it does not. Mormon and Moroni clearly understand much about the narrative they are writing but not everything—particularly what meaning others can find in it.

Furthermore, after Moroni had received the plates from his father and was in the process of adding to them, he laments both his father's "weakness in writing" as well as his own. As he says, the Lord "hast made *us* mighty in word by faith, but [he] hast not made *us* mighty in writing" (Ether 12:23). Moroni is concerned that the Gentiles in particular will "stumble because of the placing of our words" and mock their work (v. 25). God, however, comforts Moroni and explains that he will make strong the work that Moroni sees as weak and will show unto his readers through that work "that faith, hope and charity bringeth unto [God]— the fountain of all righteousness" (vv. 27–28). In other words, the Book of Mormon is not limited to Moroni's or Mormon's abilities or understandings. As Moroni affirms, those who read the Book of Mormon and "shall not condemn it because of the imperfections which are in it, the same shall know of greater things than these" (Morm. 8:12).

Mormon and Moroni Also Encourage Readers to Eclipse Them

In this way, Mormon and Moroni function like rabbinic commentators. Not only do they reach out to their readers and teach them by providing helpful examples of what readers can see in the Book of Mormon, but both of them encourage their readers to engage them and see more than they currently see in the Book of Mormon. Immediately after Moroni receives comfort from God concerning his writings, he continues with his work, summarizing the prophecies of Ether "from the beginning of man" until the coming of "a new heaven and a new earth" (Ether 13:2–11). Little wonder then that at the end of his writings, Moroni similarly exhorts his readers to "remember how merciful the Lord hath been unto the children of men, from the creation of Adam even down until the time that [they] shall receive these things, and ponder it in [their] hearts" (Moro. 10:3). According to Moroni, God is ultimately the author of the Book of Mormon, and God himself will help its readers understand it just as he helped Moroni finish it—provided they ask him. Consequently, Moroni exhorts his readers again to "ask God, the Eternal Father, in the name of Christ, if these things are not true" and has faith that God will "manifest the truth of it unto [them], by the power of the Holy Ghost." For "by the power of the Holy Ghost [they] may know the truth of *all things*" (vv. 4–5)—including messages in the Book of Mormon that Mormon and Moroni did not include or know of.

Judging Every Person in a Favorable Light

In this way, Mormon and Moroni, as well as Nephi and all of the other authors of the Book of Mormon, fulfill the last of Rabbi Joshua ben Perachiah's suggestions. By functioning as Rashi-like teachers who lay the foundation for serious study but do not construct an interpretive ceiling for them, these authors very much judge their readers "in a favorable light," as Rabbi Joshua recommended. Nephi, for instance, states plainly that he has "charity for the Jew" as well as for the Gentiles (2 Ne. 33:8–9) and prays regularly that many of his readers "if not all, may be saved in [God's] kingdom" (v. 12). Enos similarly prays for his people as well as his people's enemies, the Lamanites, and receives an assurance from God that "at some future day" the descendants of these people "might be brought unto salvation" (Enos 1:13). And indeed not only does Moroni pray for his readers, but he sees his work as a way of improving their lives by laying before them his people's imperfections so that they "may learn to be more wise than we have been" (Morm. 9:31). As Moroni tells his future readers: "it is wisdom in God that these things should be shown unto you, that thereby ye may repent of your sins, and suffer not that these murderous combinations shall get above you" (Ether 8:23).

Indeed repentance, the ability to change and improve, is a constant theme of the Book of Mormon. The book begins with "many prophets, prophesying unto the people that they must repent, or the great city Jerusalem must be destroyed" (1 Ne. 1:4) and ends with a plea for that same Jerusalem to "awake, and arise from the dust," to put on its "beautiful garments," and to no more be confounded (Moro. 10:31). In between, there are calls for Laman and Lemuel to repent (1 Ne. 16:39; 18:10), appeals for the Gentiles to repent (2 Ne. 28:32), appeals for Jacob's people to repent (Jacob 3:4), as well as for King Benjamin's people (Mosiah 4:10), King Noah's people (Mosiah 11:25), the Zarahemlaites (Alma 5:51), the Ammonihahites (Alma 8:29), the Amalekites (Alma 21:6), the Zoramites (Alma 34:31), and many other -ites. Some of these people fail to repent in any meaningful way, but many do. The Anti-Nephi-Lehites, for instance, despite committing many grievous sins and murders, repented sufficiently before God that he took away their stain (Alma 24:11), and, after they buried their weapons of war, "they began to be a righteous people; and they did walk in the ways of the Lord, and did observe to keep his commandments and his statutes" (25:14).

In this way, the writers of the Book of Mormon demonstrate an almost irrepressible optimism that is essential for effective teachers and helpful *chavrutot*. Despite conveying dire prophecies, describing numerous set-backs, and relating a story book that ends with a once great and glorious civilization being utterly destroyed because of wickedness, they all remain hopeful about their readers. As Moroni addresses them at the end of the Book of Mormon:

> Yea, come unto Christ, and be perfected in him, and deny yourselves of all ungodliness; and if ye shall deny yourselves of all ungodliness, and love God with all your might, mind and strength, then is his grace sufficient for you, that by his grace ye may be perfect in Christ; and if by the grace of God ye are perfect in Christ, ye can in nowise deny the power of God.
>
> And again, if ye by the grace of God are perfect in Christ, and deny not his power, then are ye sanctified in Christ by the grace of God, through the shedding of the blood of Christ, which is in the covenant of the Father unto the remission of your sins, that ye become holy, without spot.
>
> And now I bid unto all, farewell. I soon go to rest in the paradise of God, until my spirit and body shall again reunite, and I am brought forth triumphant through the air, to meet you before the pleasing bar of the great Jehovah, the Eternal Judge of both quick and dead. Amen. (Moro. 10:32–34)

In the end, how could Moroni judge his readers more favorably? Even Rabbi Joshua ben Perachiah might be tempted to join with him in his final amen.

Part 2

Appreciating the Roots

Chapter Five

Roots and Branches

Wherefore, let us take of the branches of these which I have planted in the nethermost parts of my vineyard, and let us graft them into the tree from whence they came; and let us pluck from the tree those branches whose fruit is most bitter, and graft in the natural branches of the tree in the stead thereof.

And this will I do that the tree may not perish, that, perhaps, I may preserve unto myself the roots thereof for mine own purpose.

And, behold, the roots of the natural branches of the tree which I planted whithersoever I would are yet alive; wherefore, that I may preserve them also for mine own purpose, I will take of the branches of this tree, and I will graft them in unto them. Yea, I will graft in unto them the branches of their mother tree, that I may preserve the roots also unto mine own self, that when they shall be sufficiently strong perhaps they may bring forth good fruit unto me, and I may yet have glory in the fruit of my vineyard. (Jacob 5:52–54)

Approaching the Book of Mormon rabbinically clearly involves reading it in levels, paying close attention to its phrasing, and studying it with others. However, such an approach must also connect with the larger corpus of the Hebrew Scriptures as well. After all, the Hebrew Scriptures are the foundation of the rabbinic tradition—the roots from which the Talmud, the Mishnah, the Tosefta, and all of their various offshoots sprang. These scriptures provide many of the issues, problems, and conundrums the rabbinic tradition attempts to solve, and they also furnish the quotations, stories, and perspectives this tradition used to solve them. No rabbinic activity exists outside of the overall context of the Hebrew Scriptures. They supply the spiritual atmosphere, the historical environment, even the religious ecosystem upon which all of these activities depend. Even the study of the Torah, a subset of the Hebrew Scriptures, is inseparably connected to the other books in the Jewish canon. As Cohen writes, scriptural "intertextuality lies at the core of Torah learning."[1] Not only did the Talmudic rabbis understand this, but they sought to foster it by discovering "new meanings, exposing the interpretive relationships already evident in the Bible, as well as shaping new ties among verses by revealing linguistic and thematic connections heretofore unrecognized."[2]

For them, this intertextuality was especially apparent between the Torah and the Prophets, so much so that within rabbinic Judaism these two biblical sections form a close dialogic relationship, a kind of scriptural *chavrutah*, which is clearly evident in Jewish Sabbath worship services. There, in these services, the way the Torah and the Prophets are presented, a related selection from one read immediately after a portion from the other, and interpreted together reveals and reinforces a resonantal link between the two that vividly illustrates just how the Hebrew Scriptures and the Book of Mormon are linked.

The Rabbinic Connection between the Torah and the Prophets

In Jewish Sabbath services (more properly *Shabbat* services) the Torah reigns supreme, but it is not without its dependencies. According to Robinson, the Shabbat morning service begins with the congregants praising God and thanking him for the regal gift of the Torah. Afterwards,

> the congregants rise and the prayer leader or leaders go to the *Aron ha-Kodesh Holy Ark*. The entire body of worshippers chant or sing the verses from Numbers in which Moses spoke as the Ark of the Covenant moved forward, then a verse from Isaiah, ". . . *From out of Zion Torah shall go forth, and the word of Adonai from Jerusalem.*" The cantor or reader takes the *Sefer Torah/ Scroll of the Law* from the Ark. . . . Everyone echoes the cantor's recitation of the *Sh'ma*, and as the Torah is carried around the room . . . hymns to the greatness of Adonai are sung, while congregants bow to or kiss the *Sefer Torah* as it passes by. The scroll is returned to the *amudah*, the reading table at the front of the congregation, and the worshippers are seated.[3]

At this point, the royal crown, sash, and robes in which the Torah was dressed are removed, and the Torah is partially unrolled so that it can be read. Then, using a *yad*, or pointer, so as not to smudge its letters

---

1. Norman J. Cohen, *The Way Into Torah*, 87.

2. Ibid., 88.

3. George Robinson, *Essential Judaism: A Complete Guide to Beliefs, Rituals, and Customs*, 42.

or otherwise defile it, a member of the congregation chants the weekly *parashah* loudly and with great feeling. Those who read Hebrew follow along in their *chumashim* while those who cannot listen intently to the attendant translation. After the reading, the Torah scroll is held up, high overhead, and turned, solemnly, reverentially, in its unrolled state, toward the congregation so that its words can be admired by each member of the congregation. At this point, the congregation chants "This is the Torah that Moses placed before the Children of Israel by the command of Adonai" (Deut. 4:44), and the scroll is subsequently laid down again on the *amudah*, where it is rerolled, redressed, and finally returned to its Ark—all while the congregation sings *Etz Chaim*, "[The Torah] is a tree of life to those who hold fast to it."[4]

As is clear from this treatment, the Torah is unquestionably the king of Shabbat, as it is of rabbinic Judaism in general, and its reading is not simply a verbal exercise. It is a kind of coronation, a ceremonial celebration where the congregation dramatically reenthrones the Torah as the monarch of their lives and redeclares their allegiance to it.[5] However, despite its unchallenged sovereignty, the Torah still requires help in carrying out its royal role. Soon after the weekly *parashah* is read, there is a sermon or *derashah*. This *derashah* (pl. *derashot*), a word related to *derash*, is not just a speech or simply an oration based on the most current controversy or notable event of the day. Also known as a *d'var torah* or "word of Torah,"[6] the *derashah* is delivered by a *darshan* or "interpreter." This *darshan* then, true to the meaning of this title, proceeds to *interpret* the day's reading "in the light of tradition, theology, or historical circumstance" but does so in terms understandable and applicable to the congregation.[7] Even when that reading deals with a seemingly uninteresting, anachronistic, or politically incorrect subject, the *darshan* remains focused on the text at hand. Just as the Talmudic rabbis, according to Rabbi Donin, attempted to explain Torah passages anciently using parables to "vividly bring home the lesson of the Scriptural text in its application to the daily life of the people,"[8] so *darshanim* (pl. of *darshan*) add, according

---

4. Ibid., 43.

5. Ibid., 42.

6. Michael Strassfeld, *A Book Life: Embracing Judaism as a Spiritual Practice*, 121.

7. Michael Fishbane, *The JPS Bible Commentary: Haftarot*, xix.

8. Rabbi Hayim Halevy Donin, *To Pray as a Jew: A Guide to the Prayer Book and the Synagogue Service*, 232.

to Fishbane, "human words" to divine ones "in order to make [the Torah's] ongoing relevance and significance clear and immediate."[9]

Thus, the Torah, despite its powerful position, is not completely self-sufficient. It requires help in getting out its message—and not just from interpretive sermons but from readings from other scriptural works as well. In between the Torah readings and the *derashot* come readings from the Prophets. Called *haftarot* (sing. *haftarah*, an Aramaic word meaning "conclusion" or "epilogue"),[10] these prophetic readings complement rather than compete with their respective *parashot*. Much like respectful colleagues presenting papers at a conference, they do not comment directly on the Torah portion or impose an overt interpretation upon it. They instead present images, events, and figures that resonate with the Torah readings in a more subtle, respectful, and associative manner. In this way, *haftarot*, according to Rabbi Wayne Dosick, unite with their *parashot* to add "depth of meaning and understanding to the weekly Torah lesson."[11]

Sometimes this resonance is fairly obvious. For example, the *parashah* Numbers 13:1–15:41 and its *haftarah* Joshua 2:1–24 both deal with spies entering Palestine in preparation for Israelite invasions. However, the *parashah* tells the story of faithless spies whose report kept the Children of Israel wandering while the *haftarah* relates how faithful spies paved the way for the children of those Children to enter the Promised Land. The situational similarities in these stories serve to highlight their differences, bringing into striking relief the main points of both. Other *haftarot* connect with their *parashot* in ways that are much less evident. Exodus 13:17–17:16 and Judges 4:4–5:31, for instance, seem similar only in the fact that both contain victory songs, one Moses's Song of the Sea and the other the Song of Deborah. Nonetheless, despite sometimes tenuous connections, Fishbane and others still find within these two kinds of readings subtle commonalities that serve to enhance the meaning of both. Obvious or not, the point of these readings is for congregants to meditate on all the possible ways these two readings could relate and find meaning in their disconnections as well as in their connections. As Rabbi J. H. Hertz writes: "there is always some similarity between the [*parashah*] and the Prophetic selection. Even when the [*haftarah*] does not contain an explicit

---

9. Fishbane, *Haftarot*, xix.

10. Stephen Gabriel Rosenberg, *The Haphtara Cycle: A Handbook to the Haphtaroth of the Jewish Year*, xx.

11. Rabbi Wayne Dosick, *Living Judaism: The Complete Guide to Jewish Belief, Tradition, & Practice*, 78.

reference to the events of the Sedrah, it reinforces the teaching of the weekly Reading upon the mind of the worshipper."[12]

No one knows for sure when or why this practice of reading selections from the Prophets began. Traditionally, *haftarot* readings are said to have originated during the second century B.C.E, when Antiochus Epiphanes IV, a Greek Seleucid king, imposed harsh restrictions on Jewish worship, including banning the reading of the Torah. Jews at this time, so the theory goes, resorted to reading related material from the Prophets as a reminder of the Torah portion they would have ordinarily read on that day.[13] Other scholars feel that *haftarot* were later innovations affirming the place of the prophets in response to the Samaritans and Sadducees, both of whom denied prophetic authority.[14]

Regardless of the circumstance of their origin, it is clear that *haftarot* readings were firmly established by the time of the Talmudic rabbis and that this practice was actively promoted by them. The tractate Megillah in the Mishnah, for example, contains several references to the *haftarot*, or what Neusner calls the "reading of a prophetic lection" (MI Megillah 4:2–5, 10),[15] and the later Talmudic commentary to that section adds many more (BT Megillah, 31a). The official emphasis, as Rabbi Hertz writes, may indeed have been on how the Prophets reinforce the Torah, but it is evident from the experience itself that this reinforcement goes both ways. Clearly the Talmudic rabbis felt, as Rabbi Donin writes, that the "books of the Prophets, though a part of the Bible, are not equal to Torah" and for this reason the Rabbis "fixed the rule that the reading of the Haftarah could not be done independently of the Torah reading." Indeed these rabbis mandated that a *haftarah* must immediately succeed its *parashah* and that the *maftir*, or *haftarah* reader, must repeat the last few lines of the Torah portion before he or she begins reading (BT Megillah, 32a). However, as Rabbi Strassfeld writes, despite their difference from the Torah and their dependency upon it, the prophetic writings are still believed to be "the word of God,"[16] and approaching them as if they were theologically inferior significantly undermines the entire *parashah-haftarah* dialogue as well as the benefits that are derived from that dialogue. As Fishbane writes, reading from the Prophets as well as the Torah instead

---

12. J. H. Hertz, ed., *The Pentateuch and Haftorahs*, 20.

13. Ibid.

14. Rosenberg, *Haphtara Cycle*, xxii.

15. Jacob Neusner, *The Mishnah: A New Translation*, 322–24.

16. Strassfeld, *A Book of Life*, 143.

stresses the unity of the Hebrew Scriptures and their interdependence. Its dominant concern is not to divide these scriptural sections but "to establish the historical symmetries between events, persons, or institutions and thus to show various types of continuities and correlations" within them.[17]

Haftarot may indeed consist of prophetic reflections of the Torah, images that do not originate from the Torah itself, but still each *haftarah* has a look of its own even if the original image is only reversed or otherwise changed by its human "mirror," and it is those differences between these two equally valid images that bring out the beauty and power of both. As Donin notes, these public readings from the Prophets are "meant to strengthen the loyalty of the people to the teachings of the Torah" and, by their connection to similar readings from the Torah, are intended "to strengthen Jewish faith in the sanctity of the prophetic writings, in the holiness of Jerusalem, and in the messianic destiny of the Davidic dynasty."[18] In other words, the flow of enhanced meaning and increased significance goes both ways. The *haftarot* support and reinforce the Torah, and the *parashot* verify and authorize the Prophets. Consequently the Hebrew Scriptures as a whole are benefited from the vibrant, symbiotic, respectful relationship between these two significant scriptural sections.

The Connection between the Book of Mormon and the Hebrew Scriptures

Although the term *haftarah*, like *pardes* and *peshat*, never actually occurs in the Book of Mormon, an interdependent, *haftarah*-like relationship with the Prophets and the Torah is very much promoted by it. Clearly, a close connection to the Prophets is suggested by the Book of Mormon's inclusion of twenty-one complete chapters from Isaiah as well as by the way it frequently alludes to these chapters and lauds them. "Great are the words of Isaiah," Jesus says in 3 Nephi, commanding his audience explicitly to "search these things," including the words of other Hebrew prophets (23:1, 5).

The Book of Mormon also assumes a thorough understanding of the Torah. Obscure figures from Genesis such as Nimrod and Melchizedek as well as the more familiar Adam and Eve, Cain and Abel, Noah, Abraham, Isaac, and Jacob are all referred to in the Book of Mormon without explanation or elaboration. Brief references to Moses—his dividing of the Red Sea,

17. Fishbane, *Haftarot*, xxix.
18. Donin, *To Pray as a Jew*, 243, 247.

Table 5.1 Genesis *Parashot* and their *Haftarot*

Parashot	Haftarot
Genesis 1:1–6:8	Isaiah 42:5–43:10
Genesis 6:9–11:32	Isaiah 54:1–55:5
Genesis 12:1–17:27	Isaiah 40:27–41:16
Genesis 18:1–22:24	2 Kings 4:1–37
Genesis 23:1–25:18	1 Kings 1:1–31
Genesis 25:19–28:9	Malachi 1:1–2:7
Genesis 28:10–32:3	Hosea 12:13–14:10
Genesis 32:4–36:43	Hosea 11:7–12:12 or Obadiah 1:1–21
Genesis 37:1–40:23	Amos 2:6–3:8
Genesis 41:1–44:17	1 Kings 3:15–4:1
Genesis 44:18–47:27	Ezekiel 37:15–28
Genesis 47:28–50:26	1 Kings 2:1–12

his smiting of the rock to produce water, his raising of the brazen serpent in the wilderness—similarly figure prominently in the Book of Mormon. Indeed, one wonders how anyone without an extensive knowledge of the Hebrew Scriptures could understand the Book of Mormon at all.

However, recognizing and appreciating the linkages between the Book of Mormon and the Hebrew Scriptures is more than simply a requirement for a working understanding of the Book of Mormon; it is the gateway to a deeper level of comprehension and appreciation of both of these sacred volumes. Unlike traditional *haftarot*, the Book of Mormon connects to both the Torah and the Prophets, and it does so in an extremely organized, sequential way. Reversing the major periods of Hebraic history, as they are presented in Jewish versions of the Hebrew Scriptures, the Book of Mormon unites with them chiastically, moving backwards, period by period, from the Captivity to the Creation, in a particularly productive, respectful, and resonantal way. In this way, the Book of Mormon actually "out-*haftarahs*" the *haftarot*, linking to the Hebrew Scriptures much as hinges do in a door—not selectively—here a quotation and there a quota-

Table 5.2 Non-hagiographic Biblical Books
and their Jewish Groupings

Group	Books
Torah	Genesis Exodus Leviticus Numbers Deuteronomy
Former Prophets	Joshua Judges 1 Samuel 2 Samuel 1 Kings 2 Kings
Later Prophets	Isaiah Jeremiah Ezekiel Minor prophets (Hosea, Amos, etc.)

tion—but point by point, progressively, comprehensively for the mutual support of both.

As has been noted, traditional *haftarot* link to their *parashot* in a somewhat haphazard fashion—a connection Fishbane diplomatically calls "discontinuous."[19] They consist of selections from all of the Former Prophets (Joshua, Judges, 1 & 2 Samuel, and 1 & 2 Kings) as well as from most of the Later Prophets (Isaiah, Jeremiah, Ezekiel, Hosea, etc.).[20] However, as can be seen from examples in Table 5.1, they follow no discernable order—chronological, historical, or biblical.[21] They seem to be simply chosen because of their connection to the section of the Torah being read without any regard for when they were written, by whom, or in what order they appear in the Bible.

The Book of Mormon, however, is structured so as to connect with the Torah and the Prophets in order, as these sections are arranged in the Jewish version of the Hebrew Scriptures. Following the Masoretic text

19. Fishbane, *Haftarot*, xix.
20. Rosenberg, *The Haphtara Cycle*, xix–xx.
21. W. Gunther Plaut, *The Haftarah Commentary*, xi.

Table 5.3 Historical Periods in Relation to
the Biblical Books and Groupings

Grouping	Books	Periods
Torah	Genesis	Patriarchal Period
	Exodus Leviticus Numbers Deuteronomy	Mosaic Period
Early or Former Prophets	Joshua Judges	Confederacy Period
	1 Samuel 2 Samuel 1 Kings 2 Kings	Monarchic Period
Later or Literary Prophets	Isaiah Jeremiah Ezekiel	Prophetic Period

rather than the Greek Septuagint, Jewish versions of the Torah and the Prophets group the non-hagiographic books as shown in Table 5.2.[22]

This arrangement coincides, for the most part, with the four standard periods of pre-exilic Israelite history,[23] particularly if the Later Prophets are set off into a period of their own. Such a division is justified since although this Prophetic Period occurs while kings rule Israel and Judah and therefore is part of the Monarchic Period, these books treat history so differently and look at it from such a different point of view that they seem not to fit into that era as a genre. Adding the periods of pre-exilic history produces a table such as Table 5.3.

The Book of Mormon follows this same basic sequence—but in reverse, with the first period last and the last period first. For instance, 1 and 2 Nephi contain wholesale quotations from Isaiah and describe its main prophets, Lehi and Nephi, in terms that recall the major prophets of the

22. Biblical books such as Ruth, Chronicles, Esther, and Daniel, which frequently appear in between these books in the Christian Old Testament, are placed in the Writings (or Hagiographa) section in Jewish versions of the Hebrew Scriptures.

23. Bernard W. Anderson, *Understanding the Old Testament*, 21.

Table 5.4 Book of Mormon Books in Relation to
Biblical Books and Periods

Hebrew Books	Periods	Mormon Books
Genesis	Period of Origins	Ether Mormon
Exodus Leviticus Numbers Deuteronomy	Period of Receiving the Law	4 Nephi 3 Nephi
Joshua Judges	Period of Judges	Helaman Alma
1 Samuel 2 Samuel 1 Kings 2 Kings	Period of Kings	Words of Mormon Mosiah
Isaiah Jeremiah Ezekiel Minor prophets	Period of Prophets	Omni Jarom Enos Jacob 2 Nephi 1 Nephi

Prophetic Period. Mosiah is an account of two sets of three kings, some righteous and some wicked, described in ways very similar to the three main kings of the Monarchic Period. Judges rule in Alma and Helaman, and heroes dominate just as they do during the Confederacy Period. Much as Moses does during the Mosaic Period, Jesus descends from on high to give the specifics of his Law right after wicked people are miraculously destroyed and the remainder assembles at a mountain-temple. Finally, the books of Mormon and Ether present a world where chaos and profound darkness dominate, much like the beginning of the Creation story in Genesis. In these books, massive migrations also occur, a great tower is built, and a great sea journey is undertaken—all events similar to those that occurred during the Patriarchal Period. If these periods are expressed more generally, a clear correlation is apparent, as shown in Table 5.4.

This relationship, however, appears most meaningfully when arranged as a chiasm, an inverted sequential parallelism, intersecting at the destruction of the First Temple and the resulting dispersion of the Jews (as shown in Table 5.5).

Table 5.5 Books of the Book of Mormon and the Hebrew Scriptures
Arranged Chiastically by Period

Period of Origins: Genesis

    Period of Receiving the Law: Exodus, Leviticus, Number, Deuteronomy

        Period of Judges: Joshua, Judges

            Period of Kings: 1 & 2 Samuel, 1 & 2 Kings

                Period of Prophets: Isaiah, Jeremiah, Ezekiel, Minor Prophets

                The Diaspora

                Period of Prophets: 1 & 2 Nephi, Jacob, Enos, Jarom, Omni

            Period of Kings: Words of Mormon, Mosiah

        Period of Judges: Helaman, Alma

    Period of Receiving the Law: 3 & 4 Nephi

Period of Origins: Mormon, Ether

The connection between the Book of Mormon and the Torah and the Prophets therefore is more of a piece than that between the Torah and the Prophets alone. It seems more purposeful, more unified, more intentionally integral than the relationship between traditional *haftarot* and their *parashot*. It therefore invites a more literary approach to all these books and fairly begs for large-scale comparisons and contrasts. However, this linkage is more than simply a general, macro-level connection. As the subsequent chapters show, this tie is reinforced by numerous micro-level details that together create a sophisticated dialogue between the Book of Mormon and the Hebrew Scriptures. Together they form a kind of scriptural "conversation" that enhances readers' appreciation of both of these books, and they do so in classic *haftarah*-like ways: reinforcing main points, rendering academic points applicable in a modern setting, increasing the significance of points, as well as providing prophetic hope.

Hope is, after all, what J. H. Hertz sees as the primary purpose of a *haftarah-parashah* relationship, and it is also the ultimate result of the

Book of Mormon's structural connection to the Hebrew Scriptures. By presenting their historical periods in reverse and by providing positive examples, the Book of Mormon counters the negative examples that dominate the Hebrew Scriptures. In other words, just as the Torah and the Prophets move "downward," describing period-by-period the mistakes that accumulate gradually, building inexorably to the final, wide-spread dispersion of the Israelite people, so the Book of Mormon moves upward, reiterating the gravity of those mistakes, to be sure, but also providing examples of people making better choices and assuring its readers that the consequences of those historical mistakes are neither everlasting nor permanently part of their situation, as shown in Table 5.6.

In this way, the Hebrew Scriptures are themselves redeemed, saved step-by-step from the consequences of the long descent they describe. Much as Genesis repeats, in order, the events that preceded God's decision to flood the earth—a cataclysmic creation, an attempt by God to speak to a man, a description of that man's sons, an account of human development at that time, a listing of ten generations, and a story of the downfall of a powerful group—in order to cast that decision as a new beginning for the world instead of an ending, so the Book of Mormon similarly changes the finality of the Diaspora into a temporary setback by reversing the order of those events that led up to it.

In other words, these mistakes can be undone, Moses's "kingdom of priests" can yet be established (Ex. 19:6), prophets can yet be heeded, kings can rule in righteousness, judges can judge justly, and the Law can at last be welcomed. God's presence can also be apparent and a "holy nation" can yet be established on the earth. By connecting to the Hebrew Scriptures chiastically, the Book of Mormon transforms the destruction of the First Temple and its resultant dispersion of the Jews from an endpoint into a turning point. It is the event where these two sets of scripture meet and as such becomes a fulcrum for change, a pivot both for its readers as well as for the overall story.

"Turn away from your sins," Jacob pleads, "shake off the chains of him that would bind you fast; come unto that God who is the rock of your salvation" (2 Ne. 9:45). "Turn to the Lord with full purpose of heart, and put your trust in him," Limhi similarly entreats, and he will "deliver you out of bondage" (Mosiah 7:33). "Turn ye, turn ye unto the Lord your God," a later Nephi implores (Hel. 7:17), and Mormon, too, speaking directly to his future readers, asks them beseechingly, "how can ye stand before the power of God, except ye shall repent and turn from your evil ways? Know ye not

Table 5.6 Positive Incidents from the Book of Mormon
in Contrast with Negative Incidences from the Bible.

Negative Biblical Incident	Positive Book of Mormon Incident
The majority of Jews ignore their prophets, are captured by the Babylonians, and are carried off into captivity.	A family of Jews (the Lehites) heed their prophet, avoid captivity, and go off to freedom in a promised land.
Fallen kings (Saul, David, Solomon) and wicked despots frequently rule Israel and promote idolatry within their kingdoms.	Righteous Israelite servant-kings (Benjamin, Mosiah) reign and under their rule the people shun idolatry.
Faithless Israelites during Samuel's era choose an earthly king over a heavenly king and renounce the leadership of charismatic judges.	Faithful Israelites during King Mosiah's reign renounce the rule of dynastic kings and move to a system of people-appointed judges, with God as their ultimate king.
Murmuring children of Israel fail to wait for Moses when he ascends Mt. Sinai, disobey his law, and fashion a golden calf; when it is time to enter the Promised Land, they refuse out of fear and consequently wander in the desert for forty years.	Loyal children of Israel patiently await a Moses-like figure (Jesus) who finally comes down from on high in power and glory; and they so completely embrace his law that their promised land enjoys a two-hundred year period of peace and prosperity.
One man (Adam) transgresses God's law, brings about the Fall, and is cast out of God's presence.	One man (the brother of Jared) is so faithful to God that he is personally redeemed from the Fall, and is welcomed back into God's presence.

that ye are in the hands of God? Know ye not that he hath all power, and at his great command the earth shall be rolled together as a scroll? Therefore, repent ye, and humble yourselves before him, lest he shall come out in justice against you" (Morm. 5:22–24). In this way, the Book of Mormon embodies the *haftarah* tradition. Not only does it "conclude" the Torah and the Prophets with fine words, reiterating and reaffirming their most important points and providing prophetic encouragement to its readers, but its chiastic connection with those scriptures reinforces their words structurally, providing a tightly linked "epilogue" to them that points the way upward, to God. The Book of Mormon in effect mirrors the Torah and the Prophets so that their readers can see their lessons more clearly and apply those lessons more readily. As its title page states, one of the principal purposes of the Book of Mormon is to "show unto the remnant of the House of Israel what great things the Lord hath done for their fathers; and that they may know the covenants of the Lord, that they are not cast off forever." This the Book of Mormon very much provides for both Jews and Gentiles.

Chapter Six

Reinforcing a Point

And after it had come forth unto them I beheld other books, which came forth by the power of the Lamb, from the Gentiles unto them, unto the convincing of the Gentiles and the remnant of the seed of my brethren, and also the Jews who were scattered upon all the face of the earth, that the records of the prophets and of the twelve apostles of the Lamb are true. (1 Ne. 13:39)

One of the simplest and most straightforward ways a *haftarah* connects to a *parashah* is by reinforcing a main point. In this way, the *haftarah* serves as a kind of "second witness" or literary mirror that reflects a central idea of that *parashah* and in so doing helps establish it as valid, recurring pattern. This is one of the main ways Jeremiah 1:1–2:3, for instance, functions (in the Sephardic tradition) with respect to Exodus 1:1–6:1, a *parashah* entitled *Shemot* in Jewish versions of the Hebrew Scriptures. As a *haftarah*, this selection from the book of Jeremiah places the prophetic commissioning of Jeremiah alongside that of Moses to better reveal what Fishbane calls, "a common pattern of divine address, human resistance, and divine assurance."[1] In this way the similarities between the events of Jeremiah's life to those in Moses's not only fortify Moses's position as a prophet but buttress Jeremiah's as well. The two witnesses combine, in other words, to mutually vouch for each other. The *haftarah* verifies the *parashah*, and the *parashah* provides the foundation for the *haftarah*. By being read together, these passages link Moses and Jeremiah, and, as Fishbane writes, a "chain of prophetic messengers is thus formed across the generations, dramatizing God's involvement in Israel's destiny."[2] The books 1 Nephi, 2 Nephi, and Jacob connect with the major prophets of the Period of Prophets in a similar way. Read as a *haftarah* to Isaiah,

---

1. Michael Fishbane, *The JPS Bible Commentary: Haftarot*, 86.
2. Ibid.

Jeremiah, and Ezekiel, these first three books in the Book of Mormon help support those prophets and establish a common pattern of prophetic relevance, mission, and benefit.

Addressing the Period of Prophets

As mentioned previously, the Period of Prophets in the Hebrew Scriptures, for the purposes of this study, coincides chronologically with the last part of the Period of the Reign of Kings (the reigns of Jeroboam II and Uzziah on). In the Hebrew Scriptures, this period is marked by the many troubles of the Northern and Southern Kingdoms, where idolatrous practices as well as political and cultural dependence upon other nations continually pull their people away from the ways of God. At this time, various prophets—notably Isaiah, Jeremiah, and Ezekiel—appear, calling the people back to a greater reliance upon God and to a more strict observance of his laws. For the most part, these prophetic warnings go unheeded, and both kingdoms are eventually conquered: the Northern Kingdom by the Assyrians in 722 B.C.E. and the Southern Kingdom by the Babylonians in 586 B.C.E.

Given these prophets' lack of success, it is natural to question their value—both then, in their own day, as well as now, in a time long after their deaths. If they could not save their own people with their swelling words and outlandish acts, what value could they possibly have today? Are their words worth the effort to read, study, and apply them to our time? Even Rabbi Bernard Bamberger, who very much believes that "all human history has been fundamentally changed by" these prophets and that "they still have a vital message for all humanity," concedes that "in their day, by their own testimony, the prophets were failures." As he continues, "Some of them were disregarded, some were laughed at as lunatics, and some provoked popular resentment or official ire to the point of persecution and martyrdom."[3]

Such questions strike at the very heart of the *haftarah* tradition. They challenge the point of prophets as well as the utility of the Hebrew Scriptures as a whole, since the Former and Later Prophets take up over half of its pages. It is therefore appropriate that the Book of Mormon answers these questions using both the traditional *haftarah* approach as well as providing an additional *haftarah* of its own. In other words, not

---

3. Bernard J. Bamberger, *The Story of Judaism*, 24.

only do Nephi and Jacob support the importance and relevance of Isaiah, Jeremiah, and Ezekiel by including readings from these prophets and by following them with *derashah*-style homilies, but they also offer a narrative that resonates with these prophets in a way that both affirms their relevance and enhances their status in the eyes of its readers. In this way, these first three books in the Book of Mormon use traditional Jewish methods to promote a traditionally Jewish respect and reverence for the great literary prophets.

The Book of Mormon accomplishes this complex task by first setting up a situation that connects both with that of the great literary prophets as well as with that of many modern Jewish readers. 1 Nephi begins by starting its story just before the destruction of the First Temple and the resultant scattering of Judah, a time when Jeremiah, Ezekiel, and other prophets were warning Judah about the coming catastrophe. As Nephi writes, "For it came to pass in the commencement of the first year of the reign of Zedekiah, king of Judah . . . there came many prophets, prophesying unto the people that they must repent, or the great city Jerusalem must be destroyed" (1:4). Lehi, Nephi's father, has a vision "concerning Jerusalem—that it should be destroyed, and the inhabitants thereof; many should perish by the sword, and many should be carried away captive into Babylon" (v. 13)—and he becomes one of those "many prophets." The people, however, "were angry with him" when he told them to repent "and they also sought his life, that they might take it away" (v. 20). As a result, Lehi and his family flee into the desert, preempting a forced exile from Jerusalem by leaving the city voluntarily on their own in hopes of finding a better "land of their inheritance."

Although living in tents in the middle of an Arabian desert on their way to an unknown promised land may seem more like a plot for a fantasy novel than a real-life situation, for many Jews during the last two and a half millennia it is not all that different from normal life. Certainly the circumstances are extreme, but it is still the story of a family—with all the complexity of relationships that that entails—living away from familiar surroundings. They are a small vulnerable group amongst a multitude of foreigners, trying their best to survive and maintain their religious traditions against all odds. Danger lurks on the horizon. No place is permanent. Moving is a way of life. Questions as to why this happened to them and what they are to do about it dominate their conversations.

In other words, Lehi and his family are Diaspora Jews. Many of the details of their situation may be different, but their situation itself is fundamentally the same as that of countless Jews—as are the questions. For generations, Jews wondered in print and in private why Jerusalem was destroyed, why they were scattered, when they will return, and, most importantly, what they are to do now. It is in this light, in these very real and very relevant situations, that the words of these great biblical prophets are quoted and explained in the Book of Mormon.

Affirming the Words of the Prophets

After his great vision of the future of the House of Israel, Nephi returns to the "tent of [his] father" (1 Ne. 15:1), and it is there, in this fitting image of a dispersed and wandering people, that he shows Isaiah's continued relevance. His brothers are arguing when he arrives. They do not understand "the words which [their] father hath spoken concerning the natural branches of the [Israelite] olive-tree" (v. 7). After he recovers his strength, Nephi joins in on the discussion and, apparently without having any writings in front of him, rehearses to them from memory "the words of Isaiah, who spake concerning the restoration of the Jews" and how, "after they were restored they should no more be confounded, neither should they be scattered again." Nephi does not list his sources or otherwise describe what exactly he quoted from Isaiah; he only says that his brothers "were pacified and did humble themselves before the Lord" (v. 20).

This incident seems to be set up to pique his readers' curiosity. What exactly did Nephi read to them to produce such a response? Fortunately his readers do not have to wait long for an answer. Soon Nephi returns again to Isaiah and addresses this topic in a much more thorough and seemingly formal way. Perhaps he and his family are engaged in an ancient Shabbat worship service. It is not clear. However, Nephi does indeed follow the traditional Torah-*haftarah-derashah* sequence used in synagogues, and his use of this sequence very much affirms the continuing relevance and importance of the Prophets. First, Nephi reads to his brothers many things "which were written in the books of Moses." He then follows his readings with "that which was written by the prophet Isaiah" (1 Ne. 19:23). Last, he delivers to them an extended homily in which he explains the meaning of the chapters he has read to them.

Nephi does not record the reaction of his brothers. However, since he includes all of Isaiah 48 and 49—chapters he knows will be available to his future readers—as well as the complete text of his homily, the point seems more to include his future readers in on the experience and enable them to understand, in a very real way, both the power and the relevance of prophetic writings. Consequently, when his brothers ask the meaning of "these things which [he has] read," he is also speaking to his future readers when he testifies that "by the Spirit are all things made known unto the prophets" (1 Ne. 22:1–2). He then backs up his testimony with a lengthy explanation as to just what these chapters from Isaiah are saying and what it means to them. As he says, "the things of which I have read are things pertaining to things both temporal and spiritual; for it appears that the house of Israel, sooner or later, will be scattered upon all the face of the earth, and also among all nations" (v. 3). However, eventually, with the help of the Gentiles, they "shall be gathered together to the lands of their inheritance; and they shall be brought out of obscurity and out of darkness; and they shall know that the Lord is their Savior and their Redeemer, the Mighty One of Israel" (v. 12). Nephi's homily, as well as his inclusion of the two Isaiah chapters, seems designed to reveal the continued value of Isaiah and the other writings from the Hebrew prophets—a point Nephi makes plain at the end of his sermon. As he says, "the things which have been written upon the plates of brass [the Hebrew Scriptures] are true and they testify that a man must be obedient to the commandments of God" (v. 30).

Under Nephi's direction, Jacob also honors Isaiah. In a setting that may also be a Shabbat service, Jacob first addresses his people formally and explains why he is standing before them, what he is about to read to them, and why he has chosen these chapters to read to them:

> Behold, my beloved brethren, I, Jacob, having been called of God, and ordained after the manner of his holy order, and having been consecrated by my brother Nephi, unto whom ye look as a king or a protector, and on whom ye depend for safety, behold ye know that I have spoken unto you exceedingly many things. Nevertheless, I speak unto you again; for I am desirous for the welfare of your souls. Yea, mine anxiety is great for you; and ye yourselves know that it ever has been. For I have exhorted you with all diligence; and I have taught you the words of my father; and I have spoken unto you concerning all things which are written, from the creation of the world. And now, behold, I would speak unto you concerning things which are, and which are to come; wherefore, I will read you the words of Isaiah. And they are the words which my brother has desired that I should speak unto you. And I speak unto you for your sakes, that ye may learn and glorify the name of your God. And now, the words which I shall read are they which Isaiah spake concerning all the house of Israel; wherefore, they may be likened unto you, for ye are of the house of Israel. And there are many things

which have been spoken by Isaiah which may be likened unto you, because ye are of the house of Israel. (2 Ne. 6:2–5)

Jacob then reads Isaiah 49, 50, and 51, possibly as a *haftarah* to the "things which are written, from the creation of the world." And again, like Nephi, he includes these chapters in their entirety, enabling his readers to experience his *haftarah* as though they were present. Jacob next follows his reading with a *derashah*-style sermon. In this sermon, Jacob addresses the issue of exile as it relates to his future readers as well as to his original audience, and again he stresses the power of the prophets:

> And now, my beloved brethren, I have read these things that ye might know concerning the covenants of the Lord that he has covenanted with all the house of Israel—That he has spoken unto the Jews, by the mouth of his holy prophets, even from the beginning down, from generation to generation, until the time comes that they shall be restored to the true church and fold of God; when they shall be gathered home to the lands of their inheritance, and shall be established in all their lands of promise. (2 Ne. 9:1–2)

Jacob elaborates on just how this gathering will take place—first spiritually and then temporally—and affirms the relevance of these prophetic words, sounding much like Isaiah (particularly in Isaiah 5). Jacob tells his people,

> But wo unto the rich, who are rich as to the things of the world. For because they are rich they despise the poor, and they persecute the meek, and their hearts are upon their treasures; wherefore, their treasure is their God. And behold, their treasure shall perish with them also.
>
> And wo unto the deaf that will not hear; for they shall perish.
>
> Wo unto the blind that will not see; for they shall perish also.
>
> Wo unto the uncircumcised of heart, for a knowledge of their iniquities shall smite them at the last day.
>
> Wo unto the liar, for he shall be thrust down to hell.
>
> Wo unto the murderer who deliberately killeth, for he shall die.
>
> Wo unto them who commit whoredoms, for they shall be thrust down to hell. (2 Ne. 9:30–36)

Nephi follows Jacob's sermon with still "more of the words of Isaiah" (2 Ne. 11:2), in fact thirteen chapters of them, which, one hopes, were not read out loud in one formal worship service. However, despite a length unheard of in traditional *haftarah* readings, Nephi again follows this reading with *derashah*-style homily. Although the size of this quotation is extreme, this approach reinforces the relevance and importance of the words of this prophet. They are so important that they bear repeating even though they can be had in the Hebrew Scriptures themselves and are not changed significantly. In addition Nephi does not break the reading up with minute verse-by-verse or even chapter-by-chapter interpretations. The impression he leaves is that Isaiah can speak for himself, and nothing should interfere in his one-to-one connection with his readers. It is no surprise then that after quoting so many chapters, Nephi exclaims that his soul "delighteth in the words of Isaiah" (2 Ne. 25:5). While he concedes that Isaiah "spake many things which were hard for many of [Nephi's] people to understand" (v. 1), Nephi, however, considers the meaning of Isaiah's words to be "plain unto all those that are filled with the spirit of prophecy" and notes that at least the "Jews do understand the things of the prophets" (vv. 4–5).

Given this praise as well as the way Isaiah is treated by Nephi and Jacob, it is clear that the first three books in the Book of Mormon affirm both the general validity of the book of Isaiah as well as the value of reading and studying it in detail. If the simple act of including nineteen chapters of Isaiah was not proof enough, Nephi also testifies that "the prophecies of Isaiah shall be fulfilled" (2 Ne. 25:7). To him, a deep understanding of Isaiah is not only useful in his day, but it is important in later times as well. After reading passages from Isaiah to his people, Nephi says that he did "liken all scriptures unto us, that it might be for our profit and learning" (1 Ne. 19:23). Later on, he does the same thing, explaining that "there are many things which have been spoken by Isaiah which may be likened unto *you*," a pronoun that seems to include all of "ye who are of the house of Israel"—past, present, and future (2 Ne. 6:5). And again, five chapters later he writes, "I will liken his words unto my people, and I will send them forth unto all my children" (2 Ne. 11:2). There can be no doubt that Nephi finds Isaiah not just interesting in the past, but vital in the here and now as well.

Affirming the Position of the Prophets

The first three books of the Book of Mormon, however, do not just affirm the words of Isaiah and, by implication, the words of the other literary prophets. Nephi especially supports the ongoing relevance and validity of the position of prophets, something that was needed when he and Jacob lived as well as now. As the Jewish scholar Stephen Gabriel Rosenberg writes, prophets have a very specific function in the Hebrew Scriptures, a function that the English word does not always convey:

The term *navi* (plural *nevi'im*) is loosely translated as "prophet" but that gives the impression of someone who mainly foretells the future, which is not the case. *Navi* is a biblical word from the root *n-b-a*, which means "to bubble up" . . . and by extension to speak words that bubble up spontaneously. . . . In more general terms it implies that the subject is speaking words that well up inside him, as if implanted by an outside source. . . . The noun *navi* itself therefore indicates one who carries or conveys a special or divine message rather than prophecy.[4]

According to Rosenberg, Hebrew prophets are more "messengers" than predictors of the future, and the message they carry comes from God, not from themselves. As Rabbi W. Gunther Plaut writes, "A true prophet did not convey a personal opinion, but rather proclaimed a divinely initiated message."[5] This is precisely the kind of prophet the Book of Mormon presents, reinforcing this idea with distinct similarities to specific Hebrew prophets.

Lehi

In keeping with the era portrayed in the books of Ezekiel and Jeremiah, the Book of Mormon begins in Jerusalem during "the reign of Zedekiah," a place and a time when there are many such prophetic messengers "prophesying unto the people that they must repent, or the great city Jerusalem must be destroyed" (1 Ne. 1:4). The first prophet mentioned in the Book of Mormon, Lehi, becomes one of these messengers when he "pray[s] unto the Lord" (v. 5) and is given a message in a manner almost identical to the way Ezekiel receives his. After Lehi's first vision in which "there came a pillar of fire" and he "saw and heard much," Lehi returns home and "being overcome with the Spirit" experiences another vision where "the heavens open, and he thought he saw God sitting upon his throne, surrounded with numberless concourses of angels" (vv. 6–8). This account echoes the experience of Ezekiel when he, out of "the midst of the fire," sees the "likeness of four living creatures" (Ezek. 1:4–5). He witnesses God's chariot throne descend and then beholds "the appearance of the likeness of the glory of the Lord" sitting upon a throne "the colour of amber, as the appearance of fire" (vv. 26–28). Lehi is subsequently given a book to read (1 Ne. 1:11) just as Ezekiel is given "a roll of a book" to ingest (Ezek. 2:9; 3:1).

---

4. Stephen Gabriel Rosenberg, *The Haphtara Cycle: A Handbook to the Haphtaroth of the Jewish Year*, xx.

5. W. Gunther Plaut, *The Haftarah Commentary*, xxix.

In Lehi's vision, he sees "Jerusalem—that it should be destroyed, and the inhabitants thereof; many should perish by the sword, and many should be carried away captive into Babylon." He then addresses his fellow Jerusalemites and begins "to prophesy and to declare unto them concerning the things which he had both seen and heard" (1 Ne. 1:5–18). It is not as clear what Ezekiel saw or even that he actually *saw* anything. However, "lamentations, and mourning, and woe" were written on the book he was given (Ezek. 2:10), and the message he was told to give, though inscribed on a tile, is remarkably similar to Lehi's:

> Thou also, son of man, take thee a tile, and lay it before thee, and portray upon it the city, even Jerusalem: And lay siege against it, and build a fort against it, and cast a mount against it; set the camp also against it, and set battering rams against it round about. Moreover take thou unto thee an iron pan, and set it for a wall of iron between thee and the city: and set thy face against it, and it shall be besieged, and thou shalt lay siege against it. This shall be a sign to the house of Israel. (Ezek. 4:1–3)

In addition to Ezekiel, the Book of Mormon also connects Lehi with other Hebrew prophets of the time, especially Jeremiah. It likens the angry reaction Lehi received to that given the "the prophets of old" (1 Ne. 1:20) and later couples the way the people "sought to take away the life of [his] father" to the way the people similarly "rejected the prophets, and Jeremiah have they cast into prison" (7:14).

Nephi

Nephi too is a *navi*, a person who receives a message from God and delivers it at great personal peril. At least twice, his brothers sought to take away his life after he had prophesied unto them (1 Ne. 7:16; 17:48). Following the chiastic pattern which reaches further back into Israelite history as the Book of Mormon progresses, he is more like Isaiah than Ezekiel. Early in Isaiah's career as a prophet, before Ezekiel and Jeremiah, he has a vision of a heavenly temple where "the Lord [is] sitting upon a throne, high and lifted up, and his train filled the temple" (Isa. 6:1). Angels surround the throne and sing to each other, "holy, holy, holy, is the Lord of hosts: the whole earth is full of his glory" (v. 3). Isaiah is naturally in awe and exclaims "Woe is me! for I am undone; because I am a man of unclean lips, and I dwell in the midst of a people of unclean lips: for mine eyes have seen the King, the Lord of hosts" (v. 5). One of the angels then flies down to him, touches his lips with a live coal and takes away his iniquity (v. 7). The Lord then tells Isaiah to "Go, and tell this people, Hear ye indeed, but understand not; and see ye indeed, but perceive not" (v. 9). This vision is considered essentially Isaiah's call to be a prophet and serves as a preface to the rest of his writings.

Nephi has a similar vision where he is "caught away in the Spirit of the Lord . . . into an exceedingly high mountain" (1 Ne. 11:1), a holy place much like the heavenly temple in Isaiah 6. There an angel similarly ministers to him and at one point exclaims, "Hosanna to the Lord, the most high God; for he is God over all the earth, yea, even above all" (v. 6). Nephi is naturally awed by this experience, just as Isaiah is, and confesses that although he knows that God "loveth his children" he does not know "the meaning of all things" (v. 17). With Nephi now humbled, the angel proceeds to educate Nephi, both through his words and through a vision. After his vision, Nephi is commanded to write down on metallic plates specific sections of that vision as well other sacred experiences— what Nephi calls "the ministry and the prophecies"—for "the instruction of [his] people, . . . and also for other wise purposes, which purposes are known unto the Lord" (19:3). Like Isaiah, Nephi is therefore instructed to record specific messages for his people and future readers in a very specific way. For example, he is told to record "a greater account of the wars and contentions and destructions of [his] people" (v. 4) on his other plates, and he was instructed to not include the section of his vision that dealt with the end of the world (14:25).

In addition, Nephi has a close personal affinity with and reverence for Isaiah, almost to the exclusion of all other prophets. After the close of his sweeping vision, Nephi joins in a discussion with his brothers concerning the scattering and gathering of Israel. During the course of the discussion, he rehearses "unto them the words of Isaiah, who spake concerning the restoration of the Jews, or of the house of Israel" (1 Ne. 15:20). Later on he teaches his brothers by reading to them "that which was written by the prophet Isaiah" (19:23). Given these examples, it comes as no surprise that Nephi explains that his soul "delighteth" in the words of Isaiah (2 Ne. 11:2). In fact he feels so strongly that Isaiah's words will similarly delight his readers and induce them to "lift up their hearts and rejoice for all men" (2 Ne. 11:8) that he quotes, in their entirety, thirteen chapters and spends several chapters expounding upon Isaianic themes, especially the scattering and gathering of Israel.

As does Lehi, Nephi makes his connection with the Hebrew prophets explicit. He claims that the Lord has shown him visions of the

Jerusalemites "even as he had prophets of old" (1 Ne. 19:20). He also says that, like these prophets, he writes scriptures similar to those which his soul "delighteth in" (2 Ne. 4:15) and states that they will be "kept and preserved" and "handed down unto [his] seed, from generation to generation" (25:21). While Nephi may say several times that he writes "according to [his] plainness; in the which I know that no man can err" (v. 7), seemingly in a style distinct from Isaiah's poetic expressions, he, however, also laces his sermons with language taken directly from Isaiah and uses complex Hebraic poetic forms, most notably in the so-called "Psalm of Nephi." As Richard D. Rust points out, this psalm, found in 2 Nephi 4:15–35, "is both a supplication ('a poetic cry of distress to the Lord in time of critical need') and a psalm of praise."[6] It is arranged chiastically, artistically organized using parallelism, just as Isaiah does.

Jacob

Unlike Lehi and Nephi, Jacob does not connect as specifically with one prophet in the Hebrew Scriptures. In fact, not much is known about him. Unlike his older brothers, Jacob has no connection to Jerusalem and does not figure prominently in the journey from that city. He was born in the wilderness with his brother Joseph, where he was "grieved because of the afflictions of [his] mother" as well as by his own "afflictions and much sorrow, because of the rudeness of [his] brethren" (1 Ne. 18:7, 19; 2 Ne. 2:1). However, just what those afflictions were is not clear. Later on Jacob and his brother Joseph are consecrated by Nephi to be "priests and teachers over the land of [their] people" (2 Ne. 5:26). This was obviously an important role since many of his teachings when he was a priest are included in the Book of Mormon. However, not much is said about how he did this or what he went through during this era. While Nephi writes that Jacob saw the "Redeemer" (2 Ne. 11:2–3) and that he gave Jacob his plates with a commandment to write upon them (Jacob 1:1–2), clearly showing that he thinks highly of his brother, he mysteriously appoints another "man to be a king and a ruler over his people" (v. 9).

Nevertheless, Jacob is very much a *navi*, according to Rosenberg's description. Jacob does not speak on his own authority or from his own point of view. Before he quotes several chapters of Isaiah and then teaches his people from them, he establishes first that he was "called of God, and

6. Richard Dilworth Rust, *Feasting on the Word: The Literary Testimony of the Book of Mormon*, 71.

ordained after the manner of his holy order" and states that he speaks the words his prophet-brother Nephi "desired that [he] should speak" (2 Ne. 6:2, 4). And again, at the start of his own book, Jacob makes it clear that before he taught he "first obtained [his] errand from the Lord" (Jacob 1:17). In addition, he similarly bases his words on the Scriptures, specifically quoting those chapters from Isaiah and an extended allegory from the nonbiblical prophet Zenos. Although this may seem to fit more into the role of a teacher or commentator, biblical prophets may also very well have had passages from the Hebrew Scriptures read before they spoke. As Rosenberg writes:

> The *nevi'im*, who were orators, revolutionaries, and agents-provocateurs, had to *speak* their message, and presumably did so on those occasions when the people were gathered and assembled. I believe that some of these events would have included the public reading of some parts of the Torah and that after the reading the *navi* would deliver his message of criticism and hope. What would be more natural then, that *navi* after *navi* starts his speeches and diatribes with the words "*Koh amar Hashem,*" "thus says God"?[7]

Jacob's quoting of scriptural passages and subsequent teaching from them may not be as dramatic as the visions of Nephi and Lehi. However, it is very much consistent with what a *navi* does: deliver messages from God. In other words, Jacob is being just as much a prophet of God when he says that "this is my prophecy—that the things which this prophet Zenos spake, concerning the house of Israel, in the which he likened them unto a tame olive-tree, must surely come to pass" (Jacob 6:1) as he would have been if he had given that allegory himself. The point, in the end, is that the words of the prophet are not original to him. They come from God, whether spoken or written.

Subsequent Prophets

These three prophets—Lehi, Nephi, and Jacob—set a pattern for the rest of the prophets in the Book of Mormon and help set up the books in the Book of Mormon as prophetic *haftarot*. In all cases, these later prophets function in a manner consistent with the Hebrew *nevi'im*. Their methods and situations may vary, but they all give messages from God, not from themselves. Like Lehi, Abinadi is commanded to tell his people that God has "seen their abominations, and their wickedness, and their

---

7. Rosenberg, *The Haphtara Cycle*, xxviii.

whoredoms; and except they repent [he] will visit them in [his] anger" (Mosiah 11:20). Samuel the Lamanite says that he must "speak the words of the Lord which he doth put into [his] heart" and state that "the sword of justice hangeth over this people" (Hel. 13:5). A later Nephi preaches with "great power and authority," because such authority had been given to him from God that he might speak (Hel. 5:18). Alma too is told what to "cry into this people" by the Spirit of the Lord and commanded by an angel to "return to the city of Ammonihah, and . . . say unto them, except they repent the Lord God will destroy them" (Alma 7:9, 8:16).

Oftentimes these prophetic messages are unpopular, much as Lehi's and Nephi's were. Abinadi, for instance, goes forth amongst the Nephites and begins to prophesy. However, the people are angry with him, and he must flee for his life. Two years later, he returns in disguise, but is discovered and burned alive. Samuel the Lamanite also speaks prophetically to the Nephites and is cast out. He starts for his land but is constrained by the Lord. He then comes again to the capital of the Nephites, is forbidden to enter, and ends up delivering his message from atop an outer wall, all while soldiers shoot arrows at him. Alma, along with the sons of Mosiah, was cast into prison as well (Alma 14:17).

Furthermore, these Book of Mormon prophets not only act like biblical prophets, but they also sound like them. The hallmark phrase of the *navi*, according to Rosenberg, "thus saith the Lord," appears in the Book of Mormon thirty-six times—including twenty-two times just in the first three books, where Lehi, Nephi, and Jacob address topics that concern Isaiah, Jeremiah, and Ezekiel, especially the scattering and gathering of Israel; they do so in a way that is relevant to their listeners' current behavior. Similar to the way Plaut characterizes the message of the Hebrew prophets, their message is usually: "*If* you continue on your current paths and disregard God's ways, *then* disaster lies ahead." However, if you "turn from your evil ways you will live and enjoy God's favor."[8] In this way, as Plaut continues, "The prophetic challenges remain relevant today. They apply to all human beings and to all societies, and with special urgency they address Jews, who are the inheritors of the Covenant, which demands devotion to God and Torah and carries its own rewards. It is fitting, therefore, that Torah readings are concluded with prophetic haftarot."[9]

---

8. Plaut, *The Haftarah Commentary*, xxix.
9. Ibid., xxx.

Affirming the Value of Prophets

The Book of Mormon confirms that Judah was indeed taken captive by the Babylonians as the prophets predicted would happen if the people did not repent, and in many ways its main figures mirror the plight of the ancient Judahites. As Lehi and his family leave Jerusalem, his family splits into two figurative camps: one, headed by Laman and Lemuel, goes grudgingly, not really obeying their father, only conforming to his wishes; the other, headed by Nephi, sees in this journey the hand of the Lord and goes willingly, often enthusiastically, and with full purpose of heart. The Laman and Lemuel camp is very much like the Judahites Lehi left behind. In fact, Nephi states explicitly that "they were like unto the Jews who were at Jerusalem, who sought to take away the life of my father" (1 Ne. 2:13), and then portrays them, like the Jews at Jerusalem, as mocking their prophet-father, ignoring him, and even attempting to kill him. Lehi, like Jeremiah, continues to plead with them to change, saying things like "O that thou mightest be like unto this river, continually running into the fountain of all righteousness!" and "O that thou mightest be like unto this valley, firm and steadfast, and immovable in keeping the commandments of the Lord!" (vv. 9–10). But they remain unmoved, and eventually separate from Nephi and his followers. They are "cut off from the presence of the Lord" and experience "a sore cursing" so much so that the light of the Lord's countenance no longer shines on or in them, and they become spiritually "dark, and loathsome," "a filthy people, full of idleness and all manner of abominations" (12:20–21, 23). Lehi goes on to prophesy that if they continue in their evil ways that, as with the Judahites just before the Babylonian Captivity, the Lord "will take away from them the lands of their possessions, and he will cause them to be scattered and smitten" (2 Ne. 1:11).

The other group, following Nephi's example, obeys Lehi explicitly, observing "to keep the law of Moses and the sabbath day holy unto the Lord" (Jarom 1:5). Although they too are led from Jerusalem and driven from the original land of their inheritance, they wax strong in their new world and become "exceedingly rich in gold, and in silver, and in precious things, and in fine workmanship of wood, in buildings, and in machinery, and also in iron and copper, and brass and steel" (Jarom 1:5, 8). In general, they continue, as they began, to "prosper exceedingly, and to multiply in the land" (2 Ne. 5:13).

Through the example of the Lamanites and Nephites then, the Book of Mormon shows not only the consequences of not following the prophets—a consequence abundantly shown in the Hebrew Scriptures—but also the benefits of following them, something not described very well in those same scriptures. Thus, the Book of Mormon supplies a positive example to reinforce the negative one. It suggests how modern Jews should deal with their dispersed state. Some ancient Jews were essentially forced out of Jerusalem like Laman and Lemuel and some may have been led out for their own safety and for a higher purpose like Nephi. Regardless of the ancient reason, the best plan now is to obey the Lord, keep his commandments, and prosperity in all of its forms will come.

This initial story of Lehi connects the Book of Mormon with a crucial point in the Hebrew Scriptures and establishes a pattern for the subsequent *haftarot*. The pattern is certainly simplified, and there is more to those connections than it can point out. Nevertheless, this pattern is a helpful tool that enables readers to explore the connections in other ways. The Book of Mormon works as a *haftarah* by, first, connecting with an era in the Hebrew Scriptures; second, by literarily exploring its problems through characters, plots, and other means; and last, by elaborating upon these ideas in a similar manner that presents other approaches that are applicable to the modern reader's situation. This pattern works in the subsequent *haftarot* in the Book of Mormon.

In this way, the first three books of the Book of Mormon support and affirm the teachings, the station, and the benefit of prophets. By having their readers read these prophets' writings, discuss their messages, and see positive examples of how their words actually benefited someone, these books provide additional testimony and evidence of the validity and contemporary value of the prophets. Since the validity of all *haftarot* is dependent upon their originating from "true and just" prophets, it is fitting and perhaps fundamental that the first period the Book of Mormon addresses is the Period of Prophets. By first connecting to this period, the Book of Mormon affirms and enhances the importance of the great "literary" prophets of the Hebrew Scriptures and it helps establish its own writers as great prophets in their own right, setting up the books in the Book of Mormon as suitable *haftarot*. In this way, the Book of Mormon not only sets the tone of its relationship to the Hebrew Scriptures, but it establishes the basis on which that relationship is founded.

Chapter Seven

Rendering an Academic Point Applicable

Nevertheless, if it were possible that ye could always have just men to be your kings it would be well for you to have a king.

But remember the iniquity of king Noah and his priests; and I myself was caught in a snare, and did many things which were abominable in the sight of the Lord, which caused me sore repentance; Nevertheless, after much tribulation, the Lord did hear my cries, and did answer my prayers, and has made me an instrument in his hands in bringing so many of you to a knowledge of his truth. (Mosiah 23:8–10)

In addition to supporting the main idea of a *parashah*, another way a *haftarah* connects to a *parashah* is by applying its more academic points to circumstances modern readers experience. This approach is traditionally most helpful for practices associated with Mosaic priests and sacrifices, which cannot be performed without a temple but still must contain some relevance to life without a temple. For instance, the relationship between the *parashah Emor* (Lev. 21:1–24:23) and its *haftarah* (Ezek. 44:15–31), according to Fishbane, "exemplifies the process of tradition and change—the need to maintain continuity with the sacred practices of the past, and the desire to innovate for new times."[1] This *haftarah* presents this point by connecting Ezekiel's laws for the "reincorporation" of priests to those concerning their ritual defilement. Neither of these sets of laws can be followed without a working temple. However, since a number of priestly regulations promulgated by Ezekiel contradict their counterparts in the Torah, they show how ancient ideas can be updated for more contemporary times. In other words, when these two readings are put together, they, as Fishbane explains, explore an important point that is applicable to all:

---

1. Michael Fishbane, *The JPS Bible Commentary: Haftarot*, 197.

"Inevitable conflicts arise between religious duties and social or familial obligations. Devotion to God may require separation from natural and communal forms that would betray one's integrity and religious path; at the same time, there are forms of social contact and acts of care that take precedence over personal practices and considerations."[2]

The Book of Mormon connects in a similar way to the Hebrew Scriptures, both by affirming them as they are and by broadening their relevance temporally. For the Period of Kings, the books of Omni and Mosiah, as well as the Words of Mormon, connect to the kingly books in the Hebrew Scriptures—1 Samuel, 2 Samuel, 1 Kings, and 2 Kings—by confirming the good and evil that kings can do as well as by expanding the implications of these actions beyond the influence of kings to general principles that people can employ today.

Addressing the Period of Kings

The question of kings and their ultimate effect on society is left somewhat unresolved in the Hebrew Scriptures. According to Rabbi Samuel Sandmel, "viewpoints in Samuel–Kings [on this issue] clash and contradict each other."[3] Much is said in favor of kings as well as against them. For instance, the book placed just before these books in the Jewish canon, the book of Judges, seems fairly pro-king. Many of the judges, like Samson, are ineffectual or, like Deborah and Gideon, achieve only temporary results despite the fact that they themselves are individually impressive. In addition, the sentence "In those days there was no king in Israel, but every man did that which was right in his own eyes" (Judg. 17:6) precedes several somewhat chaotic and unfortunate acts: Micah having a house of graven images and consecrating his son and a Levite to be their priests (vv. 5, 12); Danites wandering about in search of a land of inheritance as well as images, which they took (18:1); concubines being raped and killed (19:24–27); and Jabesh-gilead being attacked in order to provide wives for the severely depopulated tribe of Benjamin (21:12–15). The thrust of these incidents in Judges seems to be that the kind of order and stability kings bring would have prevented these problems and therefore constitute a better social situation.

---

2. Ibid.

3. Samuel Sandmel, *The Hebrew Scriptures: An Introduction to Their Literature and Religious Ideas*, 442–43.

Furthermore, this favorable opinion of kings is not limited to Judges. The later books, where actual kings appear, seem to bear out this idea, at least initially. King Saul makes headway against the enemies of Israel, the Ammonites and the Philistines, when the judges could not. King David finally defeats these enemies and makes the land secure. King Solomon brings an era of peace and prosperity and is at last able to build a lavish temple to the Lord. Nonetheless, there is an equally deep countercurrent against kings. Back in the book of Judges, Gideon, a judge, is asked to be king, and he declines, telling his people that it is better that "the Lord shall rule over [them]" (Judg. 8:23). In other words, having a human king, by definition, supplants God as the true king and therefore cannot be countenanced. This idea comes up again in 1 Samuel 8 when the people plead with Samuel to "Give us a king to judge us." Here, too, the Lord sees this request as an indication that they desire "that he should not reign over them" and takes it as a rejection (v. 6). The Lord's plan for Israel also seems to be thwarted by this plea. He wants to transform them into "a peculiar treasure . . . above all people," even a "kingdom of priests, and an holy nation" (Ex. 19:5–6); however, they want to "be like all the nations" and have an earthly king (1 Sam. 8:20). To help his people understand what they are asking for, the Lord has Samuel explain to all Israel the disadvantages of having such a king:

> This will be the manner of the king that shall reign over you: He will take your sons, and appoint them for himself, for his chariots, and to be his horsemen; and some shall run before his chariots.
>
> And he will appoint him captains over thousands, and captains over fifties; and will set them to ear his ground, and to reap his harvest, and to make his instruments of war, and instruments of his chariots.
>
> And he will take your daughters to be confectionaries, and to be cooks, and to be bakers.
>
> And he will take your fields, and your vineyards, and your oliveyards, even the best of them, and give them to his servants.
>
> And he will take the tenth of your seed, and of your vineyards, and give to his officers, and to his servants.
>
> And he will take your menservants, and your maidservants, and your goodliest young men, and your asses, and put them to his work.
>
> He will take the tenth of your sheep: and ye shall be his servants. (1 Sam. 8:11–17)

Nonetheless, the people persist in their desire—despite Samuel's warning that when these events occur "the Lord will not hear [them] in that day" when they cry out for relief (1 Sam. 8:18). Consequently, both the Lord and Samuel set a king over Israel "whom [they] have desired" and give them a promise that if they "will fear the Lord, and serve him, and obey his voice, and not rebel against the commandment of the Lord, then shall both [they] and also the king that reigneth over [them] continue following the Lord" (1 Sam. 12:13–14); but if they disobey, "then shall the hand of the Lord be against [them]," and they will "perceive and see that [their] wickedness is great, which [they] have done in the sight of the Lord, in asking for themselves a king" (1 Sam. 12:15–17).

The history of kings in the Hebrew Scriptures seems to bear cruel witness to the truth of these predictions. Saul may have started off "little in [his] own sight" when "the Lord anointed [him] king over Israel," but he changed; he did not obey "the voice of the Lord" and instead did "evil in the sight of the Lord" (1 Sam. 15:17, 19). David may have been brave and faithful to God when he stood up to Goliath in the field of battle, but he was cowardly and faithless when he sent Uriah into another battlefield in order to cover up his own sins. Solomon too may have begun his reign asking only for an "understanding heart to judge [his] people, that [he] may discern between good and bad" (1 Kgs. 3:9). However, he ends up, despite the Lord's warning, allowing his "seven hundred wives, princesses, and three hundred concubines" to turn away his heart after other gods and consequently does, as Samuel warned, "evil in the sight of the Lord" (11:3–4, 6). Judah, Nadab, Baasha, Omri, Ahab, Ahaziah, Jehoram, and many other kings of both Israel and Judah follow suit, similarly doing "evil in the sight of the Lord" (1 Kgs. 14:22; 15:26, 34; 16:19, 30; 22:52; 2 Kgs. 3:2; 8:18, 27). Eventually both kingdoms, the southern as well as the northern, are destroyed by invading armies, and their people are enslaved. That fact alone would seem to indicate that there is a profound flaw in the notion of kings. Nevertheless, it cannot be denied that there are indications that kings can do much good. In the end, it is difficult to say what side of the king debate the Hebrew Scriptures come down upon.

Affirming the Danger and Benefit of Kings

The book of Mosiah, as a *haftarah* to the books of 1 Samuel, 2 Samuel, 1 Kings, and 2 Kings, resolves this dilemma in such a way that makes sense of the two seemingly contradicting positions in the Hebrew Scriptures. However, it first affirms both the danger and benefit of kings by showing them in action. Nephi may have been "desirous that [his people] should have no king" (2 Ne. 5:18) and therefore refused to become one, but his successors did not (Jacob 1:9). Two of these New World kings in particular seem to dramatically affirm the worst and the best of biblical kings: King Noah and King Benjamin.

King Noah

King Noah is the epitome of all the problems Samuel predicted that kings would bring. To "support himself, and his wives and his concubines" as well as his priests and their families in "many elegant and spacious buildings," he lays a heavy tax burden on his people, even "one fifth part of all they possessed" (Mosiah 11:3–4, 8). He is lazy and idolatrous. Not only does he require his people to "labor exceedingly to support iniquity," but he deceives them with his "vain and flattering words" and in this way causes them "to commit sin" (vv. 2, 6–7). In addition, he plants "vineyards round about in the land" as well as "wine-presses," and thus he becomes a "wine-bibber" as well (v. 15). In stark contrast to the Lord's counsel to Solomon (1 Kgs. 3:14), King Noah does not "walk in the ways of his father" but instead walks "after the desires of his own heart." Echoing the most common biblical phrase connected with evil kings, the Book of Mormon states that he does "that which was abominable in the sight of the Lord" (Mosiah 11:1–2).

King Benjamin

King Benjamin, on the other hand, seems more like a biblical "anti-king," something entirely different from what Samuel predicted. Unlike King Noah and most of the kings in the Hebrew Scriptures, he does not seek for "gold nor silver nor any manner of riches." He does not command that his people "be confined in dungeons" or become "slaves one of another." He does not allow his people to "murder, or plunder, or steal, or commit adultery" or "commit any manner of wickedness." He also does not raise taxes for his own personal gain but instead labors "with [his] own hands . . . that [his people] should not be laden with taxes" (Mosiah 2:12–14).

King Benjamin is instead an amalgam of kingly virtues, a consistent example of attributes Israelite kings demonstrate only occasionally. When his people were attacked, King Benjamin, like Saul before his fall, "gathered together his armies, and he did stand against them; and he did fight with the strength of his own arm" (W of M 1:13). Like David before his problems with Bathsheba and Absalom, King Benjamin makes decisions "with the assistance of the holy prophets" and punishes people "according to their crimes" (W of M 1:16). Like Solomon before he is religiously seduced by his many wives and concubines, King Benjamin is a "holy man," laboring "with all the might of his body and the faculty of his whole soul . . . [to] establish peace in the land" (W of M 1:17–18). In fine, King Benjamin is worthy of the ultimate compliment for a biblical king: "he did reign over his people in righteousness" (v. 17).

Resolving the Scriptural Issue

With the quandary regarding kings now firmly in its readers' minds, the book of Mosiah attempts to resolve it. Just before he dies, King Mosiah, the son of King Benjamin, does not name a successor. Instead he dissolves the monarchy entirely and reverts back to the original biblical system of judges. King Mosiah justifies his decision by explaining that the problem with kings centers not on whether they can do good—they can—but on the uncertainty of their moral and spiritual condition. Kings who are just, like King Benjamin, can work much righteousness, even by God's standards, but unjust kings, like King Noah, can produce widespread wickedness and suffering. The problem is that no one knows when a king is crowned what kind of king he will be, and it is precisely that uncertainty that makes monarchy undesirable. As King Mosiah explains:

> Therefore, if it were possible that you could have just men to be your kings, who would establish the laws of God, and judge this people according to his commandments . . . I say unto you, if this could always be the case then it would be expedient that ye should always have kings to rule over you. . . . [However], because all men are not just it is not expedient that ye should have a king or kings to rule over you. (Mosiah 29:13, 16)

Here King Mosiah concedes the point put forth in Judges and supported by King Benjamin. Kings can indeed "establish peace throughout the land" and ensure "that there should be no wars nor contentions, no stealing, nor plundering, nor murdering, nor any manner of iniquity" (Mosiah 29:14). However, he also admits that kings can, as evidenced by the books of 1 and 2 Kings as well as by King Noah, produce "much iniquity" and "great destruction" (Mosiah 29:17). To resolve this dilemma, Mosiah suggests that they do away with the kingly approach altogether and rely instead on God as their ruler. As he says "it is better that a man should be judged of God than of man, for the judgments of God are *always* just, but the judgments of man are *not always* just" (v. 12). In this way, Mosiah acknowledges the temporary benefits of kings, but in the end he sides with Samuel by affirming that the source of these benefits is, ultimately, their "heavenly King" (2:19) and that it is he who deserves to rule.

Expanding the Idea into a Principle

Nonetheless, interesting as these points may be regarding kings, they have little relevance to readers in today's world. Not many are in a position to choose whether they are to be governed by kings or not. The kingdoms of Judah and Israel are no more and are not likely to reappear. Even when the state of Israel was established in 1948, there was no debate about the possibility of establishing a king over the land. For the most part, having a king or a queen as a real, functioning leader is a thoroughly outdated idea. Democracy, in one form or another, has won the day in most parts of the developed and developing world.

To speak to the concerns of modern readers, the book of Mosiah therefore shifts the discussion early on to a question more fundamental than whether or not kings should rule, a question all humans can relate to regardless of their position or political situation: how does one serve God? Building upon passages from the kingly period in the Hebrew Scriptures, the book of Mosiah delves more deeply into the question of governance to find an overarching principle. It connects to David's and Solomon's frequent description of themselves as "servants" of God to produce a kind of meditation on what it means for a king to serve God (1 Sam. 23:10–11, 1 Kgs. 3:7). The main mechanism the book of Mosiah uses to expand this idea into a principle is King Benjamin, the acme of everything good in a king.

Given what happens in the Hebrew Scriptures to kings such as Saul, David, and Solomon, all of whom begin well but succumb in one way or another to the temptations of power later on, one has to wonder how King Benjamin manages to avoid a similar fate. What is his secret? And the answer that resoundingly comes is that instead of attempting to rule his people in typical kingly fashion, King Benjamin tries to serve them. Instead of seeking riches, he desires to "spend [his] days in [their] *service.*" Instead of imprisoning them, he teaches them "that [they] should keep the commandments of the Lord." Instead of burdening them with taxes, he labors "with [his] own hands that [he] might *serve* [them]" (Mosiah 2:12–14).

According to King Benjamin, serving one's people is the key to being a righteous, and therefore ideal, king. However, King Benjamin takes this principle at least one step further. After he details his desires to serve his people instead of merely ruling over them, he explains that he did all this not to brag or otherwise aggrandize himself but to be "in the service of God" (Mosiah 2:16). In other words, serving God and serving humanity are inherently intertwined. They cannot be extricated from each other. This is evidenced even in the language he uses to describe his calling as king to serve his people:

> I have been chosen by this people, and consecrated by my father, and was suffered by the hand of the Lord that I should be a ruler and a king over this people; and have been kept and preserved by his matchless power, to serve you with all the might, mind and strength which the Lord hath granted unto me. (Mosiah 2:11)

Here King Benjamin's words echo those used in Deuteronomy to indicate how an Israelite is to act toward God. In Deuteronomy 6, God commands each Israelite to "serve" the Lord (Deut. 6:13) and love him "with all thy heart, and with all thy soul, and with all thy might" (v. 5). By also using "mind" and "strength" to describe the depth of his efforts to serve his people, King Benjamin connects these efforts with the more general commandment to serve God. All in all, King Benjamin's actions, teachings, and even word choice combine to expand the idea suggested somewhat obliquely in the Hebrew Scriptures that a righteous king is first and foremost a servant of God. King Benjamin provides an example of this principle by serving people.

Applying the Principle

Discovering a deeper principle behind this monarchical question helps make the Period of Kings more relevant and applicable to modern readers. They can then extrapolate it and relate it to their own presidents and prime ministers as well as to their own leadership styles at work and in the home. This kind of extrapolation may seem adventurous (or even dangerous). However, the book of Mosiah actually encourages it by emphasizing that this is not just a *governmental* principle; it is a basic *theological* question that must be answered by all. The question is not really "which government is best?" or even "how can a king serve God?" It is more "how can *anyone* serve God?" The book of Mosiah, in other words, in the best *haftarah* fashion, takes these academic, historical questions and transforms them into a question of universal relevance. King Benjamin may be an ideal king, an even more powerful and righteous version of Saul, David, and Solomon. However, the source of his power comes not from his regal office but from his individual character. Again, King Benjamin is described as a "holy *man*," not as a holy king or righteous ruler; his holiness, not his governmental brilliance, is put forth as the reason "he did reign over his people in righteousness" (W of M 1:17). Reinforcing this distinction, his people give thanks that they have a "just *man* to be their king" and credit his personal character, which taught them "to keep the commandments of God" and to have "love towards God and all men," as the source of his ability to establish "peace in the land of Zarahemla" (Mosiah 2:4).

Emphasizing his humanity, King Benjamin plays down his royal position in his final address to his people and instead stresses his status as a common servant: "I have not commanded you to come up hither that ye should fear me, or that ye should think that I of myself am more than a mortal man. But I am like as yourselves, subject to all manner of infirmities in body and mind" (Mosiah 2:10–11). He later tells his people that he is "no better than ye yourselves are; for I am also of the dust" (v. 26). In other words, King Benjamin is different from his subjects (and his readers) only in the office in which he serves and not in his abilities or obligations. All should serve God by serving people, not just kings. As King Benjamin tells his hearers directly, using a second-person plural pronoun: "when *ye* are in the service of your fellow beings *ye* are only in the service of your God" (Mosiah 2:17). Interestingly this interpretation is consistent with Jewish thought. As Noson Gurary writes:

> According to the Torah, a Jewish king was not an object of worship but a role model, a person who was totally dedicated to God. A Jewish king such as Moses or King David was the epitome of humility and self-effacement. They saw their roles as the servants of God, and their greatness was a product of their humility; the greatness of a holy person is that he is totally subservient to God and has no ego. He sees his role as actualizing God's will on earth.[4]

As a *haftarah* to the kingly books in the Hebrew Scriptures, the kingly books in the Book of Mormon—Omni, Words of Mormon, and Mosiah—connect to 1 Samuel, 2 Samuel, 1 Kings, and 2 Kings to affirm the benefits as well as the problems of kings. They explain how kings can and should serve God and expand upon these ideas in order to help readers better serve God and humanity. Finally, they take Samuel's admonition that people, even when they have a king, are to serve God first (1 Sam. 12:14), and they explore what that admonition really means, what are the reasons for it, and what consequences come from following it. In this way, these books in the Book of Mormon render otherwise academic points about ancient Israelite kings relevant and applicable to readers today.

---

4. Noson Gurary, *Thirteen Principles of Faith: A Chasidic Viewpoint*, 204.

Chapter Eight

Translating an Ancient Situation into Modern Terms

And it came to pass in the eighth year of the reign of the judges, that the people of the church began to wax proud, because of their exceeding riches, and their fine silks, and their fine-twined linen, and because of their many flocks and herds, and their gold and their silver, and all manner of precious things, which they had obtained by their industry; and in all these things were they lifted up in the pride of their eyes, for they began to wear very costly apparel. (Alma 4:6)

Not all "impractical" points in the Hebrew Scriptures are academic in the sense that they cannot be implemented in modern times. Some apply specifically to ancient matters, which require updating in order to be relevant to today. A *haftarah* can help in this effort as well by translating these matters into terms that modern readers can understand and benefit from. For instance, the *parashah Va'yikra* (Lev. 1:1–5:26) lists many laws concerning the nature and implementation of various temple sacrifices. Since a Mosaic temple no longer exists in which to perform these sacrifices, this *parashah* would seem to have little relevance today. However, according to Plaut, Isaiah 43:21–44:23, its *haftarah*, renders it relevant by reminding its listeners that Isaiah urged the people of his time "to bring God their offerings of the heart."[1] For Plaut, Isaiah's condemnation of Israel for failing to call upon God and to honor him with sacrifices when there was no temple (Isa. 43:22–23) is both an affirmation of the commandment to offer these sacrifices as written in the *parashah* as well as an alteration of what is to be sacrificed. As Plaut sees it, the connections between these two readings indicate that although offering sacrifices are vital, when a temple is not available "prayers and good deeds" suffice.[2]

---

1. W. Gunther Plaut, *The Haftarah Commentary*, 232.
2. Ibid., 233.

Plaut makes nearly the same point concerning the connection between the next *parashah* from Leviticus, chapters 6 through 8 (*Tzav*) and its *haftarah*, Jeremiah 7:21–8:3 and 9:22–23. As he writes, "the weekly portion speaks of sacrifices, and so does the haftarah. The Prophet warns his people not to believe that sacrifices by themselves will please the Almighty; they must be accompanied by godly deeds."[3] In general then the connections between the prophetic readings and the readings in the Torah not only serve to reinforce Torah teachings as they are, but they also extend their applicability to situations not explicitly treated by the *parashah* itself.

This is another way the Book of Mormon respectfully relates to the Hebrew Scriptures. It both affirms them as they are as well as broadens their relevance for modern readers. For the Period of Judges, the books of Alma and Helaman connect to Joshua and Judges in this way. They confirm the struggles that Israel must go through to establish a righteous society. However, they also expand and deepen the problems Israelites encounter so that modern readers can relate to them and solve them.

Addressing the Period of Judges

Much of the anti-king material mentioned in the previous chapter comes from the book of Judges. However, Judges is not fundamentally so much a political book as it is a spiritual book. It does not, for instance, offer a clear description—much less criticism—of the governmental system used during the time of the judges. It contains no information whatsoever concerning the laws, statutes, rulings, appointments, or policies that specifies what Israel could have done that would have improved the situation. The main argument for a king in the book of Judges is circumstantial, based on two simple facts: first, there is near constant chaos during this time, and, secondly, "there was no king in Israel" (Judg. 21:25). The implication it presents, and this is tenuous, is that if there were a king there would not have been as much social commotion.

However, as Samuel Sandmel points out, this chaos is more of a "religious anarchy" than a political one.[4] There are many tumultuous events in Judges—wars mostly—resulting in temporary captivity or momentary liberation. However, the book of Judges continually states that the outward situation of Israel is dependent upon its inward situation. In other words, rulers, be they foreign or domestic, are not actually controlling

---

3. Ibid., 244.
4. Samuel Sandmel, *The Hebrew Scriptures*, 431.

Israel or determining its condition. The Israelites themselves are, through their spiritual choices. These wars and periods of captivity are therefore not events in themselves so much as expressions of the spiritual conflict going on inside Israel's soul, a conflict between their devotion to God and their fascination with idolatry.

Time and time again in Judges, wars are preceded by the statement, "the children of Israel did evil in the sight of the Lord" (Judg. 2:1, 3:7, 3:12, 4:1, 6:1, 10:6, 13:1). This statement is then quickly followed by some indication of the Lord's displeasure and his resultant action. For instance, Judges 3:7–8 reads: "And the children of Israel did evil in the sight of the Lord, and forgat the Lord their God, and served Baalim and the groves. Therefore the anger of the Lord was hot against Israel, and he sold them into the hand of Chushanrishathaim king of Mesopotamia: and the children of Israel served Chushanrishathaim eight years."

The Lord's anger is not always mentioned though. Judges 6:1, for example, simply says that "the children of Israel did evil in the sight of the Lord: and the Lord delivered them into the hand of Midian seven years." However, in each case the position of these two statements makes it clear that the evil that Israel does offends God and causes him to punish them in some way. Judges 3:12 even expresses this as a direct causality: "And the children of Israel did evil again in the sight of the Lord: and the Lord strengthened Eglon the king of Moab against Israel, *because* they had done evil in the sight of the Lord." In other words, although Judges and Joshua contain many heroic men and women who perform dramatic military feats and unite the different tribes for a time, the problem is not the lack of a system where kings govern and great people are continuously in charge. The real problem is that Israelites themselves continue to lust after idols despite the Lord's best efforts to woo them to him by giving them difficulties and then delivering them from those difficulties.

Consequently, throughout the book of Judges, Israel is locked into a cycle of sin. During the days of Joshua, "the people served the Lord" (Judg. 2:7), but as soon as Joshua dies, "the children of Israel did evil in the sight of the Lord, and served Baalim" (v. 11). To help the situation, the Lord raises up judges, who "delivered them out of the hand of those that spoiled them" (v. 16). However, the effects of the judges are not permanent. As Judges summarizes,

> And when the Lord raised them up judges, then the Lord was with the judge, and delivered them out of the hand of their enemies all the days of the judge:

for it repented the Lord because of their groanings by reason of them that oppressed them and vexed them.

And it came to pass, when the judge was dead, that they returned, and corrupted themselves more than their fathers, in following other gods to serve them, and to bow down unto them; they ceased not from their own doings, nor from their stubborn way. (Judg. 2:18–19)

And this pattern continues with relentless regularity throughout the book of Judges. After Joshua, "the children of Israel did evil in the sight of the Lord, and forgat the Lord their God, and served Baalim and the groves," they are sold "into the hand of Chushanrishathaim king of Mesopotamia," they cry out "unto the Lord," and the Lord raised up Othniel to deliver them (Judg. 3:7–9). After Othniel "the children of Israel did evil again in the sight of the Lord," the Lord allows Eglon the king of Moab to afflict them, "the children of Israel cried unto the Lord," and the Lord raises up Ehud "the son of Gera, a Benjamite" to deliver them, which he does in a particularly graphic way (vv. 12, 15–30). After Ehud dies, "the children of Israel again did evil in the sight of the Lord" (4:1), and the pattern continues with Deborah, Gideon, Jephthah, and Samson.

Given the preponderance of this pattern and the lack of any political detail, the main purpose of Judges seems to have little to do with Israel's having or not having kings. It seems to make the case instead that the causes of Israel's problems are spiritual, not governmental, and that if the inward conditions changed so would their outward circumstances. In other words, the books of Joshua and Judges may contain many military battles and use the language of warfare—swords, shields, spears, and such—but these are merely expressions of Israel's spiritual struggles. The warfare these books are really addressing is the warfare of the spirit, a kind of seesaw battle where an inclination for idolatry is contending against the worship of God.

Affirming the Cycle of Sin

The books of Alma and Helaman describe a similar cycle and stress it just as relentlessly, although in a somewhat more refined and more clearly articulated way. This cycle follows the same basic steps and causality outlined by Sandmel: "Prosperity, according to the authors, led to license, and license was equivalent to apostasy from Yahve, and Yahve punished the disobedient by having them harassed or conquered. Then a Great

Deliverer arose who destroyed the enemy."[5] Then, after the Great Deliverer destroys the enemy, prosperity returns, which starts the cycle rolling again.

The problem for modern readers is that these steps—prosperity, license, punishment, and deliverance, as they are expressed in Judges—do not easily apply to their situation. Prosperity in Judges is described cursorily, in vague terms: the land "resting" for a time (Judg. 3:11, 30; 5:31). License seems to be limited to ancient idolatry: serving "Baalim and the groves," making "Baalberith their god," and worshiping "the gods of Syria, and the gods of Zidon" (3:7, 8:33, 10:6). Punishment comes almost always in some form of physical captivity: delivering them into "the hands of the spoilers," selling them into "the hand of Chushanrishathaim," and smiting Israel with "the children of Ammon and Amalek" (2:14; 3:8, 13). Deliverance then appears in the form of a dynamic military leader who fights dramatic battles: Ehud knifing the king of the Moabites in the stomach, Deborah defeating Sisera's "nine hundred chariots of iron," and Gideon's miniscule army of "three hundred men" outwitting the hosts of Midian with trumpets, pots, and torches (3:21, 4:13, 7:16).

Although these stories are all memorable and motivating in some sense, modern readers may have trouble relating to them. These readers do not have the same problems or need the same solutions. They therefore must somehow dress up these ancient situations in more current garb, so to speak, before they can apply their lessons—a task that though possible is not easily done. The books of Alma and Helaman, however, though nearly just as ancient, have no such problem. In them each step in the cycle of sin is well defined and described in terms that modern readers can better relate to.

Developing the Concept of Prosperity

In the book of Alma, the cycle starts with prosperity, just as it does in the book of Judges. However, unlike Judges, Alma lays bare the roots of prosperity. He first describes how the people were "steadfast and immovable in keeping the commandments of God" (Alma 1:25) and then explains that it is precisely because of their steadiness and immovability that they began to be "exceedingly rich, having abundance of all things whatsoever they stood in need." Indeed, this abundance is described in some detail: "an abundance of flocks and herds, and fatlings of every kind,

---

5. Ibid., 431.

and also abundance of grain, and of gold, and of silver, and of precious things, and abundance of silk and fine-twined linen, and all manner of good homely cloth" (v. 29). However, the reason for their riches is more than a simple affirmation of belief. It involves a spiritually rooted work ethic that cuts across all classes—eliminating class and its outward manifestations altogether. As Alma explains:

> And when the priests left their labor to impart the word of God unto the people, the people also left their labors to hear the word of God. And when the priest had imparted unto them the word of God they all returned again diligently unto their labors; and the priest, not esteeming himself above his hearers, for the preacher was no better than the hearer, neither was the teacher any better than the learner; and thus they were all equal, and they did all labor, every man according to his strength. And they did impart of their substance, every man according to that which he had, to the poor, and the needy, and the sick, and the afflicted; and they did not wear costly apparel, yet they were neat and comely. (Alma 1:26–27)

Generosity toward others is therefore an integral component of this kind of God-given prosperity. It is not simply an expression of religious charity; it actually contributes to the viability of their economy:

> And thus, in their prosperous circumstances, they did not send away any who were naked, or that were hungry, or that were athirst, or that were sick, or that had not been nourished; and they did not set their hearts upon riches; therefore they were liberal to all, both old and young, both bond and free, both male and female, whether out of the church or in the church, having no respect to persons as to those who stood in need. And thus they did prosper. (Alma 1:30–31)

In the book of Alma, prosperity brings with it a responsibility to help others—a responsibility, which if left unfulfilled, brings poverty. This description of prosperity is not so specific as to be temporally or culturally limited, and yet it is detailed enough for modern readers to readily understand and see its causes and dependencies clearly. Prosperity in the Book of Mormon is inextricably tied to specific attitudes and actions toward God and humanity in general that are required for the land to have "rest." This sets up the other steps of the cycle by clearly showing what prosperity involves and what modern readers must do to avoid losing it.

Updating the Idea of License

The next step in this cycle is "license," which for the book of Judges means idolatry. No real cause and effect is given or even implied for this behavior in Judges. The children of Israel simply begin to do "evil in the sight of the Lord" and forsake "the Lord God of their fathers" (Judg. 2:11–12). Modern readers often have trouble understanding why something as ludicrous (in their eyes) as worshiping a stone statue would be attractive to the ancient Israelites and therefore have trouble relating to this section of the sin cycle. This is not a problem in the books of Alma and Helaman. There the "license" that must be avoided is pride, a problem that is both understandable to modern readers and, unfortunately, a frequent outgrowth of prosperity.

Prosperity for both the Book of Mormon and the Hebrew Scriptures is not something incidental or capricious. It does not pop up for no reason nor is it simply a product of human industry. Prosperity, which includes social serenity and personal peace as well as material wealth, is presented as a natural consequence of righteous living. Again and again, the Book of Mormon asserts that those who keep the commandments of God "shall *prosper* in the land" (2 Ne. 1:20, 4:4, etc.). The same is true for the Hebrew Scriptures. Abraham is "very rich in cattle, in silver, and in gold" (Gen. 13:2). Jacob is blessed with "the fatness of the earth, and plenty of corn and wine" (27:28). Everything Joseph undertakes the Lord causes to "prosper in his hand" (39:3). So prevalent is this idea that Deut. 29:9 reads, almost as a summary, "Keep therefore the words of this covenant, and do them, that ye may prosper in all that ye do"—a concept that is repeated by Joshua (Josh. 1:7) as well as by King David (1 Kgs. 2:3).

In addition, prosperity in both the Book of Mormon and the Hebrew Scriptures has a larger purpose. Abram receives a blessing that he and his descendants would be "a great nation," and in the same sentence he is commanded to "be a blessing" such that "all families of the earth [should] be blessed" (Gen. 12:2–3). This charge is repeated several times in the Hebrew Scriptures (Gen. 18:18, 22:18, 26:4, 28:14) as well as in the Book of Mormon (1 Ne. 15:18; 19:17, 22:9, etc.) The problem is that people often forget the origin as well as the purpose of this prosperity. Without this perspective, many are tempted to think of prosperity, especially its material manifestations, as proof of their superiority and therefore it becomes a personal toy to do with as they please. They may see it as solely the fruit of their own labor, unconnected to God or social responsibility. Unlike ancient idolatry, this prideful tendency is something modern readers see around them in abundance and know from their own experience. So, when the books of Alma and Helaman present statements such as this, modern readers are not surprised:

> And it came to pass in the eighth year of the reign of the judges, that the people of the church began to wax proud, because of their exceeding riches, and their fine silks, and their fine-twined linen, and because of their many flocks and herds, and their gold and their silver, and all manner of precious things, which they had obtained by their industry; and in all these things were they lifted up in the pride of their eyes, for they began to wear very costly apparel. (Alma 4:6)

However modern readers may be surprised at how vigorously and thoroughly Alma and Helaman explore this problem. Pride, and its avoidance, is a central topic in both of these books—in fact, in all the books of the Book of Mormon. It is introduced immediately, in the first chapter of Alma and sets the stage for the rest of the book. In this chapter, Nehor appears "declaring unto the people that every priest and teacher ought to become popular; and they ought not to labor with their hands, but that they ought to be supported by the people" (Alma 1:3). He and his message are so well received that "many did believe on his words, even so many that they began to support him and give him money." This causes him to be "lifted up in the pride of his heart, and to wear very costly apparel." As he declares his message, Nehor meets a man of a different opinion. Nehor begins to "contend with him sharply," at first with words but eventually he draws "his sword and began to smite him." The man subsequently dies, and Nehor is brought before the judge for murder (vv. 5–10). In a nutshell, this initial incident shows the fundamental problem with pride: that it divides people into classes, which breed disunity, contention, and, eventually, violence.

As the rest of the book of Alma elaborates, pride is not just a matter of outward show but a change in inward direction. It causes people to set "their hearts upon riches and upon the vain things of the world" (Alma 4:8). It can be rooted in differences in material goods, but it also can grow out of differences in "their chances for learning" (3 Ne. 6:12). It affects both those who openly rebel against God (Alma 1:32) as well as those who profess to follow him (Alma 4:8). Pride also profoundly influences how people treat each other, prompting them to disobey the cardinal rule of prosperity and become "scornful, one towards another" and "persecute those that did not believe according to their own will and pleasure." It leads to "great contentions" based on "envyings, and strife, and malice even among those who deem themselves followers of God" (Alma 4:8–9).

Carried to its logical conclusion, as it is in the Book of Mormon, pride can rip entire societies apart, creating a "great inequality among the people" (Alma 4:12) and tearing at the fundamental fabric that binds them together. People are subsequently "distinguished by ranks" (3 Ne. 6:12) and segregated "because of the coarseness of their apparel" (Alma 32:2). In the book of Alma, pride is blamed for destroying the generosity required for a truly prosperous society and for causing people instead to turn their backs "upon the needy and the naked and those who were hungry, and those who were athirst, and those who were sick and afflicted" (Alma 4:12). This "oppression to the poor" (Hel. 4:12) leads to "great contentions among the people" (Alma 4:9). So great a problem is pride that, according to Alma, it eventually brings on the "destruction of the people" (v. 11), an idea that is ultimately proved correct by the history of the Book of Mormon people as well as that of the kingdom of Judah (Jer. 13:9).

Pride possesses all the problems now that idolatry did anciently. Not only do they both bring about the destruction of their people, but both are born of the same impulse. In the book of Alma, pride arises because the people no longer remember "how many times [the Lord] delivered [their] fathers out of the hands of their enemies, and preserved them from being destroyed" (Alma 9:10), just as idolatry in Judges is caused by the people forsaking "the Lord God of their fathers, which brought them out of the land of Egypt" (Judg. 2:12). Thus, pride is a valid and helpful update for idolatry. It is a kind of modern idolatry, the worship of self in place of the worship of God. In this way, the substitution of "pride" for idolatry in the book of Alma, far from breaking with Judges, actually works with it, updating its application while preserving its core message and retaining all its implications of divine betrayal, ultimate destruction, and even absurdity. In this way Alma works together with Judges to expand, deepen, and update its message. It helps modern readers of Judges "translate" these ancient stone gods of Syria, Zidon, and Moab into problems they can relate to and avoid.

Modernizing the Form of Punishment

In Judges, when Israel turns to idolatry, "the anger of the Lord [becomes] hot against Israel" (Judg. 2:14, 3:8, 10:7), and the Lord chastises them, usually by allowing them to experience some sort of physical captivity enforced by a nearby nation. Punishment is then the next step in the cycle of sin. However, since modern readers no longer have to deal with spear-wielding Moabites, Amalekites, or Philistines, they must update these ancient oppressors by giving them appropriate modern names or by substituting them with personal enemies. This approach can be useful and is occasionally appropriate. However, it is not always easy or accurate. Physical captivity is not something many modern readers experience and the connection between sin and more subtle oppressions is not always clear. The books of Alma and Helaman, however, ease this process of updating the situation in Judges first by showing a natural connection between pride and social problems (captivity being one of them) and second by illustrating how pride can be its own punishment.

A Natural Connection

In Judges, the neighboring nations of Israel—the Moabites, the Amalekites, the Philistines, and so forth—serve, in a sense, as God's enforcers. They lurk beyond the borders of Israel, armed and ready for the Lord to give them the go-ahead to oppress his chosen people. There is no reason for their attacks or justification for their success other than Israel waxes wicked and God is angry with it. As Judges 2:21–22 reads, "I [the Lord] also will not henceforth drive out any from before them of the nations which Joshua left when he died: That through them I may prove Israel, whether they will keep the way of the Lord to walk therein, as their fathers did keep it, or not."

The Lamanites function in a similar way in the Book of Mormon. As Nephi records, "And the Lord God said unto me: [The Lamanites] shall be a scourge unto thy seed, to stir them up in remembrance of me; and inasmuch as [thy people] will not remember me, and hearken unto my words, [the Lamanites] shall scourge them even unto destruction" (2 Ne. 5:25). Nevertheless, despite this similarity, in the Book of Mormon the Lamanites take more of a passive role. They are always there, like the Philistines, in the periphery, a distant presence like a dark cloud on the horizon, but they get involved only when the Nephites actually invite them in. In this way, the books of Alma and Helaman build upon the book of Judges by showing how sin actually brings its own punishment. Consequently, if their readers wish to avoid captivity, they will shun the pride that causes it. For instance, in the fourth chapter of the book of Helaman, a peaceful time among the Nephites is disturbed by "many dissensions" from within, a typical problem caused by pride. These dissensions escalate until there is "a contention among the people" and then "much bloodshed" (Hel. 4:1). The defeated Nephite rebels, however, angrily seek to punish their opponents and go to the Lamanites where they "endeavor to stir up the

Lamanites to war against the Nephites" (v. 3). After much effort, they eventually succeed, and a bloody land grab ensues where the Lamanites capture a sizable chunk of Nephite territory. Several battles then follow where some of the Nephite land is regained but only at the expense of a "great slaughter" of Nephites, even those who professed to be followers of God (v. 11).

After relating this event, Mormon, the compiler/commentator of these books, explains in detail just how pride caused this tragedy:

> And it was because of the pride of their hearts, because of their exceeding riches, yea, it was because of their oppression to the poor, withholding their food from the hungry, withholding their clothing from the naked, and smiting their humble brethren upon the cheek, making a mock of that which was sacred, denying the spirit of prophecy and of revelation, murdering, plundering, lying, stealing, committing adultery, rising up in great contentions, and deserting away into the land of Nephi, among the Lamanites— And because of this their great wickedness, and their boastings in their own strength, they were left in their own strength; therefore they did not prosper, but were afflicted and smitten, and driven before the Lamanites, until they had lost possession of almost all their lands. (Hel. 4:12–13)

Even without this explanation, modern readers can easily see in the description of this episode itself why this tragedy occurred. Pride causes dissention; dissention causes conflict; conflict causes combat; combat causes war; and war brings about captivity and death. It is inevitable. It is not a divine whim. God does not arbitrarily decide to punish prideful people because it suits him. People undermine their own prosperity by impoverishing segments of their population and by setting up a society where each member competes with the other without consideration of the group as a whole or compassion for its people as individuals. Such societies are doomed to destruction naturally, by definition, without divine interference. In this way, Helaman builds upon the lessons of Judges by making clear the causes of the captivity it describes and by helping its readers avoid them. Just as the Lamanites attacked the Nephites only when the Nephites invited them into their country, so punishment comes when people invite pride into their hearts. Avoiding captivity is therefore as simple as avoiding pride.

A Self-imposed Punishment

In addition to showing that punishment is a natural consequence of pride, the book of Helaman deepens the lessons of Judges by illustrating how such punishment comes from within—that it is not imposed from the outside. In a sense, pride brings its own punishment. In Helaman 6, for example, the "outside" oppressors are not outside of Nephite society at all. They come from within. At this point in the book of Helaman, a group of criminals arises among the Nephites called the Gadianton robbers. They are a secret organization whose purpose is to "murder, and plunder, and steal, and commit whoredoms and all manner of wickedness" (Hel. 6:23) in order to get gain. Their goal is the captivity of the Nephites, and they accomplish this goal, not by capturing the Nephites bodily or militarily, but by getting "hold upon the hearts of the Nephites." This they do to such a degree that the Nephites are "turned out of the way of righteousness," "trample under their feet the commandments of God," and, in a way eerily reminiscent of the Israelites in Judges, "build up unto themselves idols of their gold and their silver" (v. 31).

The Gadianton robbers are so successful that they "overspread all the land of the Nephites, and had seduced the more part of the righteous until they had come to believe in their works and partake of their spoils, and to join with them in their secret murders and combinations" (Hel. 6:38). These robbers even take over the "sole management of the government" and use this power to "trample under their feet and smite and rend and turn their backs upon the poor and the meek, and the humble followers of God" (v. 39). Although the Gadianton group comes from within the Nephite society, they capture that nation just as effectively as any outside enemy, and they do so not through force but by getting the Nephites to buy into their schemes and profit from their crimes. The Nephites, then, through their pride have become their own oppressors and in so doing are, like all sinful societies in the Book of Mormon or in the Hebrew Scriptures, "ripening for an everlasting destruction" (v. 40).

As if this conclusion were not plain enough, Nephi, a descendant of the original Nephi, reiterates that pride is the cause of his people's captivity. In the next chapter, he explains to his people that their actions, like those of the Israelites in the book of Judges, "have provoked [the Lord] to anger against [them]" and claims that their behavior has demonstrated that they too have "forgotten [their] God" (Hel. 7:18–20). However, unlike those ancient Israelites, they strayed not because of idolatry but "because of that pride which [they] have suffered to enter [their] hearts" and because they have united themselves with "that secret band which was established by Gadianton" (vv. 25–26).

Demilitarizing the Method of Deliverance

In the book of Judges, after having been punished for their idolatry, the Israelites often cry "unto the Lord" (Judg. 3:9, 4:3, 6:7, 10:10), and the Lord raises up a deliverer who defeats their current captor. They are then free—that is, until the Israelites again begin to serve other gods and the cycle of sin begins anew. Although Israel does not always seem to merit these deliverers or benefit from them in any lasting way, they and their military exploits form the main focus of the book of Judges. In fact, according to Sandmel, "the Book of Judges could appropriately be called 'The Book of the Great Deliverers.'"[6]

Consequently, again, as it is with the sins and punishments of Israel in Judges, modern readers would generally have problems relating to these deliverers—violent people who stab kings in the belly, hammer nails through opponents' temples, scare enemy soldiers into killing themselves, and slay hundreds of Philistines with the jawbone of an ass (Judg. 3:21, 4:21, 7:22, 15:16). This kind of behavior is clearly not something that we typically experience today or regard as practical solutions to our problems, and again the books of Alma and Helaman help translate the idea of a deliverer into terms modern readers can understand and relate to. Like the book of Judges, these books present many such deliverers. However, most of them are not military heroes, and those that are fight more with their words than with their swords, frequently pleading with their people to repent and become worthy of deliverance. In this way, the deliverers in Alma and Helaman are easier for modern readers to relate to, and the deliverance they offer is more clearly connected to their situation, particularly as it relates to pride.

Alma

In the first example of pride discussed in the book of Alma, Alma's people have lost a fair amount of land to the Lamanites and remain "greatly afflicted for the loss of their brethren, and also for the loss of their flocks and herds, and also for the loss of their fields of grain, which

---

6. Ibid., 430.

were trodden under foot and destroyed by the Lamanites" (Alma 4:2). However, Alma, as their chief judge, does not mount a dramatic military campaign to expel the Lamanites. Instead he "deliver[s] the judgment seat unto Nephihah" and sets out among the people "that he might preach the word of God unto them, to stir them up in remembrance of their duty, and that he might pull down, by the word of God, all the pride and craftiness and all the contentions which were among his people, seeing no way that he might reclaim them save it were in bearing down in pure testimony against them" (vv. 18–19).

Alma, in other words, initiates a kind of internal crusade, a campaign to deliver his own people from their sinful behavior, believing that deliverance from external captivity will follow. As Alma sees it, he is striking at the roots of what oppresses the Nephites—their pride—rather than hacking at its leaves and branches—their enemies. Appropriately then, since the deliverance Alma offers includes deliverance from many kinds of bondage, he uses the word often and in different ways, as if to emphasize the scope of his purpose. Alma, for instance, goes off to "*deliver* the word of God unto the people"; he speaks about how his father and his people "were *delivered* out of the hands of the people of king Noah, by the mercy and power of God"; and he explains how, when they were later captured by the Lamanites, "the Lord did *deliver* them out of bondage by the power of his word" (5:1, 4–5). In other words, Alma is very much the deliverer like Ehud and Othniel. However, his efforts are aimed more at eradicating internal sins than at expelling external oppressors.

During his first sermon to his people, Alma comes quickly to this point:

> Behold, are ye stripped of pride? I say unto you, if ye are not ye are not prepared to meet God. Behold ye must prepare quickly; for the kingdom of heaven is soon at hand, and such an one hath not eternal life. Behold, I say, is there one among you who is not stripped of envy? I say unto you that such an one is not prepared; and I would that he should prepare quickly, for the hour is close at hand, and he knoweth not when the time shall come; for such an one is not found guiltless. And again I say unto you, is there one among you that doth make a mock of his brother, or that heapeth upon him persecutions? Wo unto such an one, for he is not prepared, and the time is at hand that he must repent or he cannot be saved! Yea, even wo unto all ye workers of iniquity; repent, repent, for the Lord God hath spoken it! (Alma 5:28–32)

Much of what Alma has to say, in this speech and in others later on, centers on how humility governs one's future in the next life. However, this quality also controls the here and now. In effect, humility produces prosperity. As Alma blesses those who gave "exceeding diligence and heed" to his words, "And now, may the peace of God rest upon you, and upon your houses and lands, and upon your flocks and herds, and all that you possess, your women and your children, according to your faith and good works, from this time forth and forever" (7:27).

Deliverance from pride is a theme that Alma comes back to again and again in his preaching. When he comes to the city of Ammonihah—a Nephite city that, in a typically prideful way, did "study at this time that they may destroy the liberty of [all the Nephites]" (8:17)—Alma attempts to humble them by reminding them of how their ancestors had been "delivered of God out of the land of Jerusalem," (again, the word *delivered*), were "brought out of bondage time after time," and "prospered until they are rich in all manner of things" (9:22). However the Ammonihahites did "wax more gross in their iniquities," and Alma is charged "to testify against them concerning their iniquities" (8:25, 28). More pointedly, he is commanded to tell them "to repent, or [the Lord] will utterly destroy [them] from off the face of the earth" (9:12).

During Alma's mission to the Ammonihahites, he, like a hero from the book of Judges, engages in several one-on-one battles but with words, not swords. Along with his companion, Amulek, Alma first engages Zeezrom, a wealthy lawyer and "one of the most expert" among those who opposed him (10:31). Zeezrom begins his attack on Alma by feinting with a bribe, tempting Amulek to "deny the existence of a Supreme Being" for six onties of silver (11:22). Amulek, however, does not fall for this ploy and keeps his balance. Zeezrom then counters with an extended questioning session where the answers and response come so quickly that it resembles the lightning-like thrust-and-parry rhythm of a fencing match (11:26–37). Finally, after "the words of Amulek had silenced Zeezrom" (12:1), Alma enters the fray, returning to his theme of deliverance from captivity. He exposes Zeezrom's arguments as "a snare of the adversary, which he has laid to catch this people, that he might bring [them] into subjection unto him, that he might encircle [them] about with his chains, that he might chain [them] down to everlasting destruction, according to the power of his captivity" (v. 6).

Zeezrom at this point is convinced, surrenders to Alma and Amulek, and humbly requests that they teach him more concerning their message. Unfortunately, the Ammonihahites remain resistant. They cast Zeezrom out, bind Alma and Amulek with "strong cords," place the two missionaries in prison, and taunt them, saying "If ye have the power of God deliver yourselves from these bands, and then we will believe that the Lord will destroy this people according to your words" (14:24). Alma then prays and, just as Samson broke the new cords of the Philistines (Judg. 15:14), he breaks "the cords with which they were bound" (Alma 14:26). The earth shakes, and again, just as the prison collapsed around Samson and his captors (Judg. 15:13–14), the "walls of [Alma and Amulek's] prison were rent in twain" (Alma 14:27), and all those who withstood Alma and Amulek are killed in the collapse, while Alma and Amulek go free.

Alma's encounter with Zeezrom, goes far in checking the pride of those in Sidom (Alma 15:17). However, in the person of Korihor he appears to "duel" with pride directly and in terms that modern readers can relate to. Here Korihor is a kind of false deliverer—a mock judge, an able orator who attempts to liberate the Nephites from the "foolish traditions of [their] fathers." Sounding at once like an empiricist, a humanist, and finally a Social Darwinist, he claims that they "are bound down under a foolish and a vain hope," and he therefore attempts to set them free by stating that human beings "cannot know of things which [they] do not see" and therefore they "cannot know that there shall be a Christ" (30:13–15). Korihor then rails against repentance as well as revelation, preaching instead that "every man, fare[s] in this life according to the management of the creature," prospering "according to his genius," and conquering "according to his strength" (v. 17). In this way, Korihor both exemplifies and preaches pride, telling others that "whatsoever a man did was no crime" and causing many, in Mormon's terms, "to lift up their heads in their wickedness" (vv. 17–18).

Korihor and Alma spar verbally for quite some time (30:30–44) with neither gaining much of an advantage. Korihor finally demands a sign and is struck dumb (v. 50). At this point Korihor, true to his philosophical roots, freely acknowledges that he is indeed mute, "for [he] cannot speak," but he also admits that he "always knew that there was a God" (v. 52). After his confession, Korihor pleads to have his curse removed, but Alma refuses, telling him, "if this curse should be taken from thee thou wouldst again lead away the hearts of this people; therefore, it shall be unto thee even as the Lord will" (v. 55). Pride, in the person of Korihor, has been defeated with a finality all the military heroes in Judges would be jealous of.

At the conclusion of his encounter with Korihor, Alma in all his efforts acknowledges that it is the Lord who actually delivers, not him. Nowhere is this more evident than in his dealings with the Zoramites. After his battle of words with Korihor, Alma goes "among the Zoramites, to preach unto them the word" (31:7). There he finds them, as part of their worship, ascending "a place for standing, which was high above the head" and which "would only admit one person" (v. 13). There, each worshiper would "stretch forth his hands towards heaven" and utter the same prayer (v. 20), a poem in praise of pride:

> Holy, holy God; we believe that thou art God, and we believe that thou art holy, and that thou wast a spirit, and that thou art a spirit, and that thou wilt be a spirit forever. Holy God, we believe that thou hast separated us from our brethren; and we do not believe in the tradition of our brethren, which was handed down to them by the childishness of their fathers; but we believe that thou hast elected us to be thy holy children; and also thou hast made it known unto us that there shall be no Christ. But thou art the same yesterday, today, and forever; and thou hast elected us that we shall be saved, whilst all around us are elected to be cast by thy wrath down to hell; for the which holiness, O God, we thank thee; and we also thank thee that thou hast elected us, that we may not be led away after the foolish traditions of our brethren, which doth bind them down to a belief of Christ, which doth lead their hearts to wander far from thee, our God. And again we thank thee, O God, that we are a chosen and a holy people. Amen. (Alma 31:15–18)

After hearing this prayer, Alma is grieved because of the wickedness of the Zoramites and because their hearts are "lifted up unto great boasting, in their pride" (Alma 31:24–25), and he therefore attacks it. However, again Alma does not fight with weapons but with words, holy words. He quickly counters this prayer of pride with a prayer of his own, in which he asks the Lord to "comfort [his] soul, and give unto [him] success, and also [his] fellow laborers who are with [him]" (v. 32). Rather than distancing himself from them or claiming superiority as the Zoramites do in their prayer, Alma stresses his connections to them, saying that "their souls are precious, and many of them are our brethren." He then asks God for "power and wisdom that [he] may bring these, our brethren, again unto [him]" (v. 35).

Alma's success is mixed. The Ammonihahites do not repent and are later destroyed (Alma 16:3). However, he does manage to see to it "that the people [in other parts of their land] were checked as to the pride of their hearts." These people "began to humble themselves before God" (15:17), and so when the Lamanites come upon them again and take captive some of their people, they humbly approach Alma and desire to know "whither the Lord would that they should go into the wilderness in search of their brethren, who had been taken captive by the Lamanites" (16:5). The Nephites end up following Alma's instructions, retaking "their brethren who had been taken captive by the Lamanites," and driving the Lamanites "out of the land" (vv. 8–9).

Captain Moroni

Captain Moroni is another deliverer in the book of Alma, and, as his title implies, he is very much a military leader. He is not a judge; he is not a civil administrator. He is more of a hero, someone along the lines of Barak, Deborah's great general, or Gideon, and as such, he dominates nearly one-third of the book of Alma with his exploits—fighting off the much larger forces of Zerahemnah, Amalickiah, and Ammoron—all of whom are determined to "gain power over the Nephites by bringing them into bondage" (Alma 43:8, 48:4). Captain Moroni's part of the book of Alma is full of dazzling military details: spies, forces secreted in hidden areas, strategically placed archers and slingers, and a variety of creative baiting tactics used to coax enemies out of their fortifications (43:23, 29–31; 49:22).

Militarily, Moroni is the master of preparing his people with the latest weapons and equipment. He is the first to equip them with "breastplates and with arm-shields," "shields to defend their heads," and thick clothing; when his enemies also acquire these things, he seemingly invents "small forts, or places of resort; throwing up banks of earth round about to enclose his armies, and also building walls of stone to encircle them about, round about their cities and the borders of their lands" (43:19, 48:8). Moroni always seems several steps ahead of his foes. However, Moroni is more than just a supreme strategist. He is also a religious leader, and he therefore prepares his people spiritually with religious instruction as well as militarily through weapons. He knows that it is ultimately the Lord who delivers his enemies into his hands (44:3, 9; 48:16; 50:22). Consequently, Moroni also readies "the minds of the people to be faithful unto the Lord their God" by preaching to them "the word of God" and by making sure that they fight, not for pride or power, but "to support their liberty, their lands, and their wives, and their children, and their peace" (48:7, 10, 19).

This anti-pride message of Moroni's is a constant theme of this section of Alma. Moroni preaches it to his soldiers, inspiring "their hearts with these thoughts" and leading them to victory (Alma 43:48). However, when triumph on the battlefield is followed by dissension, he returns to this theme again in order to unite his people in humility. At this point, Moroni dramatically tears off a piece of his coat and writes on it "In memory of our God, our religion, and freedom, and our peace, our wives, and our children" (46:12). He then fastens this "title of liberty" to a pole and rallies his people around it. He even has his words hoisted up as banners "upon every tower which was in all the land" (vv. 13, 36). As a result of his labors as well as those of his like-minded lieutenants, the people get the message and "humble themselves because of [his] words." They become again "highly favored of the Lord" and are "free from wars and contentions among themselves . . . for the space of four years" (48:20). Even when a group of proud people later on attempt to establish a king, Moroni campaigns against them on both levels, militarily and spiritually, and pulls "down their pride and their nobility" (51:18).

Moroni does not ultimately succeed, however; his people are not completely freed from the cycle of sin. After his death, they again become prideful, and the cycle begins once again. However, his success is more long-lasting and deeply rooted than anything in Judges. At the end of the book of Alma, when Moroni's career is almost over, his people "prosper again in the land," waxing "exceedingly strong again" and becoming "exceedingly rich" (Alma 62:48). Nonetheless despite this abundance, they are "not lifted up in the pride of their eyes" and do not forget "how great things the Lord had done for them, that he had delivered them from death, and from bonds, and from prisons, and from all manner of afflictions and he had delivered them out of the hands of their enemies" (v. 50). They "pray unto the Lord their God continually, insomuch that the Lord did bless them, according to his word, so that they did wax strong and prosper in the land" (62:51).

Captain Moroni may not have been "*the* Deliverer," the hero who brings them permanent peace. However, as "*a* deliverer" his impact was deep and widespread during his lifetime. According to Mormon, Captain Moroni was not merely a "mighty man of valour," like Gideon or Jephthah (Judg. 6:12, 11:1); he was "a man of a perfect understanding; yea, a man that did not delight in bloodshed; a man whose soul did joy in the liberty and the freedom of his country, and his brethren from bondage and slavery" (Alma 48:11). Consequently, Captain Moroni labored "exceedingly for the welfare and safety of his people" not only by rescuing them from external oppression but by attempting to save them from the internal imprisonment caused by pride.

Teancum

If Captain Moroni is a radical departure from the Judges-style hero, Teancum is a minor modification. He is much more the standard, no-nonsense warrior, a man of action, killing outward enemies through physical strength and skill, than the prophet-leader who campaigns verbally against inward pride. However, for all his military prowess, Teancum never really strikes at the heart of the matter or makes much of a difference. In this way,

Teancum serves as a commentary on the Judges-style hero, a way of showing the inferiority of that approach compared to Alma's and Moroni's.

Teancum's connection to Ehud and Gideon is clear. Like these judges, his military deeds are spectacular, even legendary. He slays Morianton and defeats his army, taking a sizable portion of his soldiers prisoner (Alma 50:35). He saves the land Bountiful by repelling Amalickiah when it seemed certain that the Lamanites would take it (51:29–31). He wisely decides against attacking a group of heavily fortified Lamanites head on and instead tricks them into leaving their fortifications by marching out with a "small number of men" and then leads the much larger force away until Moroni can "march forth into the city, and take possession of it" (52:19–24). All in all, Teancum is the most mentioned military leader other than Moroni in the entire Book of Mormon. He fulfills every mission he is given and does it with efficiency, courage, and creativity. His soldiers are described as "great warriors" and it is said that "every man of Teancum did exceed the Lamanites in their strength and in their skill of war" (51:31)—a fitting tribute to his leadership and ability to train and motivate his men.

However, when Teancum performs his most heroic acts—his most Judges-like feats—the results are very un-Judges-like. In fact, they are almost negligible. Just as Ehud takes it upon himself to personally rid his people of their oppressor, Teancum and his servant steal forth by night "into the tent of the [Lamanite] king, and put a javelin to his heart" (Alma 51:34). However, unlike Ehud, this action accomplishes nothing. King Amalickiah is dead, to be sure, but his brother, Ammoron, immediately takes over and the Nephites are delivered neither from their enemies nor from their own pride. Teancum, ever the hero, repeats his exploit by killing Ammoron in the same way. However, this time he is killed in the process. The next day, Moroni marches against the now kingless Lamanites and does indeed defeat them. However, in the long run, there is no indication that Teancum's deed affected the Lamanites in any meaningful way. They still hate the Nephites, and they return again to attack them but with a larger, better armed and better prepared force. At most, Teancum's heroics buys the Nephites time but little else.

Mormon seems to highlight the ineffectiveness of Teancum's approach. When Teancum's death is discovered, he describes Captain Moroni and his army as "exceedingly sorrowful" and pays tribute to Teancum as "a man who had fought valiantly for his country, yea, a true friend to liberty." However, in the end, Mormon writes simply that Teancum "was dead, and had gone the way of all the earth" (Alma 62:37). This short epitaph coupled with the fact that Mormon records none of Teancum's words seems to undermine any importance one might associate with Teancum's Judges-like exploits—a concision that is well-supported in the book of Judges itself. There the dazzling deeds of Ehud, Gideon, Samson, and others are presented as being exciting, perhaps even inspiring but they have no lasting value. In the end, the people in Judges repented temporarily, superficially, and "when the judge was dead, . . . they returned, and corrupted themselves more than their fathers" (Judg. 2:19). Military deliverance, though dramatic, seems limited in both the books of Judges and Alma.

End Result

All in all, the books of Alma and Helaman make it very clear that the cycle of sin as described in the book of Judges continues to thrive in the modern era. However, the "license" it describes is no longer idolatry per sé but pride, a sin which both includes and is included in the ancient sin of idolatry. Pride exists in many forms but each one of them originates in an erroneous understanding of the causes of prosperity and in an unwillingness to accept its responsibilities. Pride undermines the "engine" of prosperity and so naturally brings about dissention, division, poverty, war, and captivity. Deliverance from the effects of pride, although somewhat mitigated by heroic deeds, can only come from an inward change where a people humble themselves, repent, and return to the principles upon which prosperity is founded.

The books of Alma and Helaman combine with the book of Judges to show that outward force—be it military or otherwise—is not fundamentally effective in combating the problems created by pride since it does not treat the cause: pride itself. Outward force may create a situation where such an inner change can take place, for, as Alma tells his people, "a man sometimes, if he is compelled to be humble, seeketh repentance." However, as Alma continues, more blessed are those who "truly humble themselves because of the word" and are "without stubbornness of heart" or "are compelled to be humble because of their exceeding poverty" because "he that truly humbleth himself, and repenteth of his sins, and endureth to the end, the same shall be blessed" (Alma 32:13–15).

Chapter Nine

Increasing Significance

Behold, I am he that gave the law, and I am he who covenanted with my people Israel; therefore, the law in me is fulfilled, for I have come to fulfil the law; therefore it hath an end. Behold, I do not destroy the prophets, for as many as have not been fulfilled in me, verily I say unto you, shall all be fulfilled. And because I said unto you that old things have passed away, I do not destroy that which hath been spoken concerning things which are to come. For behold, the covenant which I have made with my people is not all fulfilled; but the law which was given unto Moses hath an end in me. (3 Ne. 15:5–8)

All *haftarot* enhance or support in some way their *parashot*. This is the dominant direction in which this interscriptural relationship flows. However, it is not the only direction. A *parashah* can also increase the significance of its *haftarah*. For instance, Genesis 1:1–6:8 reinforces the imagistic power of Isaiah 42:5–43:10. In this passage, Isaiah draws upon Creation imagery to reassure Israel that God will indeed redeem them and return them from their scattered and oppressed state. After all, this is not just any divine being promising to "bring [Israel's] seed from the east, and gather [them] from the west" (Isa. 43:5). This is the same God who "created the heavens," "spread forth the earth," and "giveth breath unto the people upon it" (42:5). Surely, he can be trusted to make good on his word and accomplish such a miraculous task.

Given this approach, it is easy to see how linking this passage to Genesis 1:1–6:8 in a *parashah-haftarah* relationship reinforces the power of Isaiah's imagery. First, it provides the full sweep of the creative activities that Isaiah's "heaven and earth" imagery alludes to, and second, it brings to the fore other, less obvious allusions. For example, God's pledge in Isaiah 42:16 to remove the blindness of his people Israel and "make darkness light" resonates with how he brought forth light out of darkness during the first day of

Creation (Gen. 1:2–3). Similarly, God's promise in Isaiah 43:9 to cause "all the nations [to] be gathered together" and "the people [to] be assembled" connects closely with the way He caused the "waters under the heaven [to] be gathered together" in order to form dry land on the third day (Gen. 1:9).

In addition, as Fishbane writes, when these two passages are read together, the participial form (similar to the present tense in modern English) of the Hebrew verbs used in the Isaiah passage "stands in marked contrast with the verbs of Genesis 1, which indicate past, completed action." This contrast transforms this *haftarah's* "theme of creation" into a "basis for theological reflection on God's ongoing concern for the world."[1] God's creative efforts, in other words, did not end on the seventh day. They continue as God forms and reforms Israel out of the dust and helps them multiply and replenish the earth (Isa. 43:1, 5–6; Gen. 1:28, 2:7). In this way, Genesis 1:1–6:8 increases the significance of Isa. 42:5–43:10 by supercharging its most prominent images, by empowering its less notable ones, and by revealing their ongoing potency in relation to God's people.

Several passages in the Book of Mormon similarly acquire enhanced meaning because of their links to the Hebrew Scriptures. Certainly, the book of Mosiah's connection to the biblical Period of Kings, as discussed in the previous chapter, amplifies the implications of King Mosiah's adoption of a judge-based system of government. Such a linkage transforms this act from a mere modification of a local policy into a profound correction of a very ancient and very tragic mistake. After suffering under their own flawed kings, these Israelites choose to reenthrone God as their king and desire no more to simply be "like all the nations" (1 Sam. 8:5–7). They have individually and collectively embraced their unique mission and decided, as King Mosiah said, "it is better that a man should be judged of God than of man, for the judgments of God are always just, but the judgments of man are not always just" (Mosiah 29:12).

For the Period of Receiving the Law, the many connections between the last two books of Nephi and the last four books of the Torah similarly transform Jesus's giving of the Sermon on the Mount to the Nephites from a regional "rerun" of a talk previously given in Galilee into a new, more positive version of what happened at Sinai. Just as Isaiah 42:5–43:10 draws upon Genesis 1:1–6:8, these two books from the Book of Mormon connect with these four from the Torah to show how Jesus not only can miraculously deliver his people from Egyptian-like oppression and give

---

1. Michael Fishbane, *The JPS Bible Commentary: Haftarot*, 11.

them Mosaic-like laws to live by, but how he can also make them a "holy people," just as God commanded anciently (Ex. 19:6). In this way, 3 and 4 Nephi function as a Christian *haftarah* to Exodus, Leviticus, Numbers, and Deuteronomy. They draw upon this relationship in order to portray Jesus as more than a "new Moses," as he is presented in Matthew, a Moses-like prophet who simply intensifies and internalizes Moses's Law; he is instead a "super-Moses," a divine lawgiver nearly identical to Moses but who also completes Moses's mission and the purpose of his law.

Addressing the Period of Receiving the Law

As many scholars attest, the Sermon on the Mount as it is presented in the Gospel of Matthew has close connections to Moses and to Sinai. Aaron M. Gale, for example, writes, before this sermon "Jesus, like Moses, is rescued in infancy and travels to Egypt; like Moses, after leaving Egypt, Jesus crosses water (the baptism), enters the wilderness (the temptation), and climbs a mountain before beginning his instruction (the 'Sermon on the Mount')."[2] Given these connections, it is not surprising then that Jesus subsequently states that "one jot or one tittle shall in no wise pass from the law, till all be fulfilled" (Matt. 5:18). As a "Moses figure," Jesus very much affirms the Law of Moses and consequently spends much of the Sermon on the Mount fulfilling its most prominent commandments by intensifying them, not doing away with them. As Bart D. Ehrman notes, despite the fact that the "ye have heard it of old time" statements found in the Sermon on the Mount are often called "antitheses," they do not oppose the Law of Moses. Jesus "does not say, 'You have heard it said, *You shall not commit murder*, but I say unto you that you should.' Instead Jesus urges his followers to adhere to the Law, but, to do so more rigorously than even the religious leaders of Israel."[3] In fact, according to Jacob Neusner, Jesus's effort to eliminate the causes of murder, adultery, and so forth is consistent with the long-standing attempts by ancient Mosaic Law-loving rabbis to "make a fence around the Torah" by advocating behaviors that "will avoid even the things that cause [people] to sin, not only the sin itself."[4]

The Book of Mormon also links Jesus and Moses but not in the same way or on the same subjects. Certainly, the sermon the resurrected Jesus delivers in 3 Nephi is remarkably similar to the one he presented

---

2. Aaron M. Gale, "The Gospel According to Matthew," 2.

3. Bart Ehrman, *The New Testament*, 102.

4. Jacob Neusner, *A Rabbi Talks with Jesus: An Intermillenial Interfaith Exchange*, 24.

in Matthew during his mortality. This version contains numerous small changes in wording and minor additions—such as appending "who come unto me" to the "blessed are the poor in spirit" and adding "with the Holy Ghost" after "for they shall be filled" (3 Ne. 12:3, 6)—but little else about it is different. It still contains Jesus's Moses-like endorsement of the Law of Moses, his intensifying "ye had heard it of old time" statements, as well as his condemnations of those who live the law hypocritically. Nonetheless, the sermon in 3 Nephi is not preceded by stories about Jesus's infancy or his early ministry that connect him to Moses. Nowhere in the Book of Mormon, for instance, is the death of the innocents, the flight of Joseph and Mary into Egypt, or the fast Jesus underwent for forty days in the wilderness mentioned or even alluded to. Instead, 3 Nephi links Jesus to Moses through the *people* Jesus addresses in this sermon. Their situation both before and during this sermon is very similar to that of Moses's children of Israel before and during their appearance at Sinai. However, their reaction is much more positive and yields much more productive results. In the Book of Mormon, Jesus fulfills the Mosaic Law not simply by acting like Moses but by actually accomplishing Moses's God-given task.

Connecting before Sinai

Like Exodus, 3 Nephi begins with a crisis for the people of God, the birth of their deliverer, and their deliverance from oppression. In Exodus, Israel is enslaved by the Egyptians, and, because of their growing numbers and the threat that growth implies, Pharaoh orders all of the male Israelite infants be killed (Ex. 1:9–16). In 3 Nephi, the Nephites seem to live in a similarly oppressive state where all those who await the birth of the Messiah are scheduled to be executed simply because of their beliefs (1:9). Both books however lessen these crises with the birth of a deliverer. In Exodus it is Moses, after whose birth there is no more mention of killing Israelite babies; in 3 Nephi it is Jesus, the signs of whose birth commute the sentences of those Nephites who believe in him. Both deliverers then go off, losing contact with their people, preparing in their own way to eventually rescue them. Moses grows up ignorant of his ancestry and mission in the house of the Pharaoh's daughter, eventually learns more of who he is, but must leave Egypt for Midian, where he encounters the burning bush. Jesus, meanwhile, lives far off Judea, similarly preparing himself for his mission, thousands of miles away from the Nephites.

However, while these deliverers remain in distant places, the condition of both of their people worsens for similar reasons. In Egypt, Israel sighs "by reason of the bondage" (Ex. 2:23) imposed upon them by hard-hearted pharaohs "which knew not Joseph" (1:8), while in the Americas, the civilization described in the Book of Mormon completely disintegrates (3 Ne. 7:2–7), as the people themselves started "to forget those signs and wonders which they had heard, and . . . began to be hard in their hearts, and blind in their minds, and began to disbelieve all which they had heard and seen" (2:1). Cognizant of his people's condition, God in each case sends a deliverer to help them: Moses to "bring forth [the Lord's] people the children of Israel out of Egypt" (Ex. 3:10) and Jesus to "bring redemption unto the world" (3 Ne. 9:21).

In both cases, the fulfillment of the deliverers' missions involves invoking plagues to afflict the wicked. In Exodus, Moses stretches "forth his rod toward heaven: and the Lord [sends] thunder and hail, and the fire [runs] along upon the ground" to distress the Egyptians (Ex. 9:23). In 3 Nephi, the Lord also sends down fire to destroy the wicked in that part of the world (3 Ne. 9:11). Later, Moses stretches forth his hand again "toward heaven; and there was a thick darkness in all the land of Egypt three days" (Ex. 10:22). In 3 Nephi, after a great destruction comes a "thick darkness upon all the face of the land, insomuch that the inhabitants thereof who had not fallen could feel the vapor of darkness." This darkness would allow no light: "neither candles, neither torches; neither could there be fire kindled with their fine and exceedingly dry wood," and it lasted "for the space of three days that there was no light seen" (3 Ne. 8:20–23). Finally, in the last plague in Exodus, the Lord smites "all the firstborn in the land of Egypt," and there was "a great cry in Egypt; for there was not a house where there was not one dead" (Ex. 12:29–30). Similarly, in 3 Nephi after the earthquakes and the fire and the darkness have killed many, there was also a "cry saying: O that we had repented before this great and terrible day, and then would our brethren have been spared" so much so that "the howlings of the people [were] great and terrible" (3 Ne. 8:24–25).

In the midst of all this destruction and woe, the more righteous in both Exodus and 3 Nephi are protected. Although "all the cattle of Egypt died" at Moses's command, "the cattle of the children of Israel died not one" (Ex. 9:6). The children of Israel are themselves excepted from the plagues of hail and darkness, and their firstborn are saved when each Israelite household sacrificed a lamb and took "of the blood, and [struck it] on the two side posts and on the upper door post of the houses" (9:26, 10:23, 12:7). In 3 Nephi, "the more righteous part of the people" is similarly saved by following the Lamb of God. It is "they who received the prophets and stoned them not; and it was they who had not shed the blood of the saints, who were spared" (10:12). The wicked city of Moroni, however, "did sink into the depths of the sea" while the equally wicked cities of Gadiandi, Gadiomnah, Jacob, and Gimgimno were "buried up in the depths of the earth" (8:9, 9:8) just as the Egyptian cavalry in Exodus was overthrown when the waters of the divided Red Sea returned, and they "sank as lead in the mighty waters" and "the earth swallowed them" (Ex. 15:10, 12).

Connecting at Sinai

Given the many ways the people in 3 Nephi connect to the children of Israel before they reached Sinai, it is easy to see more connections at the Mount despite several significant differences. Just as all of the children of Israel are "camped before the mount" at Sinai en masse (Ex. 19:2), "a great multitude" of Nephites are also gathered together at a Mosaic temple, a religious re-creation of the sacred mountain (3 Ne. 11:1). There, Jesus descends "out of heaven" to deliver his teachings (v. 8) just as Moses goes "down from mount Sinai with the two tables of testimony" (Ex. 34:29). Jesus at this time is "clothed in a white robe" and so startling is his appearance that those who saw him "thought it was an angel that had appeared unto them" (3 Ne. 11:8), a sight reminiscent of how the "skin of [Moses's] face shone" when he came down after talking with God (Ex. 34:30).

However, the Nephites, unlike the ancient Israelites, are not "afraid to come nigh unto" this heavenly being (Ex. 34:30). Like their forebears, they too "cry out with one accord," blessing the name of the Most High God (3 Ne. 11:16–17) and implicitly committing themselves as a unified group to obey "all that the Lord hath spoken" (Ex. 19:8; 24:3, 7). However, these New World Israelites actually keep this commitment. They do not "remove" themselves from the temple or otherwise stand "afar off" (Ex. 20:18). They instead go forth individually, as commanded, thrusting "their hands into [Jesus's] side," feeling "the prints of the nails in his hands and in his feet," bearing record "that it was he, of whom it was written by the prophets, that should come" (3 Ne. 11:15).

Even when Jesus leaves them for a time, these Nephites do not lose faith in him, build actual or figurative golden calves, or indulge in idolatrous fertility rites, as the original children of Israel did (Ex. 32:1, 6). They instead disperse to inform their neighbors that they "had seen Jesus" and explain that "he would also show himself on the morrow" (3 Ne. 19:2).

In this way, they do not "*make* [unto themselves] gods" (Ex. 32:1) but do "*labor* exceedingly all that night, that they might be on the morrow in the place where Jesus should show himself" (3 Ne. 19:3). Never did these people doubt that Jesus would return. Furthermore, their priests also act faithfully. Unlike Aaron, they do not fashion idols from gold and say unto their people, "These be thy gods, O Israel" (Ex. 32:4). Nephi and the others to whom Jesus gave authority (3 Ne. 11:21–22) instead divide those gathered at the temple the next morning into "twelve bodies," just like the camp of Israel, and cause "the multitude [to] kneel down upon the face of the earth, and [to] pray unto the Father in the name of Jesus" (19:5–6). They then baptize each other in preparation for Jesus's return, reminiscent of the way the Israelites were told to wash and sanctify themselves in preparation for meeting God at Sinai (Ex. 19:10).

Consequently, when Jesus does come down again, he stands in their midst and is neither angry nor does he upbraid them as Moses did ancient Israel (Ex. 32:19–21). Instead he affirms the goodness of what they are doing and provides them with food and drink—not water laced with the gold of their idolatry (v. 20), but bread and wine miraculously provided—a sacrament of blessing, not of punishment (3 Ne. 20:3–7). Jesus also speaks to God on their behalf, interceding for them—not as Moses did, pleading with God to be merciful and spare the lives of his "corrupted" people (Ex. 32:7, 11–14)—but praying to God, twice, thanking him for giving *his* people the Holy Ghost and for purifying them "because of their faith" (3 Ne. 19:20, 28). Jesus's disciples join him in prayer, and Jesus prays again. However, this time "so great and marvelous were the words which he prayed that they cannot be written, neither can they be uttered by man," and the hearts of the multitude "were open and they did understand in their hearts the words which he prayed" (vv. 33–34).

Connecting after Sinai

These many connections to the book of Exodus strongly suggest that these New World Israelites have been delivered from their own Egypt, that they have encountered their own Sinai, and that they have heard from their own Moses. However, unlike their Old World ancestors they have embraced this experience with great faith, and therefore they enjoy more positive results. Just as Moses desired, these Nephites sanctified themselves (Lev. 20:7) and the Lord "put his spirit upon them" (Num. 11:29). Moreover, immediately after Jesus's departure, they formed a church "in all the lands round about" and all people, both Nephites and Lamanites, were soon "converted unto the Lord" (4 Ne. 1:1–2). A two-hundred year period of righteousness, peace, and prosperity is then initiated, and these people become collectively a "holy nation" just as their ancestors were commanded to be generations before on Sinai (Ex. 19:6).

However, the holiness they exhibit is not simply general goodness, a vague quality common to all pious people everywhere; it instead corresponds closely to areas of emphasis in the "Holiness Code" of Leviticus 17–26, a group of laws that emphasizes, according to Baruch A. Levine, Israel's interdependence "in every aspect of life" as well as their "collective responsibility to seek to achieve holiness."[5] For instance, 4 Nephi describes the people at that time as dealing "justly one with another" (1:1), while the Holiness Code stipulates that Israelites should use "just balances, just weights, a just ephah, and a just hin" in their business dealings and should never defraud their neighbor, "neither rob him," even by retaining the wages a worker has earned beyond the time agreed upon for payment" (Lev. 19:13, 36). Also, 4 Nephi states that the people at that time had "all things common among them; therefore there were not rich and poor, bond and free but they were all made free, and partakers of the heavenly gift" (1:3). Similarly, the Holiness Code seems to undermine the idea of personal property by describing a variety of ways sold land reverts back to the family it was originally given to, and it justifies this approach, tellingly, by stating that "the land shall not be sold for ever: for the land is [the Lord's]" (Lev. 25:23). This code also contains a number of laws to facilitate the freeing of slaves (25:39–42) and helping the poor (19:9, 23:22). Servants, too, are to be treated with dignity and equity (25:43).

According to 4 Nephi, there were also no "whoredoms, nor lyings, nor murders, nor any manner of lasciviousness" among its people during this idyllic time (1:16). The Holiness Code likewise requires Israelites not to prostitute their daughters or cause them to be whores "lest the land fall to whoredom" (Lev. 19:29). They should also not "steal, neither deal falsely, neither lie one to another" either (v. 11). Adultery (20:10), murder (24:17), and sexual sins (18:6–24, 20:10–21) are all expressly forbidden.

In both 4 Nephi and Leviticus, social harmony is also stressed. Frequently 4 Nephi emphasizes that there was no contention in the land (1:2, 13, 15, 16) and states that there were "no envyings, nor strifes, nor tumults" there either (v. 16). The Holiness Code similarly forbids Israelites

---

5. Baruch A. Levine, *The JPS Torah Commentary: Leviticus*, 111.

from hating "thy brother in thy heart," rebuking him, or in any way suffering sin upon him. It commands Israelites not to "avenge, nor bear any grudge" against their own people or to vex the stranger that sojourns in their land. Israelites are instead required to love the stranger as well as one's neighbor "as thyself" (Lev. 19:17–18, 34). In addition, they are not to "curse the deaf, nor put a stumblingblock before the blind" (v. 14).

Both 4 Nephi and Leviticus describe the joy and blessedness resulting from such harmony. In 4 Nephi it says that the "Lord did prosper them exceedingly in the land"; these people did "wax strong, and did multiply exceedingly fast, and became an exceedingly fair and delightsome people" (1:7, 10). The Holiness Code also promises blessings to those who "walk in [God's] statutes, and keep [his] commandments, and do them." As Leviticus records God covenanting with Israel:

> I will give you rain in due season, and the land shall yield her increase, and the trees of the field shall yield their fruit. And your threshing shall reach unto the vintage, and the vintage shall reach unto the sowing time: and ye shall eat your bread to the full, and dwell in your land safely.
>
> And I will give peace in the land, and ye shall lie down, and none shall make you afraid: and I will rid evil beasts out of the land, neither shall the sword go through your land. And ye shall chase your enemies, and they shall fall before you by the sword. And five of you shall chase an hundred, and an hundred of you shall put ten thousand to flight: and your enemies shall fall before you by the sword. (Lev. 26:3–8)

Fulfilling the Law

All in all, connecting 3 and 4 Nephi to Exodus, Leviticus, Numbers, and Deuteronomy in a *haftarah-parashah* relationship greatly increases the significance of the Sermon on the Mount. It shows Jesus not merely intensifying the laws of Moses but realizing Moses's mission. Here, some Israelites actually become a "holy nation" as God commanded them through Moses. They form a cohesive socio-political unit consisting of people who truly love the Lord "with all [their] heart, and with all [their] soul, and with all [their] might" (Deut. 6:5) and similarly love their neighbors as themselves (Lev. 19:18). "Fulfilling" the Law of Moses in the Book of Mormon consequently means more than simply observing it in a manner "that gets to the reason why its demands were formulated," as Father Raymond E. Brown explains, which is an approach that seems to lessen the need for hard and fast rules and emphasizes more flexible principles.[6] It also involves more than the "higher righteousness [that] comes with the gift of God's presence," as Robert A. Spivey, D. Moody Smith, and C. Clifton Black state, a mystical approach that also undermines close observance of the laws of Moses.[7] Fulfilling the Law of Moses in this context means completing Moses's work, as prophets predicted and as God promised.

This, however, does not mean that Jesus leaves unchanged all the laws of Moses. Even before he sets foot on the American continents, Jesus, from on high, commands his people to offer up "no more the shedding of blood" and instructs them to do away with the sacrifices and burnt offerings associated with the Mosaic temple (3 Ne. 19–20). However, these few "old things" are not his primary concern. They have already "passed away" (15:3). Jesus seems most interested in the things he is still in the process of accomplishing—as is apparent in his mixing of past, future, and open-ended present tenses in the following statement:

> Behold, I say unto you that the law *is fulfilled* [present tense] that was given unto Moses.
>
> Behold, I am he that gave the law, and I am he who covenanted with my people Israel; therefore, the law in me *is fulfilled* [present tense], for I have come *to fulfil* [future tense] the law; therefore it hath an end.
>
> Behold, I do not destroy the prophets, for as many as *have not been fulfilled* [past tense] in me, verily I say unto you, *shall all be fulfilled* [future tense].
>
> And because I said unto you that old things *have passed away* [past tense], I do not destroy that which hath been spoken concerning things *which are to come* [future tense].
>
> For behold, the covenant which I *have made* [past tense] with my people *is not all fulfilled* [present tense]; but the law which was given unto Moses hath an end in me. (3 Ne. 15:4–8)

Note also how the fulfillment of the Mosaic Law for Jesus is inextricably connected to the fulfillment of God's covenant with Israel as well as with his communication with them through prophecy. The fulfillment Jesus is talking about, in other words, is a multifaceted work in progress. It is not limited to Mosaic laws nor is it confined to his past actions. Part of it has already happened, to be sure, but part of it is currently happening, and part of it has yet to happen. The more righteous Nephites have been miraculously delivered from their oppressors, they have gathered at the

---

6. Raymond E. Brown, *An Introduction to the New Testament*, 179.

7. Robert A. Spivey, D. Moody Smith Jr., and C. Clifton Black, *Anatomy of the New Testament*, 101.

temple, they are listening to Jesus, and they will soon become the kind of people God wanted them to be at Sinai. But there is more to do, and the holy state of these New World Israelites is but a foretaste of what God has in store for all Israel in the future.

Jesus further declares how he will gather Israel "in from the four quarters of the earth," much as he did the Nephites in their area around the temple, and will, in so doing, "fulfil the covenant which the Father hath made unto all the people of the house of Israel" (3 Ne. 16:5). He then describes how Israel, like the Nephites, will be delivered from their oppressors and shall be given land as their inheritance, in fulfillment of the words of Isaiah:

> Thy watchmen shall lift up the voice; with the voice together shall they sing, for they shall see eye to eye when the Lord shall bring again Zion.
>
> Break forth into joy, sing together, ye waste places of Jerusalem; for the Lord hath comforted his people, he hath redeemed Jerusalem.
>
> The Lord hath made bare his holy arm in the eyes of all the nations; and all the ends of the earth shall see the salvation of God. (3 Ne. 16:15–20; Isa. 52:8–10)

In other words, the Mosaic mission *will* be fulfilled. As prophesied by prophets, covenanted by God, and promoted by the Law of Moses, Israel *will* become "a holy people" one day. Jesus has picked up where Moses left off and succeeded, at least somewhat, where he did not. However, Jesus in 3 Nephi, makes it clear that this effort *will* not be finished until all Israel is similarly delivered, taught, and set up in their original Promised Land. As Jesus commands his Aaron-like disciple, Nephi, what he has done with these Israelites must be recorded to serve as an inspiring example to their fellow Israelites:

> And I command you that ye shall write these sayings after I am gone, that if it so be that my people at Jerusalem, they who have seen me and been with me in my ministry . . . may receive a knowledge of you by the Holy Ghost, and also of the other tribes whom they know not of, that these sayings which ye shall write shall be kept and shall be manifested unto the Gentiles, that through the fulness of the Gentiles, the remnant of their seed, who shall be scattered forth upon the face of the earth because of their unbelief, may be brought in, or may be brought to a knowledge of me, their Redeemer. And then will I gather them in from the four quarters of the earth; and then will I fulfil the covenant which the Father hath made unto all the people of the house of Israel. (3 Ne. 16:4–5)

Chapter Ten

Providing Prophetic Hope

Wherefore, the Lord commandeth you, when ye shall see these things come among you that ye shall awake to a sense of your awful situation, because of this secret combination which shall be among you; or wo be unto it, because of the blood of them who have been slain; for they cry from the dust for vengeance upon it, and also upon those who built it up. For it cometh to pass that whoso buildeth it up seeketh to overthrow the freedom of all lands, nations, and countries; and it bringeth to pass the destruction of all people, for it is built up by the devil, who is the father of all lies; even that same liar who beguiled our first parents, yea, even that same liar who hath caused man to commit murder from the beginning; who hath hardened the hearts of men that they have murdered the prophets, and stoned them, and cast them out from the beginning. (Ether 8:24–25)

Reinforcing a point, rendering an academic point applicable, translating an ancient situation into modern terms, and increasing the significance of a scriptural passage are just a few of the ways *haftarot* and *parashot* connect. There are more, many more. However, despite their diversity each of these connections combine in specific ways to provide for their hearers what Rabbi Hertz calls a "prophetic message of consolation and hope."[1] Rabbi Fishbane, for instance, finds several hopeful ties between *parashah Yitro*, Exodus 18–20, and its *haftarah*, Isaiah 6:1–13—all of which combine to offer an optimistic outlook for Israel and the world, despite historical setbacks. For one, there are thematic links between these passages that increase the significance of Isaiah's call. As Fishbane explains, Israel's encounter with God at Sinai "first presents a structure for justice and judgment (chap. 18) and then a revelation of God's instruction to the nation (chaps. 19–20)." The Isaiah passage subsequently treats these same themes "in more personal terms," bringing Exodus's message home

---

1. J. H. Hertz, ed., *The Pentateuch and Haftorahs*, 20.

and filling it with hope, as Isaiah witnesses God's majesty as well as his "promise of a new era of justice to be inaugurated by a messianic king."[2]

In this way, Isaiah 6:1–13 also translates the ancient Mosaic situation into more modern, or at least future, terms. As Fishbane continues, these passages from Exodus and Isaiah resonate from "opposite historical poles": the *parashah* gazes backward from "a past time of covenantal origins" while the *haftarah* looks forward with hope to a "future time of messianic justice. What Moses inaugurates, the prophet Isaiah may only proclaim: "a kingdom of justice under God." In Isaiah's present, "the people bidden to be a 'kingdom of priests and a holy nation' (Ex. 19:6) have failed their task and are pronounced 'unclean.'" However, they may "again become a 'holy seed,' after punishment and purgation (Isaiah 6:5, 11–13)."[3]

Such connections clearly lend hope to an otherwise hopeless situation, especially when this optimistic outlook is strengthened by specific verbal ties. As Fishbane points out, similar references to holiness as well as descriptions of inspiring winged beings, sacred smoke, and quaking door posts and mountains in these two readings reinforce the idea that God's original goal for Israel, a goal given to them by Moses but seemingly lost when Jerusalem was destroyed and its people dispersed, is still very much alive. Indeed God made an "*everlasting* covenant" with Israel (Gen. 9:16, 17:7–19; Lev. 24:8; Deut. 33:27), and though Israel may stray its people will eventually be redeemed after much tribulation. As Fishbane summarizes, this *haftarah* is, all in all, encouraging. Despite the fact that Israel will "fall like a ravaged tree," it will later "regenerate from its own stock." The "ancient promise" given in its *parashah* consequently "has hovered over the decimation of Jewish history" and therefore continues to give "hope to the present and future."[4]

Much as Isaiah 6:1–13 connects to Exodus 18–20, the books of Mormon and Ether similarly join with the book of Genesis for the same hopeful purpose. Not only do they draw significance from the first book of the Torah as they describe the final demise of their peoples, translate that ancient situation into modern terms, and reinforce one of Genesis's most important points, but they do so chiastically, combining these various connections into a powerful message of prophetic optimism and offering their readers advice as to how to avoid a similar demise. In this way, the penultimate books of the Book of Mormon constitute a kind of

---

2. Michael Fishbane, *The JPS Bible Commentary: Haftarot*, 114.

3. Ibid.

4. Ibid.

haftarah tour de force—a fitting finale that exemplifies both the reasons as well as the ways it connects to the Hebrew Scriptures.

Increasing Significance

As Jon D. Levenson writes, Genesis is fundamentally "a book about beginnings—the beginning of the natural world, the beginning of human culture, and the beginning of the people Israel."[5] Given the etiological emphasis of this first book in the Torah, it is fitting that Ether, the next to last book in the Book of Mormon, links to it by working backwards, rolling imagistically in reverse through the stories of the Great Tower and the Flood to Cain's murder in order to expose the ultimate source of the evils the Book of Mormon describes. It is also fitting that the book that precedes Ether, the book of Mormon, first connects to the event in Genesis that comes before all of these stories: the Creation.

Not only does the book of Mormon establish a linkage to Genesis, which Ether continues, but it justifies Ether's chiastic journey by using those connections to intensify the darkness of a world where these evils exist as well as to testify of God's ability to illuminate that world. In this way, the book of Mormon draws significance from the biblical Period of Origins just as 3 and 4 Nephi do from the Period of Receiving the Law. Right from the start, it is clear that the God of the book of Mormon is not a distant "watcher," a detached divinity who puts things in motion and then lets them follow their own course. Much like the God of Creation, he is personally involved in the world, forming at least one man figuratively out of "the dust of the ground," breathing "into his nostrils the breath of life," and helping him gain "dominion" over his people (Gen. 1:26, 2:7).

Mormon, whose story this is, seems very ordinary in the beginning. He starts off simply as a "sober child" whose only distinction is that he is "quick to observe" (Morm. 1:2). He grows up to be "large in stature" (2:1), but this attribute alone provides readers with no reason to expect great things of him. Mormon is not described as having any impressive societal connections or religious credentials, and there is no mention of any special educational or military preparation. Nevertheless, at "about ten years of age," Mormon is singled out by a prophet of God and chosen for the important task of recording "all the things that [he has] observed con-

---

5. Jon D. Levenson, "Genesis," 8.

cerning this people" (1:2, 4). And eventually, despite still "being young," he becomes his people's "leader, or the leader of their armies" (2:1).

It is apparent that God himself is actively involved in shaping Mormon, much as God did the earth. Not only does God provide Mormon with a divine visitation when he was "fifteen years of age," but he deals with Mormon directly—by first moving him to preach unto his people and then by forbidding him to do so because they had "willfully rebelled against their God" (Morm. 1:15–16). Furthermore, there is no one else to teach Mormon the things that he needs to know. As he says, there were no spiritual "gifts from the Lord" among his people at that time, and "the Holy Ghost did not come upon any" (v. 14). God himself is Mormon's teacher, his tutor, even his creator; and it is therefore telling that Mormon describes the great sin of his people, the one that ultimately ripens them for destruction, as "they repented not of their iniquities, but did struggle for their lives without calling upon that *Being who created them*" (5:2).

In addition to its portrayal of God, the book of Mormon also draws upon Genesis in its description of the society Mormon lives in. As he nears the end of his life and his son prepares to "finish the record of [his] father" (Morm. 8:1), Mormon and Moroni paint a pre-creational shadow over their world. Theirs is a world in which the Creation has been undone, a world that has reverted to a state of absolute chaos and disorder. As Moroni writes,

> And behold, the Lamanites have hunted my people, the Nephites, down from city to city and from place to place, even until they are no more; and great has been their fall; yea, great and marvelous is the destruction of my people, the Nephites. And behold, it is the hand of the Lord which hath done it. And behold also, the Lamanites are at war one with another; and the whole face of this land is one continual round of murder and bloodshed; and no one knoweth the end of the war. And now, behold, I say no more concerning them, for there are none save it be the Lamanites and robbers that do exist upon the face of the land. (Morm. 8:7–9)

Even worse than Genesis, where the Spirit (or wind, as it is also translated) of God is just beginning to move "upon the face of the waters" (Gen. 1:2), here "the Spirit of the Lord hath already ceased to strive with their fathers . . . and they are driven about as chaff before the wind" (Morm. 5:16). As Mormon and Moroni portray it, theirs is a world that God has deserted. Deep darkness has fallen "upon the face" of this chaotic land and whatever light it had is about to go out.

In a sense, Mormon's world has become imagistically not only an "ante-Eden," a land before the Creation, but an "anti-Eden," a mockery of that ancient paradise. And it is within this mockery that Moroni, Mormon's son, must remain alone after his father is killed. Like a misbegotten Adam, Moroni cannot be sent forth. He must instead stay where he is, by himself, laboring "in the sweat of [his] face" (Gen. 3:19) to complete "the sad tale of the destruction of [his] people" (Morm. 8:3). It is not good for Moroni to be alone, but there is no "help-meet" for him. None remain who "know the true God" (v. 10). He is therefore without assistance and companionship, knowing "not friends nor whither to go" (v. 5). Here in this dark situation Moroni, seemingly expecting to die at any moment, finishes his father's work, quickly, hopelessly, adding just a "few things" that he had been commanded by his father to write" (v. 1). He makes "an end of speaking concerning this people" (v. 13) and hides up his account "in the earth" (v. 4). Again, much like a fallen and forgotten Adam, he is preparing to return both himself and his words "unto dust" (Gen. 3:19).

Translating an Ancient Situation into Modern Terms

Just as the book of Mosiah shows how God can rescue the ancient concept of kings from the charge of irrelevance by translating it into principles modern readers can implement, so the book of Mormon similarly asserts that God can yet salvage something salvific from Moroni's dark situation. Echoing the way God brings light to the primordial darkness— powerfully and miraculously—the book of Mormon shows how Mormon and Moroni's bleak account will eventually enlighten future generations and save them from a similar fate.

After Moroni completes the seemingly lightless story of his people, he turns his attention away from his present situation to that of his future readers and begins to explain how this account of his people will be of "great worth" to them (Morm. 8:14). Again using words that resonate with the Creation, Moroni speaks in Eve-like terms of an eventual "blessed" helpmeet of his, who "shall bring this thing to light" (v. 14) just as Adam's wife is privileged to "bring forth children" (Gen. 3:16). This person will have power "given him of God" and will be instrumental in bringing Mormon and Moroni's account "out of darkness unto light, according to the word of God" (Morm. 8:16). His efforts will enable it to "shine forth out of darkness, and come unto the knowledge of the people" (v. 16). In this way, the work of Mormon and Moroni will eventually be fruitful and even replenish the earth (Gen. 1:28), much as did Adam and Eve's posterity.

And this light will be greatly needed. Moroni, having prophetically seen the world of his future readers, speaks directly to them "as if [they] were present," and he describes their "doing" using the same dark terms he uses to describe his own people's activities (Morm. 8:35). At this future time, "works of darkness" will also abound, and people will limit the intensity of heavenly light by denying "the power of God" and by being "lifted up in the pride of their hearts" (vv. 27–28). As a result, chaos, much like that in Moroni's era, will rule the land: in that day "there shall be heard of fires, and tempests, and vapors of smoke in foreign lands; And there shall also be heard of wars, rumors of wars, and earthquakes in divers places. Yea, it shall come in a day when there shall be great pollutions upon the face of the earth; there shall be murders, and robbing, and lying, and deceivings, and whoredoms, and all manner of abominations" (Morm. 8:29–31).

Given these similarities to Moroni's world, it comes as no surprise that this future era is similarly on the verge of destruction. As Moroni tells his future readers, "Behold, the sword of vengeance hangeth over you; and the time soon cometh that [the Lord] avengeth the blood of the saints upon you, for he will not suffer their cries any longer" (Morm. 8:41). In other words, Moroni's "sad tale of the destruction of [his] people" (v. 3) may eventually become the equally tragic story of his future readers if they are not careful. The same darkness that engulfs his people looms over his later readers as well. However, there is hope. There is still time for these readers to avoid the fate of Moroni's people, and to that end Moroni speaks to his readers "from the dead" and offers them the book of Ether as a warning.

Reinforcing a Point

That the world can become so corrupt that there is seemingly no hope for it is certainly not a new idea in Genesis. During Noah's time, God also "saw that the wickedness of man was great in the earth" and that their collective "heart was only evil continually." The world at that time was, much like Moroni's, "filled with violence," and this situation similarly "grieved [God] at his heart" so much that he decided to destroy all of humanity, not with war, but with a world-wide flood (Gen. 6:5–7, 13). However, not all flesh was, of course, annihilated in the flood. Noah, his wife, his three sons, and his sons' wives were all saved from destruction, along with their animals. There is indeed hope, in other words, even in this dark situation. The light comes forth again. There is to be a second creation, where these surviving couples, like new Adams and new Eves, are given dominion over "every beast of the earth, and upon every fowl of the air" and are commanded again to "be fruitful, and multiply, and replenish the earth" (9:1–3).

However, this hope is conditional. There is the sign of the rainbow and God's promise that "the waters shall no more become a flood to destroy all flesh" (Gen. 9:15). However, there are other ways of laying waste to the earth if history repeats itself and God is goaded again. As Nahum M. Sarna writes, "the destruction of the old world calls for the repopulation of the earth and the remedying of the ills that brought on the Flood. Society must henceforth rest on more secure moral foundations. New norms of human behavior must be instituted."[6] Consequently, God's command-ment against murder, an instruction not given to Adam, is significant—as is its wording. First, "blood" is emphasized. It is described as the "life thereof," and Genesis states that "whoso sheddeth man's *blood*, by man shall his *blood* be shed." Secondly, "brother" is also accentuated. As this verse continues, "At the hand of every man's brother will [God] require the life of man." Together, both of these emphases serve to clearly connect to the story of Cain and Abel. In that story, not only does "the voice of [Abel's] *blood*" cry against Cain "from the ground" (Gen. 4:10), but the word "brother" appears in connection with Abel seven times. This usage, according to Sarna, emphasizes the point that "man is indeed his brother's keeper and that all homicide is fratricide"—a point that the wording of the commandment to Noah very much affirms.[7]

In other words, God's commandment to Noah, in addition to prohib-iting murder, in a sense goes back in time, allusively, to explain precisely why such an act is forbidden as well as where and under what circum-stances it came to be. Here the unlawful taking of a human life is shown to be not simply the theft of something valuable, even irreplaceable; it is the ultimate expression of hatred toward an intimate, someone one should have loved and cared for like a member of one's family. It is a betrayal of a sacred trust, an inherently unholy act, motivated by jealousy, anger, pettiness, and greed. And it is also the cause of humanity's destruction at that time since, according to rabbinic sources, "the descendants of Cain resembled their father in his sinfulness and depravity" and eventually cor-rupted the Sethites.[8]

---

6. Nahum M. Sarna, *The JPS Torah Commentary: Genesis*, 60.

7. Ibid., 61.

8. Louis Ginzberg, *The Legends of the Jews*, 1:151–52.

Given the way the book of Mormon sets the stage for the book of Ether by connecting closely and meaningfully with Genesis, it comes as no surprise then that Ether continues this connection, descending darkly into the Period of Origins, retracing step-by-step the path that leads to the Nephites' destruction, searching for its source. And it should also come as no surprise that this journey ultimately ends with Cain and his violent rejection of familial relationships. In this way, the book of Ether connects to Genesis—just as 1 Nephi, 2 Nephi, and Jacob did to the Period of Prophets—reinforcing one of this period's most fundamental teachings so that its future readers may "give thanks unto God" and "learn to be more wise than [they] have been" (Morm. 9:30–31).

Moving Into Darkness

There can be no doubt that the book of Ether is a dark book. Earlier on in the Book of Mormon, Alma describes the plates it comes from as containing "works of darkness" including these people's murders, robbings, plunderings, and abominations, as well as other "secret works" (Alma 37:21). Alma explains that God will eventually "bring forth out of darkness unto light all their secret works and their abominations" (v. 25). He therefore advises his son to use them to "teach [his people] to abhor such wickedness and abominations and murders" (v. 29). Moroni's inclusion of this account is a fulfillment of Alma's words. And, darkness gathers as the book of Ether works its way backwards through Genesis— starting off with some light early on, during the time of the Great Tower, even displaying a burst of illumination as its people prepare, like Noah, to cross a great deep, only to show that flame flicker and die as they return symbolically to the antediluvian land of Cain.

The Tower

The first part of the book of Ether is dominated by a figure known only as the brother of Jared, a man so prominent that his people are commonly called "Jaredites," after him. He lives during the time of the Great Tower of Genesis 11 when "the Lord confounded the language of the people" (Ether 1:33) and is appropriately described in heroic Nimrod-like terms. However, he is not the "mighty one in the earth," nor is he a great king who builds the great tower and instigates a rebellious plot to "reach unto heaven" (Gen. 10:8, 11:40). The brother of Jared is instead described as a "large and mighty man" who is "highly favored of the Lord" (Ether 1:34); he is a prophet who cries unto the Lord so that he and his people might be spared God's curse for building this tower.

The Flood

And the Jaredites *are* spared. God answers the brother of Jared's prayer and the Jaredites' language is not confounded. God also leads them from inside a cloud, an image of veiled light, and sends them wandering, away from the Great Tower, back to an ancient "land of promise, which was choice above all other lands" (Ether 2:7). Retracing the steps of the "families of Noah" who, after the Flood, "journeyed from the east" to "the land of Shinar," where Nimrod ruled and the great tower was built (Gen. 10:32–11:2), the Jaredites travel through the valley of Nimrod, "into the wilderness," (presumably in the east) until they reach "that great sea which divideth the lands" (Ether 2:1, 4–5, 13).

There the brother of Jared limits his own enlightenment by failing to pray to God, and his people rest for four years by the seashore, dwelling in tents (Ether 2:13), again much as Noah and his family did after the Flood (Gen. 9:21, 27). Only after some time does the Lord come again to the brother of Jared, veiled again in an appropriately light-diminishing cloud, to chastise him for failing "to call upon the name of the Lord" (Ether 2:14). The brother of Jared immediately repents, and God just as quickly forgives him. However, echoing his words in Genesis 6:3 about the antediluvian earth, God ominously tells the brother of Jared that "[his] Spirit will not always strive with man" and then instructs him to build barges "according to the instructions of the Lord" (Ether 2:15–16), much as he told Noah to construct his ark. These instructions seem to surprise the brother of Jared and cause him great concern. Since these boats were to be "tight like unto the ark of Noah" and consequently unable to travel by "the light of fire," he worries about crossing a "great water in darkness" (Ether 2:22–23, 6:7). This time, however, the brother of Jared remembers to call upon God and presents God with his concerns; eventually, after a certain amount of initiative on the brother of Jared's part, God solves the problem by giving the brother of Jared eight miraculous stones that "shine in darkness" and "give light unto men, women, and children" so "that they might not cross the great waters in darkness" (Ether 6:3). These mysterious stones consequently provide a vivid reminder that the Lord is "the light, and the life, and the truth of the world" (Ether 4:12). Despite being "many times buried in the depths of the sea," these people "did have light continually" throughout their voyage (Ether 6:6, 10).

The Antediluvian Land

However, once Jared, his brother, and their people reenact Noah's voyage and sail to a land on the other side of the sea, this brief era of illumination quickly begins to fade. Soon, the people are given oaths from the devil, whose purpose is said explicitly "to keep them in *darkness*" (Ether 8:16). They cast their prophets into lightless pits, shut up their sons in gloomy prisons, and send many others into the night of captivity (9:7, 29; 10:14). In the end, Jared's people very much resemble Moroni's people. War becomes the norm and is present "upon all the face of the land" with "every man with his band fighting for that which he desired." Robbers too infest this society as does "all manner of wickedness" (13:25–26), so much so that

> if a man should lay his tool or his sword upon his shelf, or upon the place whither he would keep it, behold, upon the morrow, he could not find it, so great was the curse upon the land. Wherefore every man did cleave unto that which was his own, with his hands, and would not borrow neither would he lend; and every man kept the hilt of his sword in his right hand, in the defence of his property and his own life and of his wives and children. (Ether 14:1–2)

Finally, conditions deteriorate to such a degree that "all the people upon the face of the land [are] shedding blood, and there [is] none to restrain them" (Ether 13:31). They are continually fighting each other, battling so frequently and bloodily that the "whole face of the land" is eventually "covered with the bodies of the dead" (14:21). Very much like Moroni's people, they have become so wicked that they are "cut off from the presence of the Lord," the ultimate source of light. Even their last prophet, Ether, is forced to hide himself in a dark "cavity of a rock by day" to come out only at night to view "the destructions which came upon the people" (10:11, 13:13–14).

Connection to Families

This imagistic descent into darkness, however, is more than an aesthetic nicety. There is a point to it, a point very much connected to the Cain story in the first book of the Torah. Just as Jewish writings link the destruction of the antediluvian people to Cain-like fratricide in an effort to improve the behavior of their readers toward other human beings, so the book of Ether connects the demise of its people to an identical impulse for a similar purpose. Right from the start, Genesis emphasizes the familial connection to others. Tracing all of humanity to one couple certainly underscores this idea, as do the frequent genealogical listings found in Genesis. Genesis 5, for instance, presents the "generations of Adam" and names his descendants in order for ten generations, ending with Noah's sons, traditionally the ancestors of the Semites, the Africans, and the Europeans (Gen. 5:1–32). In this way, all humanity is shown to be related, not just theoretically, but in actuality, as descendants of a single couple. God's covenant also passes from father to son—from Abraham to Isaac to Jacob to Joseph—similarly emphasizing the importance of familial connections.

The genealogical list in the first chapter of Ether seemingly supports this emphasis. It too starts with Adam (although it skips many of his descendants because those details are had in the Hebrew Scriptures) and works its way through the main figures of its account. However, this list proceeds not according to descendancy—"Cainan lived seventy years, and begat Mahalaleel" (Gen. 5:12)—but ancestrally, emphasizing a person's father rather than his son: Ether "was a descendant of Coriantor. Coriantor was the son of Moron. And Moron was the son of Ethem." And so forth (Ether 1:6–32). In this way, the book of Ether seems to be signaling not only how its plot will progress—in reverse, back through Genesis chiastically—but that the true order of things is somehow upset, turned upside down. Here familial bonds may start off strong as they do in Genesis, but in the end they will be shattered, obliterated into nothingness. Consistent with this idea, Ether's beginning affirms family loyalty and love. In fact, its genealogical list concludes with a description of Jared as the man who "came forth with his brother and their *families*, with some others and their *families*, from the great tower, at the time the Lord confounded the language of the people" (v. 33).

In this context, the fact that Jared's brother is never named seems to underscore the importance of familial relationships to these people. Again, he may have been "a large and mighty man," "a man highly favored of the Lord" (Ether 1:34), even the logical choice to lead should something happen to Jared. However, his name seems to indicate that his role as a sibling was more important to him than these other roles. Jared too seems to value his brother most as a brother. Although Jared is clearly the leader of his people, a kind of early Moses, he neither approaches God himself nor does he command his brother to approach God for him. Instead, he respectfully *asks* his brother, as one would a respected peer, to pray for him and for his people, "that he will not confound [them] that [they] may not understand [their] words" (v. 34).

And this the brother of Jared does, willingly and without hesitation, and God has "compassion upon their friends and their *families* also" (Ether 1:37). Jared then grows bold and requests his brother again to pray to God, this time asking where they should go, adding "for who knoweth but the Lord will carry us forth into a land which is choice above all the earth?" (v. 38). Jared's desire proves prophetic, and soon God instructs the brother of Jared to "gather together [his] flocks, both male and female, of every kind; and also of the seed of the earth of every kind; and [his] *families*; and also Jared [his] brother and his *family*; and also [his] friends and their *families*, and the friends of Jared and their *families*" (v. 41).

And so, with the value of families firmly established and continually reiterated, the book of Ether soon moves away from a situation where this value is upheld as the people descend downward into the darkness. After they have imagistically traveled back to the antediluvian land, Jared and his brother's descendants began "to spread upon the face of the land, and to multiply," just as Adam's did in Genesis 6. They start to "till the earth; and they did wax strong in the land" (Ether 6:18). Time passes. However, before Jared and his brother "go down to the grave," another lightless image, they ask their people, including their sons and daughters, what they desire. And "the people desired of them that they should anoint one of their sons to be a king over them" (vv. 19, 22). This grieves Jared and his brother, much as Samuel mourned because of a similar request from his people (1 Sam. 8:6). However, in the end, the Jaredites, like the Israelites, prevail upon their leaders, and Orihah, one of the sons of Jared, is anointed their king (Ether 6:27).

Soon after, both Jared and his brother die, and "Orihah did walk humbly before the Lord, and did remember how great things the Lord had done for his father, and also taught his people how great things the Lord had done for their fathers" (Ether 6:30). However, under Orihah the situation begins to change. The people become "exceedingly rich" (v. 28), and the family system, which was revered previously, begins to break down. Heir-apparent sons rebel against their royal fathers (7:4), brother-princes create rival factions against each other (vv. 8–9), family feuds develop, battles ensue within clans until, like the antediluvian world, this new land becomes entirely "corrupt before God" and is continually "filled with violence" (Gen. 6:11).

At one point in particular, a prince named Jared (not the original Jared but a later one) rebels against Omer (his kingly father), draws away supporters, defeats his father in battle, and imprisons him. Two of Jared's brothers, in turn, overturn Jared and restore their father to his throne, sparing Jared's life. Jared, however, is not satisfied with this situation, and his daughter devises "a plan whereby she could redeem the kingdom unto her father" using "secret plans" from a "record which [their] fathers brought across the great deep" (Ether 8:8–9). Although these plans may seem somewhat family-oriented in the sense that the daughter of Jared uses them to help her father regain his throne, they are not. Rather than solidifying familial bonds, they set up a relational system that runs directly counter to families. The daughter of Jared initiates her plan by dancing before Omer's friend, Akish. Akish is so pleased with her that he asked Jared for her hand in marriage. Jared consents to this, provided Akish delivers unto him the head of Omer. Akish is so smitten that he eagerly agrees to Jared's demand. He therefore gathers together "all his kinsfolk" and asks them to swear unto him that they will be "faithful unto [him] in the thing" which he desires of them (v. 13). This they do, swearing ironically "by the God of heaven, and also by the heavens, and also by the earth, and by their heads, that whoso should vary from the assistance which Akish desired should lose his head; and whoso should divulge whatsoever thing Akish made known unto them, the same should lose his life" (v. 14).

Again, these oaths may appear to be somewhat supportive of families since they are given to Akish's relatives and are seemingly founded on a belief in God, but this too is not so. Rather than simply calling upon his extended family to support him as their familial bonds would require, Akish sets up a new system of relationships that both mimics and mocks those within families. It may begin with family members, but, as is soon apparent, it is not limited to them, and it certainly does not come from God. As the book of Ether continues, Moroni explains that these oaths "had been handed down even from Cain, who was a murderer from the beginning" and makes plain that "they were kept up by the power of the devil" (Ether 8:15–16). In addition, Moroni states that the purposes of these oaths were far from holy or familial. They were instead "given by them of old who also sought power" and were set up explicitly to help people who "sought power to gain power, and to murder, and to plunder, and to lie, and to commit all manner of wickedness and whoredoms" (v. 16). Armed with these oaths and the new "family" they have set up, Akish and the daughter of Jared, the person "who put it into his heart to search up these things of old" (v. 17), quickly begin using them for the purposes for which they were preserved. Akish and his accomplices—now called "his friends," not his family—attempt to murder Omer on his throne. However, Omer is warned of their plans by the Lord in a dream and departs "out of the land with his *family*" and travels many days to the place called Ablom where "he pitched his tent, and also *his sons and his daughters*, and all his household" (9:3). Jared now assumes the throne and, as promised, gives "unto Akish his daughter to wife" (v. 4).

It is at this point that the true anti-family nature of the system Akish established is revealed. Akish is not content simply to be related to the king through marriage, and so he, relying upon "those whom he had sworn by the oath of the ancients," beheads his father-in-law, and crowns himself the king (Ether 9:5–6). But now, so fragmented are families that even one's children cannot be trusted, and Akish, jealous of his own son, locks him up in prison, and there keeps "him upon little or no food until he had suffered death" (v. 7). Perhaps Akish was right to suspect his children. Nimrah, another son of Akish, becomes angry with his father for killing his brother and gathers together "a small number of men," flees to Omer (v. 9), and begins a protracted war with his father. This war lasts "for the space of many years, yea, unto the destruction of nearly all the people of the kingdom, yea, even all, save it were thirty souls" (v. 12). From this point on, the book of Ether is one continual round of intrafamilial bloodshed—Heth, another son of a king embraces "the secret plans again of old," kills his father "with his own sword," and takes the throne (vv. 26–27). The land is then cursed with famine and poisonous snakes until Shez builds up a righteous kingdom. Shez, the son of Shez, however, rebels against his father, and in due time his brother Riplakish, becomes king and, in direct contrast with Shez, lays taxes "upon men's shoulders which was grievous to be borne"—all to build "many spacious buildings" and prisons where his gold was refined and made into objects of "fine workmanship" (10:3, 5–7).

And so the book of Ether continues, back and forth, between Morianton and Kim, Levi and Corom, Kish and Lib—all the time emphasizing how greed and lust for power break up what should have been treasured familial relationships—until finally Coriantumr, the last king, leading only a handful of survivors, smites off the head of Shiz, probably a distant relation, and falls to the earth from loss of blood, looking for all the world as if he were dead (Ether 15:25–32). The book of Ether then ends with Ether, much like Moroni, alone and isolated, finishing his record, hiding it up, not knowing if he is going to be translated or suffer death. Rather than a fine posterity, this supremely dysfunctional family has imploded, leaving behind just one named descendant, a man left despondent, depressed, by himself, and without an earthly future. "It mattereth not," Ether concludes, as long as "I am saved in the kingdom of God" (Ether 15:34).

Offering Advice and Encouragement

All in all, the book of Ether is the Book of Mormon in miniature—reduced, distilled, and concentrated in such a way as to highlight its messages and methods in more intense, more vivid colors. Not only does the book of Ether connect to Genesis the way the Book of Mormon does to other books of the Hebrew Scriptures, but its basic structure is linked to the Book of Mormon as well. The Book of Mormon similarly begins with a family fleeing a wicked society. It too follows them as they traverse distant lands and great waters to a promised land. It also records the rise of the civilization they created, ending with the collapse of that civilization and the scattering of its people. And furthermore it relates all these things for the same overall purpose. Implicit within the Book of Mormon, as with the book of Ether, is the idea that modern society is going down the same dark path as the Jaredites and the Nephites. Its people are also guilty of betraying what should have been sacred fraternal ties, substituting secret oaths for more open familial covenants, and worshiping status and material gain instead of God. Consequently, it too is on the verge of destruction.

However, implicit in both the book of Ether and the broader Book of Mormon is the idea that such a future is not inevitable. It can be avoided if, as Moroni writes, modern people learn from what he calls his people's "imperfections" and become "more wise than [they] have been" (Morm. 9:31). In other words, the prophecies embodied in both of these books then are conditional. Modern people need not repeat the mistakes of the Nephites and the Jaredites. Their implosion can be prevented. However, modern people must modify their behavior for this to happen—and to that end Moroni offers plenty of explicit advice and encouragement. Like his father, Moroni does "not desire to harrow up the souls of men in casting before them such an awful scene of blood and carnage." However, since what has happened to his people is causally linked to "evil ways," Moroni, even more than Mormon, emphasizes to his future modern readers that they will not suffer a similar fate if they repent and turn from their evil ways (Morm. 5:8, 22). Early on in the book of Ether, for instance, immediately after describing how the Jaredites were led to a "land of promise," Moroni pauses to explain the conditions under which such a land may be possessed. These terms may seem stern and unbending: "whatsoever nation shall possess [this land] shall serve God, or they shall be swept off" (Ether 2:7, 9). However, bad behavior does not always result in certain or immediate destruction. People must first be "ripened in iniquity" (v. 9). Consequently, Moroni speaks to his future readers directly and passionately, pleading with them to "repent, and not continue in [their] iniquities . . . that [they] may not bring down the fulness of the wrath of God upon [them] as the inhabitants of the land have hitherto done" (v. 11).

Much like a rabbi offering a *d'var Torah* after a *haftarah* reading, Moroni frequently interrupts his narrative to deliver several short "sermonettes," small bits of counsel that describe what exactly his readers must do to be saved. After he has related how the Jaredites arrived in their new land and began to use the ancient oaths to "obtain kingdoms and great glory," Moroni stops the story to clarify what these oaths are, what they mean, and where they came from. He explains that these oaths are connected to secret combinations and are "had among all people" (Ether 8:9, 20). He then warns his future readers: "Whatsoever nation shall uphold such secret combinations . . . shall be destroyed; for the Lord will not suffer that the blood of his saints, which shall be shed by them, shall always cry unto him from the ground for vengeance upon them and yet he avenge them not" (v. 22). So dangerous are these secret societies that Moroni lingers on them and fervently appeals to his readers to "suffer not that these murderous combinations shall get above [them]" (v. 23). He also repeats the words "blood" and "cry" as if to emphasize the linkage between these societies and Cain, as Moroni implores his readers to "awake to a sense of [their] awful situation, because of this secret combination which shall be among [them; and] . . . because of the *blood* of them who have been slain; for *they cry from the dust* for vengeance" (v. 24).

Clearly Moroni connects these secret combinations with Cain's crime, both in their seriousness and in the scope of damage they can do. As he continues, these combinations "bringeth to pass the destruction of *all people*" for they are built up by "the devil, who is the father of all lies; even that same liar who beguiled our first parents, yea, even that same liar who hath *caused man to commit murder* from the beginning" (Ether 8:25). Furthermore, the elimination of these combinations will not only prevent societal destruction but will help do away with "all evil" and will help usher in the time when

"Satan may have no power upon the hearts of the children of men" and all people "may be persuaded to do good continually" (v. 26).

Such a vision of the future may not be as poetic or as sweeping as those in Isaiah, but it is still full of prophetic hope. Coupled as it is with specific advice as to what to do, or not do, to realize it, Moroni's vision promotes the possibility of real change. Furthermore, Moroni emphasizes that a more extensive vision can still be had. Just after explaining how the vision of the brother of Jared, though written down, was "forbidden to come unto the children of men" until later (Ether 4:1), he affirms that it and other visions are yet available to the faithful. "Come unto me, O ye Gentiles," he quotes the Father as saying, "and I will show unto you the greater things, the knowledge which is hid up because of unbelief. Come unto me, O ye house of Israel, and it shall be made manifest unto you how great things the Father hath laid up for you, from the foundation of the world; and it hath not come unto you, because of unbelief" (vv. 13–14). There is more in store, in other words. There is still hope.

Near the end of the book of Ether, Moroni again addresses his future readers in a hopeful manner. Despite his concerns that they will mock what he and his father have written, he has received assurances that God's "grace is sufficient for the meek" and that "they shall take no advantage of [his] weakness" (Ether 12:23, 26). Moroni therefore is comforted, prays that God would give unto his readers "grace, that they might have charity," and bids farewell to them, looking forward optimistically to the time when he and they shall meet "before the judgment-seat of Christ, where all men shall know that [Moroni's,] garments are not spotted with [their] blood" (vv. 36, 38).

In this way, the books of Mormon and Ether provide the prophetic "hope and consolation" J. H. Hertz sees as central to the *haftarah* experience. Not only do they connect with Genesis in several positive ways, all of which reinforce the biblical teaching that all humans are their brothers' keepers and that all homicide is consequently fratricide, but they offer explicit advice and personal encouragement to follow that teaching and avoid societal catastrophe.

Conclusion

And now I bid unto all, farewell. I soon go to rest in the paradise of God, until my spirit and body shall again reunite, and I am brought forth triumphant through the air, to meet you before the pleasing bar of the great Jehovah, the Eternal Judge of both quick and dead. Amen. (Moro. 10:34)

In the most fundamental sense, this chapter is misnamed. There is no conclusion to this book. It simply ends. Just as the Torah provides an "unending source of [divine] knowledge" for Cohen and exhibits a God-given "inexhaustible fertility" for Bonchek and others, so the Book of Mormon can also serve as a limitless source of inspired information for its readers.[1] The examples set forth in this book are therefore just that—*examples*, mere glimpses of the many insights readers can discover for themselves as they learn to behold the Book of Mormon and approach it rabbinically. It is therefore fitting that the final book in the Book of Mormon, the book of Moroni, is not a neatly tied-up summary of the main ideas presented in the Book of Mormon but rather bits and pieces of material centered on the Holy Ghost—brief admonitions to give the Holy Ghost to others (Moro. 2:2), cursory explanations of how priestly ordinations are dependent upon the Holy Ghost (3:4), short prayers that enable the Holy Ghost to be with Jesus's followers on an on-going basis (4:3, 5:2), and so forth.

For Moroni, the Holy Ghost is not simply a one-time cleansing power, something that baptizes believers once "with fire" (Matt. 3:11), fills them full, and is then rarely experienced again. It is an ever-present force that enables its recipients to be unceasingly "nourished by the good word of God" and kept continually "in the right way" (Moro. 6:4). In other words, through the Holy Ghost the scriptural journey goes on. It does not stop with a few scans of the Book of Mormon nor does it contract

---

1. Norman J. Cohen, *The Way Into Torah*, 108; Avigdor Bonchek, *Studying the Torah: A Guide to In-Depth Interpretation*, xv.

into a hurried scramble for easily quoted snippets. Like Nephi, Moroni believes that there is still much for his readers to learn and to do after they "have entered in by the way." They must "press forward, feasting upon the word," persistently asking questions of the Scriptures and insistently knocking on its literary doors. Only then will they be "brought into the light" (2 Ne. 31:20; 32:1, 4), and a close connection with the Holy Ghost is crucial to that process.

As Moroni presents it, the Holy Ghost is the ultimate *chavrutah* expressed in Christian terms. Not only should it be consulted frequently, like a trusted study partner, but it can confirm the veracity of scriptural insights with an authority that exceeds the ability of the most able commentator. As Moroni writes to his future readers,

> Behold, I would exhort you that when ye shall read these things, if it be wisdom in God that ye should read them, that ye would remember how merciful the Lord hath been unto the children of men, from the creation of Adam even down unto the time that ye shall receive these things, and ponder it in your hearts. And when ye shall receive these things, I would exhort you that ye would ask God, the Eternal Father, in the name of Christ, if these things are not true; and if ye shall ask with a sincere heart, with real intent, having faith in Christ, he will manifest the truth of it unto you, by the power of the Holy Ghost. (Moro. 10:3–4)

The Holy Ghost is also like Rashi, Rambam, Ibn Ezra, Redak, Ramban, and all the other Talmudic commentators rolled into one—with Abraham, Moses, Isaiah, Ezra, Peter, John, and Paul thrown in for good measure. The Holy Ghost does not eliminate the need for these learned guides; instead it augments them and amplifies them, helping readers understand the ideas they put forth—sifting those ideas, refining them, improving them, even expanding upon them and transcending them. As Moroni continues, pondering the Book of Mormon together with others and in concert with the Hebrew Scriptures is extremely important, even essential. However, it is "by the power of the Holy Ghost [that] ye may know the truth of *all* things" (Moro. 10:5). Just as Moroni's father had "the word of the Lord" revealed to him concerning religious "disputations," which were presumably unresolvable using the usual methods, so Mormon's readers too can experience "the power of the Holy Ghost" in this way, after they have done their scriptural homework (8:5–7).

In addition, the Holy Ghost is like the *Shechinah*. Not only can it enlighten students of the Scriptures, uniting them around new knowledge; it can facilitate a union with God, transforming human communication into divine communion, a state of understanding God's self as well as his words. Mormon calls this state the "rest of the Lord" and explains that it can be enjoyed not just in heaven but "from this time henceforth." Thus, he urges all "peaceable followers of Christ" to embrace what he calls "charity," or "the pure love of Christ" (Moro. 7:3, 47). This love, however, involves more than just a deep devotion to Jesus; it also includes caring just as profoundly for other human beings and expressing that love appropriately. As Mormon explains, charity "is kind, and envieth not, and is not puffed up, seeketh not her own, is not easily provoked, thinketh no evil, and rejoiceth not in iniquity but rejoiceth in the truth, beareth all things, believeth all things, hopeth all things, endureth all things" (v. 45). Charity is, simply put, loving others as God does; it is a union on the deepest level with divinity.

Mormon's description of charity is similar to Paul's, as recorded in 1 Corinthians 13:4–7. However, his description takes on greater immediacy and power when applied to those engaged in rabbinical scripture study. The same is true with Moroni's listing of spiritual gifts. His list nearly duplicates the list of spiritual gifts in 1 Corinthians 12:8–10. However, he adds to it the literary skills of the "*interpretation* of languages" as well as the *teaching* of both the "word of wisdom" and the "word of knowledge" (Moro. 10:9–10, 16). Like charity, these manifestations of the Holy Ghost take on additional meaning as they are applied to rigorous, communal scripture study. The Holy Ghost, similar to the *Shechinah*, can be present whenever two or more are gathered in such a noble pursuit.

All in all, the book of Moroni presents the Holy Ghost—whether it be as an ever-present study companion, as a timeless commentator, or as the *Shechinah* itself—as a force that fosters an unending stream of aesthetic-spiritual information flowing from divinity to humanity. And it is available to all. "These gifts," claims Moroni, "come by the Spirit of Christ; and they come unto every man severally, according as he will" (Moro. 10:17). They are limited, in other words, "*only* according to the unbelief of the children of men" (v. 19). It is therefore appropriate that Moroni concludes his book, much as synagogue-going Jews do when they complete and start again their yearly reading of the Torah: with an implied injunction to his readers to be "of strong faith and a firm mind" (7:30). One can almost hear Moroni chant: "*Hazak, hazak v'nithazek!* Be strong! Be strong! And let us be strengthened [in our efforts to read and understand the Scriptures]!"[2]

---

2. See Rabbi Hayim Halevy Donin, *To Pray as a Jew: A Guide to the Prayer Book and the Synagogue Service*, 254.

Approached rabbinically, the Book of Mormon can become a miraculous burning bush continually enlightening its readers. Read closely, on several levels, with friends, and in connection with the Hebrew Scriptures, its branches will not be "consumed by its own fire" nor will its roots be "burnt." But for those who "turn aside" and take the time to behold "this great sight," the Book of Mormon can truly become a Tree of Life, a thing of eternal beauty, an ever-growing and expanding and deepening source of divine knowledge in which angels appear, and out of the midst of which God speaks (Ex. 3:2–4).

Glossary

amudah—a stand in a synagogue upon which the Torah is placed and read.

Aron haKodesh—(Hebrew: "the sacred ark") a cabinet or another kind of secure enclosure in which Torah scrolls are stored.

chavrutah—(Aramaic: "friendship," "companionship") a partner with whom one studies the Scriptures, especially the Torah.

chiasmus—a Hebraic poetic form where significant words and ideas are repeated in reverse order.

chiddush—(Hebrew: "novelty") a new discovery or insight into the Scriptures, often solving a puzzling problem in the text.

chumash—(Hebrew: "fifth") a bound book, not a scroll, containing the Five Books of Moses frequently with commentary.

d'var torah—(Hebrew: "a word of Torah") a sermon, or scriptural insight.

darshan—(Hebrew: "interpreter") a person who delivers a *derashah*, or sermon, in a synagogue service.

derash—(Hebrew: "to seek or search out") the sermonic meaning of a scriptural text.

derashah—a sermon, particularly a sermon given in a synagogue immediately after a haftarah reading.

Gemara—(Aramaic: "to study") a later commentary on the Mishnah, written in Aramaic, published with the Mishnah in both Talmuds.

gematria—a method of scriptural interpretation based on the numerological value of Hebrew words.

haftarah—(Aramaic: "conclusion") a reading from the Prophets that complements the weekly Torah reading, or *parashah*, in some way.

hinukh—(Hebrew: "consecration") the Hebrew word for education, not limited to formal schooling but often referring to the practical training a child receives in order to make a living.

kotz—(Hebrew: "thorn") a puzzling scriptural element, which invites an ingenious interpretation or explanation.

maftir—(Hebrew: "concluder") the reader of the *haftarah* text.

midrash—from the Hebrew word *derash*. A literary genre devoted to explaining or elaborating upon elements of the Scriptures, often in an imaginative, narrative way.

Mishnah—(Hebrew: "repetition") The first attempt to write down the Jewish oral law, the Hebrew text upon which the Gemara is based.

notarikon—an effort to find hidden meanings in the letters of a word by treating it as an acronym.

parashah—(Hebrew: "portion"; pl. *parashot*) a section of the Torah assigned to be read during Sabbath services; the scriptural unit upon which a *haftarah* is based.

Pesach—Passover, a biblical Jewish holiday where unleavened bread, bitter herbs, and other symbolic foods are eaten during a *Seder*, or ordered meal that commemorates the Israelites' deliverance from slavery in Egypt. The Song of Solomon is read during this festival in the synagogue.

peshat—the plain, simple, or straightforward meaning of a scriptural text.

Pirke Avot—(Hebrew: "tractate of the Fathers" also called "the Ethics of the Fathers") the first section in the Mishnah known for its wise sayings.

Purim—(Hebrew: "lots") a non-biblical Jewish holiday where the Book of Esther is read publicly and playfully; a rowdy celebration of Jewish deliverance.

remez—the allegorical meaning of a scriptural text.

sedrah—another word for a *parashah*, where a weekly Torah portion is read in a synagogue.

Shechinah—God's immanent or indwelling presence; often characterized as female.

sod—(Hebrew: "secret") the mystical meaning of a scriptural text, often associated with *gematria* (numerology) or *notarikon.*

Succot—(Hebrew: "booths" or "huts") an eight-day Mosaic festival involving setting up and inhabiting temporary shelters in commemoration of the Israelites' wandering in the desert. Ecclesiastes is read in synagogues in conjunction with it.

synagogue—(Greek: "assembly," "gathering place") a Jewish place of worship, also called a *shul* (Yiddish: "school"), a *bet midrash* (Hebrew: "house of study"), and a *bet tefillah* (Hebrew: "house of prayer").

Talmud—(Hebrew: "learning, instruction") one of two great compilations of Jewish Law and learning put together during late antiquity. Most often the term refers to the *Talmud Bavli*, which was compiled in Babylon during the third and fifth centuries C.E. It consists of the Mishnah as well as the Gemara and other rabbinic commentaries. The *Talmud Yerushalmi* or "the Talmud of the Land of Israel" was compiled earlier, during the fourth century, in Galilee. It also contains the Mishnah as well as commentary. However, its commentary is less expansive or developed.

Tanach—a commonly used acronym for the Hebrew Scriptures formed from their three main divisions: Torah (Law), Neva'im (Prophets), Chetov'im (Writings).

Torah—(Hebrew: "instruction") the Five Books of Moses as well as Jewish teaching in general.

Tisha B'Av—(Hebrew: "ninth of Av") a non-biblical Jewish holiday mourning the destructions of the First and Second temples. On this day, the Book of Lamentations is read in traditional synagogues.

Torah lishma—studying the Torah for its own sake and not for any practical or monetary reason.

Torah—(Hebrew: "instruction") the first five books of the Hebrew Scriptures—the books of Moses: Genesis, Exodus, Leviticus, Numbers, Deuteronomy.

Tosefta—(Aramaic: "additions") a collection of Jewish law compiled slightly later than the Mishnah and seen as an extension of it.

yad—(Hebrew: "hand") a pointing instrument, often in the shape of a pointing hand on a stick, used to keep track of one's place as one reads a Torah scroll.

yeshivah—(Hebrew: "seated") a traditional Jewish institution of higher learning that focuses primarily on the Talmud and the Torah.

Yom Kippur—(Hebrew: "Day of Atonement") a biblical fast day, marking the end of the ten Days of Repentance, in which Jews typically seek to correct whatever wrongs they may have done and seek forgiveness from God as well as from those they have harmed. On this day, the Book of Jonah is read as part of the synagogue service along with the Binding of Isaac in Genesis.

Bibliography

Alter, Robert. *The Art of Biblical Narrative.* New York: Basic Books, 1981.

————. *The World of Biblical Literature.* New York: Basic Books, 1992.

Alter, Robert and Frank Kermode, eds. *The Literary Guide to the Bible.* Cambridge, Mass.: Harvard University Press, 1987.

Anderson, Bernard W. *Understanding the Old Testament.* 3rd ed. Englewood Cliffs, N.J.: Prentice-Hall, Inc., 1975.

Bamberger, Bernard J. *The Story of Judaism.* 3rd aug. ed. New York: Schocken Books, 1970.

Beer, Moshe. "Academies in Babylonia and Erez Israel." *Encyclopaedia Judaica.* Ed. Michael Berenbaum and Fred Skolnik. 2nd ed. Vol. 1. Detroit: Macmillan Reference USA, 2007.

Belnap, Daniel L., Gaye Strathearn, and Stanley A. Johnson, eds. *The Things Which My Father Saw: Approaches to Lehi's Dream and Nephi's Vision.* Salt Lake City: Deseret Book and Religious Studies Center, Brigham Young University, 2011.

Berg, Michael, ed. and comp. *The Zohar: by Rav Shimon bar Yochai: from the book of Avraham: with the Sulam commentary by Rav Yehuda Ashlag.* Rev. ed. New York: The Kabbalah Centre International, Inc. 2003.

Berkson, William. *Pirke Avot: Timeless Wisdom for Modern Life.* Philadelphia: The Jewish Publication Society, 2010.

Berlin, Adele and Marc Zvi Brettler, eds. *The Jewish Study Bible.* New York: Oxford University Press, 2004.

Bonchek, Avigdor. *Studying the Torah: A Guide to In-Depth Interpretation.* Northvale, N.J.: Jason Aronson, 1996.

————. *What's Bothering Rashi?: A Guide to In-Depth Analysis of His Torah Commentary.* New York: Feldheim Publishers, 1997.

Brettler, Marc Zvi. *How to Read the Bible.* Philadelphia: Jewish Publication Society, 2005.

Breuer, Mordechai, Simha Assaf, and Adin Steinsaltz. "Yeshivot." *Encyclopaedia Judaica.* Ed. Michael Berenbaum and Fred Skolnik. 2nd ed. Vol. 21. Detroit: Macmillan Reference USA, 2007.

Brown, Francis, with S.R. Driver and Charles A. Briggs. *The Brown-Driver-Briggs Hebrew and English Lexicon.* Peabody, Mass.: Hendrickson Publishers, 1997.

Brown, Raymond E. *An Introduction to the New Testament.* New Haven, Conn.:
    Yale University Press, 1997.

Cohen, Norman J. *The Way Into Torah.* Woodstock, Vt.: Jewish Lights Publishing, 2000.

Donin, Rabbi Hayim Halevy. *To Be a Jew: A Guide to Jewish Observance in
    Contemporary Life.* New York: BasicBooks, 1972.

———. *To Pray as a Jew: A Guide to the Prayer Book and the Synagogue Service.*
    New York: BasicBooks, 1980.

Dosick, Rabbi Wayne. *Living Judaism: The Complete Guide to Jewish Belief,
    Tradition, & Practice.* New York: HarperCollins, 1995.

Ehrman, Bart D. *The New Testament: A Historical Introduction to the Early
    Christian Writings.* 3rd ed. New York: Oxford University Press, 2004.

I. Epstein, I., ed., *The Babylonian Talmud.* London, Soncino Press, 1935.

Fackenheim, Emil L. *What Is Judaism?* New York: Summit Books, 1987.

Faulconer, James E. *Scripture Study: Tools and Suggestions.* Provo, Utah: Foundation
    for Ancient Research and Mormon Studies, 1999.

Fishbane, Michael. *The Garments of the Torah: Essays in Biblical Hermeneutics.*
    Bloomington, Ind.: Indiana University Press, 1989.

———. *The JPS Bible Commentary: Haftarot.* Philadelphia: The Jewish Publication
    Society, 2002.

———. *Sacred Attunement: A Jewish Theology.* Chicago: University of Chicago
    Press, 2008.

Friedman, Richard Elliott. *Commentary on the Torah.* New York: HarperCollins, 2001.

———. *Who Wrote the Bible?* San Francisco: HarperSanFrancisco, 1997.

Gale, Aaron M. "The Gospel According to Matthew." In *The Jewish Annotated
    New Testament,* ed. Amy-Jill Levine and Marc Zvi Brettler. Rev. ed. New
    York: Oxford Univeristy Press, 2011.

Gillman, Neil. *The Way Into Encountering God in Judaism.* Woodstock, Vt.:
    Jewish Lights, 2000.

Ginzberg, Louis. *The Legends of the Jews.* Vol 1. Philadelphia: The Jewish
    Publication Society of America, 1909.

Givens, Terryl L. *The Book of Mormon: A Very Short Introduction.* New York:
    Oxford University Press, 2009.

Grishaver, Joel Lurie. *Learning Torah: A Self-Guided Journey through the Layers of
    Jewish Learning.* New York: UAHC Press, 1990.

Gurary, Noson. *The Thirteen Principles of Faith: A Chasidic Viewpoint.* Northvale,
    N.J.: Jason Aronson, Inc., 1996.

Hardy, Grant. *Understanding the Book of Mormon: A Reader's Guide.* New York:
    Oxford University Press, 2010.

Jackson, Kent P. and Frank F. Judd Jr., eds. *How the New Testament Came to Be.* Salt Lake City:
    Deseret Book and Religious Studies Center, Brigham Young University, 2006.

Johnson, Paul. *A History of the Jews.* New York: HarperPerrennial, 1987.

Heide, A. Van der. "PARDES: Methodological Reflections on the Theory of the
    Four Senses." *Journal of Jewish Studies* 34 (Autumn 1983): 148.

Hertz, J. H., ed. *The Pentateuch and Haftorahs.* 2nd ed. London: Soncino Press, 1979.

Hoffman, Lawrence A. *The Way Into Jewish Prayer.* Woodstock, Vt.: Jewish Lights, 2000.

Kertzer, Rabbi Morris H. *What Is a Jew?: A Guide to the Beliefs, Traditions, and Practices of Judaism that Answers Questions for Both Jew and Non-Jew.* Rev. Rabbi Lawrence A. Hoffman. New York: Collier Books, 1993.

Kraemer, Joel L. *Maimonides: The Life and World of One of Civilation's Greatest Minds.* New York: Doubleday, 2008.

Kugel, James L. *The Bible as it Was.* Cambridge, Mass.: The Belnap Press, 1997.

Landesman, David. *A Practical Guide to Torah Learning.* Northvale, N.J.: Jason Aronson, 1995.

Levenson, Jon D. "Gensis." In *The Jewish Study Bible,* ed. Adele Berlin and Marc Zvi Brettler. New York: Oxford University Press, 2004.

Levine, Baruch A. *The JPS Torah Commentary: Leviticus.* Philadelphia: Jewish Publication Society, 1989.

Lieber, David L., ed. *Etz Hayim: Torah and Commentary.* New York: The Jewish Publication Society, 2001.

Ludlow, Victor. *Isaiah: Prophet, Seer, and Poet.* Salt Lake City: Deseret Book Company, 1982.

Montefiore, C.G. & H. Loewe. *A Rabbinic Anthology.* New York: Schocken Books, 1974.

Munk, Eliyaho, trans. *Hachut hameshulash: Commentaries on the Torah by Rabbeinu Chananel, Rabbi Shmuel ben Meir (Rash'bam), Rabbi David Kimchi (R'dak), Rabbi Ovadiah Seforno.* New York: Lambda Publishers, 2003.

Neusner, Jacob. *A Rabbi Talks with Jesus: An Intermillenial Interfaith Exchange.* New York: Doubleday, 1993.

———. *Judaism and Scripture: The Evidence of Leviticus Rabbah.* Chicago: The University of Chicago Press, 1986.

———. *Judaism and the Interpretation of Scripture: Introduction to the Rabbinic Midrash.* Peabody, Mass.: Hendrickson Publishers, 2004.

———. *The Mishnah: A New Translation.* New Haven, Conn.: Yale University Press, 1988.

———. *The Midrash: An Introduction.* Northvale, N.J.: Jason Aronson, 1990.

———. *The Tosefta: Translated from the Hebrew with a New Introduction.* 2 vols. Peabody, Mass.: Hendrickson Publishers, 2002.

———. *The Way of Torah: An Introduction to Judaism.* 4th ed. Belmont, Calif.: Wadsworth Publishing Company, 1988.

———. *Understanding Rabbinic Judaism.* New York: Ktav Publishing House, 1974.

Pearl, Chaim. *Rashi.* New York: Grove Press, 1988.

Pessah, Amy Grossblat, Kenneth J. Meyers, and Christopher M. Leighton. "How Do Jews and Christians Read the Bible?" In *Irreconcilable Differences?: A Learning Resource for Jews and Christians,* ed. David F. Sandmel, Rosann M. Catalono, and Christopher M. Leighton. Boulder, Colo.: Westview Press, 2001.

Plaut, W. Gunther. *The Haftarah Commentary.* New York: UAHC Press, 1996.

Robinson, George. *Essential Judaism: A Complete Guide to Beliefs, Rituals, and Customs.* New York: Pocket Books, 2000.

———. *Essential Torah: A Complete Guide to the Five Books of Moses.* New York: Schocken Books, 2006.

Rosenberg, Stephen Gabriel. *The Haphtara Cycle: A Handbook to the Haphtaroth of the Jewish Year.* Northvale, N.J.: Jason Aronson, Inc. 2000.

Rust, Richard Dilworth. *Feasting on the Word: The Literary Testimony of the Book of Mormon.* Salt Lake City: Deseret Book and FARMS, 197.

Sanders, E. P. *The Historical Figure of Jesus.* New York: Penguin Books, 1995.

Sandmel, Samuel. *The Hebrew Scriptures: An Introduction to Their Literature and Religious Ideas.* New York: Alfred A. Knopf, 1963.

Sarna, Nahum M. *The JPS Bible Commentary: Genesis.* Philadelphia: The Jewish Publication Society, 1989.

Sasso, Sandy Eisenberg. *God's Echo: Exploring Scripture with Midrash.* Brewster, Mass.: Paraclete Press, 2007.

Satlow, Michael L. *How the Bible Became Holy.* New Haven: Yale University Press, 2014.

Scholem, Gershom. *On the Kabbalah and Its Symbolisim.* New York: Schocken Books, 1965.

———. *On the Possibility of Jewish Mysticism in Our Time.* Philadelphia: Jewish Publication Society, 1997.

———. *Major Trends in Jewish Mysticism.* New York: Schocken Books, 1974.

Shereshevsky, Esra. *Rashi: The Man and His World.* Northvale, N.J.: Jason Aronson, 1996.

Shuchat, Wilfred. *The Creation According to the Midrash Rabbah.* New York: Devora Publishing Company, 2002.

———. *The Garden of Eden & The Struggle to be Human According to the Midrash Rabbah.* New York: Devora Publishing Company, 2006.

Simon, Rabbi Charles. *Understanding the Haftarot: An Everyperson's Guide.* Denver: Outskirts Press, 2012.

Spivey Robert A., D. Moody Smith Jr., and C. Clifton Black. *Anatomy of the New Testament.* 6th ed. Minneapolis: Fortress Press, 2010.

Strassfeld, Michael. *A Book of Life: Embracing Judaism as a Spiritual Practice.* New York: Schocken Books, 2001.

Welch, John W. and Donald W. Parry, eds. *The Tree of Life: From Eden to Eternity.* Salt Lake City: Deseret Book and Neal A. Maxwell Institute for Religious Scholarship, 2011.

Wylen, Stephen M. *Settings of Silver: An Introduction to Judaism.* New York: Paulist Press, 1989.

———. *The Seventy Faces of Torah: The Jewish Way of Reading the Sacred Scriptures.* New York: Paulist Press, 2005.

Scripture Index

Subject Index

Other titles in the
CONTEMPORARY STUDIES
IN SCRIPTURE series

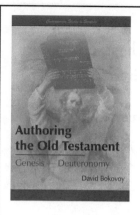

Authoring the Old Testament: Genesis–Deuteronomy

David Bokovoy

Paperback, ISBN: 978-1-58958-588-1
Hardcover, ISBN: 978-1-58958-675-8

For the last two centuries, biblical scholars have made discoveries and insights about the Old Testament that have greatly changed the way in which the authorship of these ancient scriptures has been understood. In the first of three volumes spanning the entire Hebrew Bible, David Bokovoy dives into the Pentateuch, showing how and why textual criticism has led biblical scholars today to understand the first five books of the Bible as an amalgamation of multiple texts into a single, though often complicated narrative; and he discusses what implications those have for Latter-day Saint understandings of the Bible and modern scripture.

Praise for *Authoring the Old Testament*:

"*Authoring the Old Testament* is a welcome introduction, from a faithful Latter-day Saint perspective, to the academic world of Higher Criticism of the Hebrew Bible. . . . [R]eaders will be positively served and firmly impressed by the many strengths of this book, coupled with Bokovoy's genuine dedication to learning by study and also by faith." — John W. Welch, editor, *BYU Studies Quarterly*

"Bokovoy provides a lucid, insightful lens through which disciple-students can study intelligently LDS scripture. This is first rate scholarship made accessible to a broad audience—nourishing to the heart and mind alike." — Fiona Givens, co-author, *The God Who Weeps: How Mormonism Makes Sense of Life*

"I repeat: this is one of the most important books on Mormon scripture to be published recently. . . . [*Authoring the Old Testament*] has the potential to radically expand understanding and appreciation for not only the Old Testament, but scripture in general. It's really that good. Read it. Share it with your friends. Discuss it." — David Tayman, The Improvement Era: A Mormon Blog

Re-reading Job: Understanding the Ancient World's Greatest Poem

Michael Austin

Paperback, ISBN: 978-1-58958-667-3
Hardcover, ISBN: 978-1-58958-668-0

Job is perhaps the most difficult to understand of all books in the Bible. While a cursory reading of the text seems to relay a simple story of a righteous man whose love for God was tested through life's most difficult of challenges and rewarded for his faith through those trials, a closer reading of Job presents something far more complex and challenging. The majority of the text is a work of poetry that authors and artists through the centuries have recognized as being one of--if not the--greatest poem of the ancient world.

In *Re-reading Job: Understanding the Ancient World's Greatest Poem*, author Michael Austin shows how most readers have largely misunderstood this important work of scripture and provides insights that enable us to re-read Job in a drastically new way. In doing so, he shows that the story of Job is far more than that simple story of faith, trials, and blessings that we have all come to know, but is instead a subversive and complex work of scripture meant to inspire readers to rethink all that they thought they knew about God.

Praise for *Re-reading Job*:

"In this remarkable book, Michael Austin employs his considerable skills as a commentator to shed light on the most challenging text in the entire Hebrew Bible. Without question, readers will gain a deeper appreciation for this extraordinary ancient work through Austin's learned analysis. Rereading Job signifies that Latter-day Saints are entering a new age of mature biblical scholarship. It is an exciting time, and a thrilling work." — David Bokovoy, author, *Authoring the Old Testament*

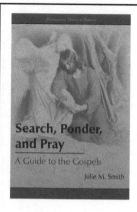

Search, Ponder, and Pray:
A Guide to the Gospels

Julie M. Smith

Paperback, ISBN: 978-1-58958-671-0
Hardcover, ISBN: 978-1-58958-672-7

From the author's preface:

During my graduate studies in theology, I came to realize that there is quite a bit of work done in the field of biblical studies that can be useful to members of the Church as they read the scriptures. Unfortunately, academic jargon usually makes these works impenetrable, and I was unable to find many publications that made this research accessible to the non-specialist. In this book, I have endeavored to present some of the most interesting insights of biblical scholars—in plain language.

It was also important to me that I not present the work of these scholars in a way that would make you feel obligated to accept their conclusions. Since scholars rarely agree with each other, I can see no reason why you should feel compelled to agree with them. My hope is that the format of this book will encourage you to view the insights of scholars as the beginning of a discussion instead of the end of an argument. In some cases, I have presented the positions of scholars (and even some critics of the Church) specifically to encourage you to develop your own responses to these arguments based on your personal scripture study. I certainly don't agree with every idea in this book.

I encourage you to read the Introduction. Although I have endeavored to keep it as short as possible, there are several issues related to the interpretation of the scriptures that should be addressed before you begin interpreting.

It is my experience that thoughtful scripture study leads to personal revelation. I hope that through the process of searching the scriptures, pondering these questions, and praying about the answers, you will be edified.

Life is full of unanswered questions. Here are over 4,500 more of them.

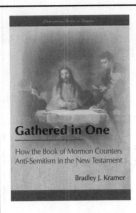

Gathered in One

How the Book of Mormon Counters
Anti-Semitism in the New Testament

Bradley J. Kramer

Gathered in One:
How the Book of Mormon Counters
Anti-Semitism in the New Testament

Bradley J. Kramer

Paperback, ISBN: 978-1-58958-709-0
Hardcover, ISBN: 978-1-58958-710-6

Since the Holocaust, a growing consensus of biblical scholars have come to recognize the unfair and misleading anti-Semitic rhetoric in the New Testament—language that has arguably contributed to centuries of violence and persecution against the Jewish people.

In *Gathered in One*, Bradley J. Kramer shows how the Book of Mormon counters anti-Semitism in the New Testament by approaching this most Christian of books on its own turf and on its own terms: literarily, by providing numerous pro-Jewish statements, portrayals, settings, and structuring devices in opposition to similar anti-Semitic elements in the New Testament; and scripturally, by connecting with it as a peer, as a divine document of equal value and authority, which can add these elements to the Christian canon (as the Gospel of John can add elements to the Gospel of Matthew) without undermining its authority or dependability.

In this way, the Book of Mormon effectively "detoxifies" the New Testament of its anti-Semitic poison without weakening its status as scripture and goes far in encouraging Christians to relate to Jews respectfully, not as enemies or opponents, but as allies, people of equal worth, importance, and value before God.

Praise for *Gathered in One*:

"His thesis is fresh, provocative, and rigorously argued. A signal contribution to Book of Mormon studies." — Terryl L. Givens, author of *By the Hand of Mormon: The American Scripture that Launched a New World Religion*

"Impressed by the book and its scholarship and attitude, I recommend it to all who are interested in the history of Christian attitudes towards the Jews, as well as those working towards interfaith reconciliation and mutual respect'" — Yaakov Ariel, professor of religious studies at the University of North Carolina at Chapel Hill and author of *Evangelizing the Chosen People: Missions to the Jews in America, 1880–2000*

Made in United States
Troutdale, OR
02/10/2024

17564835R00159